MW01043717

THE
TEXTUAL TRADITION
OF
EURIPIDES' *ORESTES*

THE
TEXTUAL TRADITION
OF
EURIPIDES' *ORESTES*

James Diggle

CLARENDON PRESS · OXFORD

1991

Oxford University Press, Walton Street, Oxford OX2 6DP
Oxford New York Toronto
Delhi Bombay Calcutta Madras Karachi
Petaling Jaya Singapore Hong Kong Tokyo
Nairobi Dar es Salaam Cape Town
Melbourne Auckland
and associated companies in
Berlin Ibadan

Oxford is a trade mark of Oxford University Press

Published in the United States
by Oxford University Press, New York

British Library Cataloguing in Publication Data
Diggle, James 1944–
The textual tradition of Euripides' Orestes.
1. Drama in Greek. Euripides.
I. Title
882.01
ISBN 0–19–814766–X

Library of Congress Cataloging in Publication Data
Diggle, James.
The textual tradition of Euripides' Orestes
1. Euripides. Orestes—Criticism, Textual.
2. Orestes (Greek mythology) in literature. I. Title.
PA3973.O73D54   1991   882'.01—dc20   90-7282
ISBN 0–19–814766–X

Text processing by Design Locker, Bristol, Avon

Printed in Great Britain by
Bookcraft (Bath) Ltd., Midsomer Norton, Avon

Preface

I RECORD with especial pleasure and gratitude my indebtedness to Professor Kjeld Matthiessen and Professor Donald Mastronarde, to whose work on the transmission of *Hecuba* and *Phoenissae* this present work is offered as a modest complement. Both were kind enough to read and comment on my typescript. In addition, Professor Matthiessen loaned me numerous microfilms, and collated for me the gnomologies gB and gE; and Professor Mastronarde gave me his photographs of Zv and answered many inquiries.

I am further indebted to Dr H. C. Günther, who allowed me to read his preliminary work on the Byzantine scholia of *Orestes*, and gave me the benefit of his advice on the dating of several manuscripts; to Professor Luigi Lehnus, who checked readings for me in manuscripts in Cremona and Milan; to Professor Rosario Pintaudi, who performed the same service with manuscripts in the Biblioteca Laurenziana; to Professsor M. Manfredi, who allowed me to see and cite an unpublished papyrus in the Istituto Papirologico 'G. Vitelli' in Florence; and to Professor G. Zuntz, who loaned me his slides of Ry. And, for information or help of various kinds, I offer my thanks to Dr R. A. Coles, Professor H. Maehler, Professor P. J. Parsons, Professor M. L. West, Dr Sir Charles Willink, and Mr N. G. Wilson.

Nor do I forget my indebtedness to the British Academy, for generous grants which enabled me to acquire copies of manuscripts and to visit foreign libraries; or to the Finance Committee of the Faculty of Classics in Cambridge, for further financial aid; or finally to my wife and children, who cheerfully bore with my absences abroad.

J. D.

Queens' College, Cambridge
September 1989

Contents

Abbreviations and References

Biehl	W. Biehl (ed.), *Euripides, Orestes* (Leipzig 1975)
Dawe, *Coll. & Inv*	R. D. Dawe, *The Collation and Investigation of Manuscripts of Aeschylus* (Cambridge 1964)
Dawe, *Studies*	R. D. Dawe, *Studies on the Text of Sophocles* (Leiden, vols. i–ii 1973, iii 1978)
Di Benedetto	V. Di Benedetto (ed.), *Euripidis Orestes* (Florence 1965)
Diggle, *Studies*	J. Diggle, *Studies on the Text of Euripides* (Oxford 1981)
Dindorf	W. Dindorf, *Scholia Graeca in Euripidis Tragoedias*, i (Oxford 1863)
Eberline	C. N. Eberline, *Studies in the MS Tradition of the Ranae of Aristophanes* (Meisenheim am Glan 1980)
Mastronarde	D. J. Mastronarde and J. M. Bremer, *The Textual Tradition of Euripides' Phoinissai* (California 1982)[1]
Matthiessen	K. Matthiessen, *Studien zur Textüberlieferung der Hekabe des Euripides* (Heidelberg 1974)
Schartau I	B. Schartau, *Observations on the Activities of the Byzantine Grammarians of the Palaeologian Era: I: Demetrius Triclinius' early Work on the Euripidean Triad* (Cahiers de l'Institut du Moyen-Âge Grec et Latin, Université de Copenhague, 4 [1970] 3–35)
Schartau II	B. Schartau, *Observations ... II: The Impact of Thomas Magistros' Introductory Matter (Vita, ὑποθέσεις) to the Euripidean Triad* (Odense 1973)
Schwartz	E. Schwartz, *Scholia in Euripidem*, i (Berlin 1887)

[1] I refer to this book by the name of Mastronarde alone, since I shall be concerned with the part for which he is solely responsible (Part I, 'Studies in the Medieval Tradition').

Smith, *Scholia*   O. L. Smith, *Scholia Metrica Anonyma in
                  Euripidis Hecubam, Orestem, Phoenissas*
                  (Copenhagen 1977)
Smith, *Studies*   O. L. Smith, *Studies in the Scholia on Aeschylus.
                  I: The Recension of Demetrius Triclinius*
                  (Leiden 1975)
Turyn   A. Turyn, *The Byzantine Manuscript Tradition
                  of the Tragedies of Euripides* (Urbana 1957)
West   M. L. West, *Euripides, Orestes, edited with
                  translation and commentary* (Warminster
                  1987)
Willink   C. W. Willink, *Euripides, Orestes, with
                  introduction and commentary* (Oxford 1986,
                  1989²)
Wilson   N. G. Wilson, *Scholars of Byzantium* (London
                  1983)
Zuntz, *Bulletin*   G. Zuntz, *Bulletin of the John Rylands Library*
                  49 (1967) 497–517
Zuntz, *Inquiry*   G. Zuntz, *An Inquiry into the Transmission of
                  the Plays of Euripides* (Cambridge 1965)

Conspectus Siglorum

General List of Manuscripts

A   Parisinus gr. 2712
Aa   Ambrosianus C 44 sup.
Ab   Ambrosianus F 74 sup.
Ad   Athous Dionysii 334
An   Parisinus suppl. gr. 393
At   Athous Vatopedii 671
B   Parisinus gr. 2713
C   Taurinensis B.IV.13
Cr   Cremonensis 130
Dr   Dresdensis Da.22
F   Marcianus gr. 468
G   Ambrosianus L 39 sup.
gB   Vaticanus Barberinianus gr. 4
gE   Escorialensis X.1.13
gV   Athous Vatopedii 36
H   Hierosolymitanus 36
J   Cantabrigiensis Nn.3.13
K   Laurentianus conv. soppr. 66
L   Laurentianus plut. 32.2
M   Marcianus gr. 471
Mn   Monacensis gr. 560
Ms   Mosquensis gr. 508
Mt   Matritensis 4677
O   Laurentianus plut. 31.10
P   Laurentianus conv. soppr. 172
Pr   Remensis 1306
R   Vaticanus gr. 1135
Rf   Laurentianus plut. 32.33
Rw   Vindobonensis phil. gr. 119
Ry   Rylandsianus 1689
S   Salamantinus 31

Sa   Vaticanus gr. 1345
T   Angelicus gr. 14
Ta   Vaticanus Urbinas gr. 142
Th   Thessalonicensis
Tp   Parmensis 154
V   Vaticanus gr. 909
Va   Vaticanus Palatinus gr. 98
X   Oxoniensis Bodleianus Auct. F.3.25
Xa   Oxoniensis Bodleianus Barocci 120
Xb   Laurentianus conv. soppr. 71
Xc   Cantabrigiensis Coll. Corp. Chr. 403
Xd   Parisinus Coislinianus 169
Xe   Parisinus gr. 2795
Xf   Parisinus gr. 2801
Xg   Parisinus gr. 2802
Xh   Parisinus gr. 2803
Z   Cantabrigiensis Nn.3.14 (ff. 1–121)
Za   Londiniensis Arundelianus 540
Zb   Vaticanus gr. 51
Zc   Hauniensis 3549
Zd   Cantabrigiensis Nn.3.14 (ff. 122–207)
Zm   Ambrosianus I 47 sup.
Zu   Uppsaliensis gr. 15
Zv   Vaticanus gr. 1824

Papyri

A list of papyri is given on pp. 115–16.

Explanation of Symbols

A^c	A after correction by an unspecified hand
A^{1c}	A after correction by the first hand
A^2	A after correction by the second hand
A^s	A *supra lineam*, by the first hand
A^{uv}	A *ut videtur*
$A^?$	A's reading is probable or possible but not certain
(A)	A with some inessential variation
[A]	A is illegible or unavailable
⟨A⟩	A's reading is based on inference
$(\sim A^c)$	A^c agrees with the other manuscripts against A
A^m	a reading in the margin of A
A^r	a reading written by the rubricator of A
A^{gl}	a gloss in A
$A^{\gamma\rho}$	a variant in A accompanied by $\gamma\rho(\acute{\alpha}\phi\epsilon\tau\alpha\iota)$
Σ^a	scholium in A
$^i\Sigma^a$	a reading implied by the scholium in A
$^l\Sigma^a$	lemma to the scholium in A
A+	A's reading is found in other unspecified manuscripts
*	an erased or obliterated letter

Where a superscript symbol precedes more than one manuscript (e.g. ^{s}ABC), the symbol applies to all these manuscripts.

CHAPTER I

Preliminaries

The foundations for all future study of the manuscripts of the Euripidean triad were laid by Turyn in *The Byzantine Manuscript Tradition of the Tragedies of Euripides* (1957).

Turyn divided the manuscripts into three classes:

(i) the *ueteres uetustiores*, which antedate the activities of scholars of the Palaeologan renaissance (roughly contemporary with the reign of Andronicus II Palaeologus, 1282–1328);

(ii) the *ueteres recentiores*, which reflect the tradition of the *uetustiores* (and, where they have scholia, have scholia which are old), but are distinguished from them by new errors of their own and (according to Turyn) by the infiltration of readings derived from Palaeologan scholars;

(iii) the *Byzantini*, which are subdivided into Moschopoulean, Thoman, and Triclinian manuscripts, according to whether they contain the scholia of the Palaeologan scholars Manuel Moschopoulos, Thomas Magister, and Demetrius Triclinius.[1]

To the first class belong five manuscripts (HMBO and the gnomology gV),[2] which were written before 1204, when Constantinople was conquered by the fourth crusade, and one more which may have been written shortly before or shortly after 1261, when the city was recaptured by the Greeks (V, 1250–80). To this class Turyn also assigned a few other manuscripts (in particular A and C) which, although probably (A) or certainly (C) written not earlier than the Palaeologan renaissance, reflect the tradition of the *uetustiores* in a purer form than do the so-called *recentiores*.

As the primary representatives of the second class Turyn chose MnPrRSSa, of which two (PrSa) are probably to be dated in the

---

[1] For the dates of these scholars see pp. 49 n. 1, 81 n. 2, 93.

[2] We now know that O belongs to this class by virtue of its date (see p. 6). Turyn (p. 312), believing it to be a fourteenth-century manuscript, assigned it to this class by virtue of its textual affiliations.

last decade of the thirteenth century, one (R) may be somewhat
earlier, and the other two (MnS) are somewhat later.

As representatives of the Moschopoulean manuscripts Turyn
chose XXaXb, which are among the earliest manuscripts containing Moschopoulean scholia. He claimed that these manuscripts
present a text in which we can see the conscious editorial policy of
Moschopoulos: namely a Moschopoulean 'edition'.

Whereas the three Moschopoulean manuscripts rarely disagree
among themselves, the Thoman manuscripts present no such uni-
formity. And Turyn claimed that they reflect successive stages in
the editorial work of Thomas. Turyn chose what he believed to be
the earliest of them, Z, and its twin Za, as representatives of what
he called the 'first edition', and Zb as the primary representative of
what he called the 'second edition'.

The work of Triclinius is represented by T, which is partly corrected and partly written by Triclinius himself. This manuscript
also contains Moschopoulean and Thoman scholia, which are
clearly distinguished from the scholia (including metrical scholia
on the lyrics) composed by Triclinius.

The scope of Turyn's work was vast, and his positive achieve-
ments are many. But his work had its limitations, and some of his
methods and conclusions were faulty. I shall define some of the
areas where he may be considered to have gone astray, so that we
may see more clearly what he left for others to do.

(i) Turyn's proposition that the manuscripts which contain
Moschopoulean scholia also contain an authenticated Moschopoulean text, and that all novel readings in these manuscripts may
be classified as Moschopoulean emendations, was stated as if it
were a self-evident fact.[3] But it is demonstrably wrong. We may
demonstrate that it is wrong by showing (*a*) that some of the readings classed as Moschopoulean emendations are found in earlier
manuscripts, (*b*) that some are found in contemporary or later
manuscripts which there is no good reason to suppose were
influenced by the Moschopoulean manuscripts, (*c*) that, while
some novel readings in the Moschopoulean manuscripts show
evidence of scholarly alertness, many are merely the product of
negligence and corruption. I shall argue that Moschopoulos did not

---

[3] 'Once we recognise different and separate sets of scholia, we shall have identified separate recensions of the poetic text as well' (p. 18).

'edit' the triad; that it is far from certain that any of the conjectures which we find in Moschopoulean manuscripts are to be ascribed to Moschopoulos himself, for there is evidence that scholars contemporary with Moschopoulos were capable of making the same kinds of conjecture (this evidence is provided primarily by K, which we have no reason to associate with Moschopoulos); and that the Moschopoulean manuscripts are sometimes witnesses to what may be regarded as inherited truth, when the truth has been lost, or all but lost, by the remainder of the tradition.

(ii) For his proposition that the Thoman manuscripts reflect not one edition but two Turyn offered no evidence at all: only the fact that the later Thoman manuscripts frequently diverge from the earliest of them. But the very notion that Thomas 'edited' the triad has even less to commend it than the notion that the triad was edited by Moschopoulos. For, while the Moschopoulean manuscripts show incontrovertible evidence of conjectural activity, the Thoman manuscripts show no such evidence. The readings which are peculiar to them give evidence of carelessness and ignorance and not of deliberate thought.

(iii) Turyn claimed that, if any reading which is not known to be old is shared by the *recentiores* and the so-called *Byzantini*, its appearance in manuscripts of the former class may be attributed to the influence on them of manuscripts of the latter class. Much the same view has been expressed, in stark and unambiguous terms, by a scholar who is the author both of an edition of *Orestes* and of a book on the manuscript tradition of Euripides: 'Nei pochi casi in cui R S Sa presentano una lezione esatta contro il resto della tradizione ci si trova di fronte a congetture, per lo più di origine moscopulea.'[4] This is very wide of the mark. There is little or no evidence for the *direct* influence of the *Byzantini* on the *recentiores*. Rather, both classes are inheritors of a medley of novelties which became current at the end of the thirteenth century. Furthermore, not every novelty first attested by the *recentiores* originated in Byzantium. In other words, the *recentiores*, no less than the *Byzantini*, preserve inherited truth which has escaped the *uetustiores*.

(iv) Turyn's investigation of the *recentiores* (or, at least, his presentation of their evidence) was inadequate. By concentrating on a

---

[4] Di Benedetto, p. x of his edition.

small selection, and by citing others only haphazardly, he denied
the reader the opportunity to see the true dissemination of many
readings. And his comparative neglect of the *recentiores* goes hand
in hand with his preoccupation with the *Byzantini*, to which he
ascribed too large a role in the formation of the later tradition.
Turyn made little attempt to study the affiliations of the *recentiores*;
and it is here that much progress can be made.[5]

This expression of my disagreements with Turyn, and of the
conclusions which I hope to establish, contains little that is new.
And I am conscious how much easier my task has been made in
analysing the tradition of *Orestes* by the work which has been done
by my predecessors: above all by Zuntz; by Matthiessen and by
Mastronarde and Bremer (in their studies of the traditions of
Hecuba and *Phoenissae*); and by Dawe (in his studies of the
Aeschylean and Sophoclean traditions). Theirs was the pioneering
work. All that remains is to alter a few more details and to repair a
few more weaknesses in that corner which has remained untouched
of the monument erected by Turyn.

---

[5] The *recentiores* which I have studied are those recommended by Matthiessen 122–3,
plus a few others. I add that Turyn's belief that none of the *recentiores* is to be dated earlier
than *c.*1300 (Turyn 323 and elsewhere) is certainly false: see especially Matthiessen, *GRBS*
10 (1969) 299–300.

CHAPTER II

The Manuscripts[1]

(i) *Manuscripts dated certainly or possibly before 1261*

H   Jerusalem, Patriarchike Bibliotheke 36. Turyn 86–7, Matthiessen 41–2, Mastronarde 2. Facsimile: S. G. Daitz, *The Jerusalem Palimpsest of Euripides. A Facsimile Edition with Commentary* (1970). Scholia (and corrigenda to the preceding work): S. G. Daitz, *The Scholia in the Jerusalem Palimpsest of Euripides. A critical Edition* (1979). A collation, made from photographs, was published by J. A. Spranger, *CQ* 32 (1938) 200–2. 10th–11th century. Lines 105–213, 313–412, 564–614, 716–66, 897–946, 1152–1200, 1356–1556. Collated from the facsimile.

M   Venice, Biblioteca Nazionale Marciana, gr. 471. Turyn 84–5, Matthiessen 48, Mastronarde 2. Facsimile: J. A. Spranger, *Euripidis quae in codice Veneto Marciano 471 inveniuntur. . .* (1935). 11th century. Collated from the facsimile and from the original.

    [Corrections were made by the original scribe and by at least two other hands, and it is often impossible to tell which hand is responsible. Corrections written in a faint grey or brown I have labelled M^2; those written in a darker grey and with a thicker stroke I have labelled M^3.]

B   Paris, Bibliothèque Nationale, gr. 2713. Turyn 87–9, Matthiessen 44, Mastronarde 1–2. Facsimile: J. A. Spranger, *Euripidis quae in codice Parisino Graeco 2713 servantur . . .* (1938). A collation, made from the facsimile, was published by Spranger, *CQ* 33 (1939) 184–92. 11th century, or even late 10th. Collated from the facsimile and from the original.

    [Most of the corrections appear to have been written by two hands: B^2 (grey) and B^3 (black). But distinction between these hands is often impossible. And it is possible that an earlier hand than these has also made corrections in an ink very close

---

[1] I do not offer full descriptions of these manuscripts, since the necessary information can be found in the authorities whom I cite. But, in the case of manuscripts which I have inspected personally, I have sometimes added a comment on hands, in order to explain my distinctions.

to the brown of the original hand (I have ascribed all such corrections to B¹ᶜ). There is a further complication: letters, words, superscript additions, and whole lines, have been re-traced by more than one of these correctors, where the original writing has become faint; and I suspect that some additions and corrections which I have ascribed to B² should have been ascribed to B, the original writing having been obliterated by the retracing of the later hand. Some corrections may have been made by even later hands than the one I have labelled B³; but I have labelled as B³ all corrections which are not certainly by B² or an earlier hand. B³ is certainly a late (Palaeologan) hand. I am not confident that B² is much earlier.]

O   Florence, Biblioteca Medicea-Laurenziana, plut. 31.10. Turyn 333–5, Matthiessen 39, Mastronarde 3, J. Irigoin in *Bizancio e l'Italia, Raccolta di Studi in Memoria di Agostino Pertusi* (1982) 132–43. Dated *c*.1175 by N. G. Wilson, *Scrittura e Civiltà* 7 (1983) 161–76. Collated from microfilm and from the original.

V   Vatican, Biblioteca Apostolica Vaticana, gr. 909. Turyn 90–1, Matthiessen 46–7, Mastronarde 3–4 and *GRBS* 26 (1985) 106–8. *c*.1250–80 (*c*.1280 Turyn, *c*.1250 N. G. Wilson, *Gnomon* 38 [1966] 342). Lines 1–1204, 1505–1693 (for the missing portion see Va below). Collated from photographs and from the original.

[I distinguish three sets of corrections: V¹ᶜ corrections made by the original scribe at the time of writing the text or the adjacent scholia; V² corrections which were made perhaps by the original scribe but are shown to have been made later by the slightly different colour of ink (the colour of ink used by the writer of the text and scholia varies throughout the manuscript); V³ corrections which are shown by the *ductus* to be by a hand different from V¹ and V². Distinction between these hands is often difficult, sometimes impossible; in cases of doubt I write Vᶜ or V¹/² or V²/³. My V³ corresponds to the hand labelled V² by Matthiessen and Mastronarde.]

(ii) *Manuscripts dated after 1261*

A   Paris, Bibliothèque Nationale, gr. 2712. Turyn 89–90, Matthiessen 43–4, Mastronarde 4, Smith, *Studies* 92 n. 70, Eberline 22. *c.*1300. Collated from microfilm and from the original.

Aa   Milan, Biblioteca Ambrosiana, C 44 sup. Turyn 340–1, Matthiessen 42, Mastronarde 4–5. 14th century. Collated from microfilm and from the original.

[There are several hands/inks. The rubricator (Aa^r), who also wrote the occasional scholia, and whose ink changes from red to purple at 645, adds many glosses and variants above the line. An (apparently) early corrector, using a faint brown ink, made a few corrections, which I have labelled Aa^2, although some at least may have been made by Aa^{1c} or even by other hands. There are many corrections in grey and black, and a few (not apparently by the rubricator) in red: all these I have labelled Aa^3.]

Ab   Milan, Biblioteca Ambrosiana, F 74 sup. Turyn 341, Matthiessen 42, Mastronarde 5. Dated *c.*1300 by Mastronarde, 1305–15 by Irigoin (see above, on O). Lines 1–959, 1087–1169, 1283–1600, 1682–93. Collated from microfilm and from the original.

[Corrections made by the second hand (Ab^2) are often difficult to distinguish from those made by the first (Ab^{1c}).]

C   Turin, Biblioteca Nazionale, B.IV.13. Turyn 85, Mastronarde 5. *c.*1300–50. Collated from microfilm.

Cr   Cremona, Biblioteca Governativa, 130. Turyn 333, Matthiessen 38, Mastronarde 5. *c.*1335. Collated from microfilm; most of the corrections checked for me in the original by Prof. Luigi Lehnus.

F   Venice, Biblioteca Nazionale Marciana, gr. 468. Turyn 360, Matthiessen 47–8, Mastronarde 5–6. *c.*1290–1300. Collated from microfilm and from the original.

[The original scribe, acting as rubricator and glossator, made many corrections and retouched many letters, in brown ink. In order to distinguish these corrections from those made *in scribendo*, I label the latter F^{1c}, the former F^2. A few corrections were made by a glossator using pink ink (F^3).]

G   Milan, Biblioteca Ambrosiana, L 39 sup. Turyn 342, Matthiessen 42–3, Mastronarde 6–7, Eberline 15–16. c.1320 (so Turyn; the date confirmed by watermarks, according to Günther). Collated from microfilm and from the original. [Corrections were made by the original scribe, both *in scribendo* and while acting as glossator and rubricator: I have labelled all these G^{1c}. A few later corrections were made by G^{2}.]

K   Florence, Biblioteca Medicea-Laurenziana, conv. soppr. 66. Turyn 338, Matthiessen 40–1, Eberline 11. c.1291 (Matthiessen, *Scriptorium* 36 [1982] 255–8). Lines 1–1681. Collated from microfilm and from the original. [All corrections are by the first hand, made either *in scribendo* or during the writing of the scholia. Many of the corrections are *in rasura*, and these are difficult to detect.]

L   Florence, Biblioteca Medicea-Laurenziana, plut. 32.2. Turyn 222–58, Matthiessen 39–40, Mastronarde 7. Facsimile: J. A. Spranger, *Euripidis quae inveniuntur in codice Laurentiano pl. XXXII, 2...* (1920). 1300–20. Collated from the facsimile and from the original. [Most of the corrections, other than those of the first hand, are made in a dark black ink (L^{2}). Towards the beginning of the play a hand using a light grey ink has added glosses and made a few corrections: I have also labelled this hand L^{2}.]

Mn   Munich, Bayerische Staatsbibliothek, gr. 560. Turyn 344, Matthiessen 128, Mastronarde 7. 14th century (first half?). Lines 1–54, 107–1693. Collated from microfilm.

Mt   Madrid, Biblioteca Nacional, 4677. Turyn 339–40, Mastronarde 7–8. c.1300 (N. G. Wilson, *JHS* 96 [1976] 172). Lines 1277–1693. Collated from microfilm.

P   Florence, Biblioteca Medicea-Laurenziana, conv. soppr. 172. Turyn 260–4, Matthiessen 41, Mastronarde 8, O. L. Smith, *Mnemosyne* 35 (1982) 326–31. Facsimile: J. A. Spranger, *Euripidis quae in codicibus Palatino Graeco inter Vaticanos 287 et Laurentiano Conv. Soppr. 172... inveniuntur* (1939–46). c.1320–5. Collated from the facsimile and from the original.

Pr   Reims, Bibliothèque de la ville, 1306. Turyn 354–5,

THE MANUSCRIPTS 9

Matthiessen 45, Mastronarde 8. *c*.1290–1300. Collated from microfilm.

R Vatican, Biblioteca Apostolica Vaticana, gr. 1135. Turyn 94–6, Matthiessen 47, Mastronarde 8–9. Middle or late 13th century. Collated from photographs and from the original. [Corrections made *in scribendo* I have labelled R^{1c}. There are many corrections and variants written by the hand which wrote glosses: I have called this hand R^2, although it is probably the hand of the original scribe. Other corrections and glosses, which may have been written by one or more further hands, I have also labelled R^2.]

Rf Florence, Biblioteca Medicea-Laurenziana, plut. 32.33. Turyn 337–8, Matthiessen 40, Mastronarde 9. *c*.1290–1300. Collated from microfilm and from the original. [A heavily corrected manuscript. Most of the corrections were made by the original scribe (Rf^{1c}), but on more than one occasion, as the varying colour of the ink indicates.]

Rw Vienna, Österreichische Nationalbibliothek, phil. gr. 119. Turyn 361–2, Matthiessen 48, Mastronarde 9. *c*.1300. Collated from microfilm.

Ry Manchester, John Rylands Library, Gaster 1689. G. Zuntz, *Latinitas* 4 (1966) 284–8 (=*Opuscula Selecta* [1972] 62–8), *Bulletin of the John Rylands Library* 49 (1967) 497–517, Schartau I. Perhaps late (Wilson, Günther) rather than middle (Zuntz) 14th century. Lines 13–156, 206–375. Collated from slides loaned by Prof. Zuntz.

S Salamanca, Biblioteca Universitaria, 31. Turyn 96, Matthiessen 45, Mastronarde 9–10. Dated 1326. Collated from microfilm. [A very carelessly written manuscript: scholia interrupt the text, lines and words are omitted, division between verses is casual, and some parts of the lyrics are written as prose.]

Sa Vatican, Biblioteca Apostolica Vaticana, gr. 1345. Turyn 96–7, Matthiessen 47, Mastronarde 10. *c*.1300. Collated from photographs and from the original. [A few corrections were made by the rubricator (Sa^r), who added (for parts of the play only) *personarum notae* and glosses. It is possible that all other corrections, glosses, and variants were written by the first hand. But I have distinguished those written at the time of writing the text (Sa¹ᶜ) from those made (as the colour of the ink indicates) later (Sa²).]

Tp Parma, Biblioteca Palatina, Fondo Parmense 154. Turyn 149–50. Transcript of the lyrics and scholia thereon: O. L. Smith, *Scholia metrica anonyma in Euripidis Hecubam, Orestem, Phoenissas* (1977). Dated *c.*1350–75 by Günther, on the basis of watermarks; *c.*1350–60 by Schartau, *ICS* 6.2 [1981] 223–4. Reports taken from Smith.

Va Vatican, Biblioteca Apostolica Vaticana, Palatinus gr. 98. Turyn 91–2, Matthiessen 45–6. 14th century. Apograph of V (but it had access to other sources: Matthiessen 126–8), containing the portion missing in V (1205–1504). Collated from photographs and from the original.

(iii) *Manuscripts with (for the most part) Moschopoulean scholia*

X Oxford, Bodleian Library, Auct. F.3.25. Turyn 42–3, Matthiessen 48, Mastronarde 10–11. *c.*1330–40. Collated from photographs and from the original.

Xa Oxford, Bodleian Library, Barocci 120. Turyn 98, Matthiessen 48, Mastronarde 11, N. G. Wilson, *Mediaeval Greek Bookhands* (1972–3) 30–1 (plates 64–5). *c.* 1320–30. Collated from photographs and from the original.

Xb Florence, Biblioteca Medicea-Laurenziana, conv. soppr. 71. Turyn 98–9, Matthiessen 48, Mastronarde 11. Early 14th century (*c.*1310–20 Günther, on the basis of watermarks). Collated from microfilm and from the original.

Xc Cambridge, Corpus Christi College, 403. Turyn 123. Late 15th century. Collated from the original.

Xd Paris, Bibliothèque Nationale, Coislin 169. Turyn 148–9, Mastronarde 172. Early 14th century (*c.*1320, according to P. Henry, *Études Plotiniennes: II, Les manuscrits des Ennéades* [1941] 97–101). Lines 1–163 (– ἐδίκαϲε), 898–1693. Collated from the original (I ignore lines 164–897, which are a later replacement).

Xe Paris, Bibliothèque Nationale, gr. 2795. Turyn 141. 14th century. Collated (for only a selection of readings) from the original.

Xf Paris, Bibliothèque Nationale, gr. 2801. Turyn 142,

Mastronarde 171. 15th century. Collated (for only a selection of readings) from the original.

Xg   Paris, Bibliothèque Nationale, gr. 2802. Turyn 142. 15th century. Collated (for only a selection of readings) from the original.

Xh   Paris, Bibliothèque Nationale, gr. 2803. Turyn 142–3. 15th century. Collated (for only a selection of readings) from the original.

Ad   Athos, Μονὴ Διονυσίου, 334. Turyn 121–2, Matthiessen 37–8, Mastronarde 13–14. 15th century or later. Collated from microfilm.

An   Paris, Bibliothèque Nationale, suppl. gr. 393. Turyn 149, Matthiessen 19, 129–30, Mastronarde 15, 172. Late 15th century. Lines 1–771, 879–1026. Collated from microfilm. This manuscript was corrected for the use of the printer of the Aldine edition (M. Sicherl, *RhM* 118 [1975] 202–25).

At   Athos, Μονὴ Βατοπεδίου, 671. Turyn 121, Mastronarde 14. 1420–43. Collated from microfilm.

Dr   Dresden, Sächsische Landesbibliothek, Da.22. Turyn 124. 15th century; now lost. Reports taken from Beck's edition, vol. iii (1788) 1032–46 (= his D).

J   Cambridge, University Library, Nn.3.13. Turyn 206–8, Matthiessen 50. 15th century. Collated from the original.

Ms   Moscow, Gosudarstvennyĭ Istoricheskiĭ Muzeĭ (*olim* Moskovskaia Sinodalnaia Biblioteka), gr. 508. Turyn 343–4, Matthiessen 43. 15th century. Reports taken from Beck's edition, vol. iii (1788) 1032–46 (= his A).

Th   Thessalonike, Γυμνάσιον, unnumbered. Turyn 151–2, Mastronarde 172–3. 16th century; now lost. Reports taken from P. N. Pappageorgiou, Ἀθήναιον 10 (1881) 286–309.

(iv) *Manuscripts with Thoman scholia*

Z   Cambridge, University Library, Nn.3.14 (ff. 1–121). Turyn 44–7, Matthiessen 50, Mastronarde 11, Smith, *Studies* 225 n. 109, *Cl&Med* 31 (1970 [1976] 27–35), *GRBS* 17 (1976) 75–80, *Cl&Med* 32 (1980) 35–43. Dated *c.*1310–20 by Smith on the evidence of watermarks, which does not appear to be conclusive. Dated *c.*1330–50 by Wilson (as reported by

Mastronarde) on the evidence of the script. Collated from the original.

[The rubricator (Z^r) added variants and glosses and made some corrections in the text. Many corrections were made, often *in rasura*, either by the original scribe or by the writer of the scholia (Z^{1c}). A few corrections were made by a later hand (Z^2).]

Za   London, British Library, Arundel 540. Turyn 99–100, Matthiessen 50–1, Schartau, *ICS* 6.2 (1981) 240 n. 7. Middle of the 15th century. A twin of Z. Collated (for only a selection of readings) from the original.

Zb   Vatican, Biblioteca Apostolica Vaticana, gr. 51. Turyn 100–1, Matthiessen 51, Mastronarde 11–12, Smith, *Studies* 81 n. 56, *Cl&Med* 23 (1981–2) 260 n. 18. *c.*1320–30. Lines 1–275a, 368–809, 863–1693. Collated from photographs and from the original.

[There are several correcting hands, which I distinguish as follows: Zb^2 the main glossator (red); Zb^3 either (*a*) a cruder hand (light brown), which also added some glosses, or (*b*) a hand using dark grey ink; Zb^4 a hand using dark black ink, which made a few corrections towards the end of the play and wrote *ιαμβικοί* in the margin at 1554 (see Matthiessen, Plate VIII). Matthiessen identifies this last hand as that of Triclinius, and it certainly looks like his; doubts are expressed by Smith, *Cl&Med* (cited above), and by Günther, who observes that pupils sometimes modelled their script on that of their master.]

Zc   Copenhagen, Det Kongelige Bibliotek, Gamle Kongelig Samling 3549. Turyn 180–1, Matthiessen 51, Mastronarde 12, Schartau I *passim*, II 52–65. *c.*1315–25 (Irigoin, Zuntz, Wilson *apud* Mastronarde) rather than *c.*1305 (Turyn, Schartau)? Lines 1–1657, 1688–93. Collated from microfilm.

Zd   Cambridge, University Library, Nn.3.14 (ff. 122–207). Turyn 180, Matthiessen 51. 15th century. Collated from the original.

Zm   Milan, Biblioteca Ambrosiana, I 47 sup. Turyn 182, Matthiessen 51, Mastronarde 12, Smith, *Cl&Med* 31 (1970 [1976]) 18 n. 21. 14th century (*c.*1310–20 Günther, on the basis of watermarks). Collated from microfilm and from the original.

[The scribe made many corrections *in scribendo*; these are often impossible to detect on microfilm, and only a much lengthier examination of the original than I was able to make would reveal their full extent. Consequently some readings which I attribute to Zm are likely to have been written by Zm^{1c}. The scribe added marginal scholia and glosses on two separate occasions (as the different colours of ink indicate) and made corrections in the text on both occasions (these also I label Zm^{1c}). A few corrections which I have labelled Zm^c or Zm^2 were not certainly, but may have been, made by the original scribe.]

Zu   Uppsala, Universitetsbibliotek, gr. 15. Turyn 185–6, Matthiessen 52, Mastronarde 12. First half of 14th century. Collated from microfilm.

Zv   Vatican, Biblioteca Apostolica Vaticana, gr. 1824. Turyn 359–60, Mastronarde, *GRBS* 26 (1985) 99–102. 14th century. Lines 1385–1591. Collated from photographs and from the original.

(v) *The edition of Triclinius*

T   Rome, Biblioteca Angelica, gr. 14. Turyn 23–52, Matthiessen 52–3, Mastronarde 13. *c.*1300–25. Collated from the original.
     [The symbol T^z designates the original scribe (*c.*1300–10), who wrote lines 1–144, 225–96, 374–771, 841–949, 1024–1239, 1576–1681. The symbol T^t designates Triclinius, the three stages of whose activity in this manuscript I distinguish as T^{t1} (*c.*1315), T^{t2} (*c.*1319–25), T^{t3} (*c.*1325). T^{t1} wrote lines 772–98, 1683–93; T^{t3} wrote lines 145–224, 297–373, 799–840, 950–1023, 1240–1575, 1682.]

Ta   Vatican, Biblioteca Apostolica Vaticana, Urbinas gr. 142. Turyn 194–6, Matthiessen 53, Mastronarde 13, Smith, *Studies* 46–7. 14th century (middle?). A copy of T, or possibly a copy of a copy of T (Mastronarde, *GRBS* 26 [1985] 104–6). Collated from photographs.

(vi) *Gnomologies*

gV   Athos, Μονὴ Βατοπεδίου, 36. Turyn 92–3, Matthiessen 37,
Mastronarde 2–3. 12th century. Reports taken from G. A.
Longman, *CQ* n.s. 9 (1959) 129–41. Lines 1–4, 70 ἄπορον–,
100, 108, 126–7, 232, 236, 251–2, 300, 340, 388, 390, 413,
424, 450–1, 454–5, 542–3, 602–6, 638–41, 666–8, 670, 737,
772, 792–ἀνδρός, 794 ὄκνος–, 823–4, 1034, 1082–3, 1155–7,
1161–2, 1175–6, 1182, 1523.

gB   Vatican, Biblioteca Apostolica Vaticana, Barberinianus gr. 4.
Turyn 93 n. 151, Matthiessen 45 and *Hermes* 93 (1965)
148–58, Mastronarde 173. *c.*1300. Collated for me from
microfilm by Prof. Matthiessen. Lines 234 μεταβολή–, 236,
279, 283, 310–ἄφιλος, 314–15, 340, 390, 393, 397 σοφόν–,
417, 424, 426 τό–, 428, 448–51, 454–5, 478 τὸ μέλλον–, 484
εἰ–, 488, 542–3, 602–6, 665–70, 694–7, 702–3, 708–10, 727
πιστός–728, 735 κοινά–, 737, 754, 768, 772–3, 786 ὡς–, 792
–ἀνδρός, 794 ὄκνος–, 804–8, 859–60, 870, 895–7, 903–4
Ἀργεῖος, 907–13, 919, 976–81, 1022–4, 1043, 1072 τί–, 1084,
1103 ὡς–, 1155–7, 1161 παύσομαι–1162, 1175–6, 1179,
1204–6, 1215, 1407 ἔρροι–ῶν, 1509, 1514, 1522–3, 1527–8,
1545 τέλος–θέληι, 1552–3 δεινὸν–πράσσοντας, 1577 ἀνάγκη–,
1590, 1659 ὁ–, 1676–7 εὐγενὴς–cύ, 1691–3.

gE   El Escorial, Real Monastero de San Lorenzo, X.1.13. Turyn
93 n. 151, Matthiessen 38 and *Hermes* 94 (1966) 398–410,
Mastronarde 174. Early 14th century. Collated for me from
microfilm by Prof. Matthiessen. Lines 1–4, 7, 10–11, 14 τί–,
16–17, 26–7, 34, 42–5, 59 εἰc–, 62, 68 ὡc–70, 75, 81 τί–, 84,
99, 126–7, 130, 132–3 πάρεισι–ξυνωιδοί, 136 ἡςύχωι–139,
170–1, 174–5, 180–1, 201–4, 213–16, 221–6, 229–30, 232,
234 μεταβολή–, 236–8, 243–4, 247–52 (om. εἰc τὸν ψόγον),
253 ὄμμα–254, 255 ἱκετεύω–256, 259, 266 τίν'–269, 271, 280,
283–4, 285 Λοξίαι–287, 297–300, 305 cὲ–306, 319–20, 328,
340, 348–51, 354 εὐτυχίαι–359, 381, 385 τί–, 387, 390, 393
φείδου–, 395–6, 397 σοφόν–398, 410, 412–13, 420, 426 τό–,
428, 450–2, 454–6, 466 (οἷc), 467–9, 482, 484–7, 504–6, 510
(εἰ φ- φ-), 511, 517, 523–5, 540–3, 546–51, 559 ἐμαυτόν–560,
572–8, 585–90, 600–4, 627 μηδὲ–628, 638 ἔcτι–639, 652–3,
665–8, 670–2 ἥκω, 678–9, 688–90, 692 εἰ–702, 706–7, 709

δεῖ–713, 715 νῦν–718, 722, 725, 727–8, 732–5, 737, 740–3, 754, 758 ὁ–, 768, 772–3, 792–3 ἐμῆς, 803–6, 816–17 προλείπει, 827–33, 856, 859–60, 870, 875–6, 883, 889 ὑπὸ–, 891–2 καλοὺς–ἐλίccων, 895–7, 902–10, 918–22, 928–9, 935 εἰ–938, 950–2 cὺν–πρόcοψιc, 979–81, 1013, 1022–4, 1031–2, 1043–4, 1049 ὦ φίλον–, 1069–71 ἕν–προcήκει, 1072, 1082, 1084–5, 1110 ἔχει–1116, 1134–42, 1153–7 (om. φεῦ), 1169–71 οὐ–ἀφήcω, 1175–6, 1200–8, 1214 πέλαc–1215, 1222 ἐπί–1223, 1244 εἷc–1245, 1257, 1287, 1302–3 ὄλλυτε, 1308 ὅθι–ἔπεcε, 1316–18, 1330, 1341–4 ἐμόν, 1345–ἐμοί, 1347 cιγᾶν–1348, 1393, 1403–7, 1483–9, 1509, 1514–15, 1523–4 cύνεcιc, 1552–3 δεινὸν–πράccοντας, 1554–5, 1576–7, 1581, 1587, 1590, 1592–3, 1599, 1613, 1614a, 1615a, 1623–5, 1627, 1650 θεοί–, 1667–70, 1675–7, 1691–3.

CHAPTER III

The *Veteres* (HMBOV) and Associates

(i) *The truth in HMBOV*

Very rarely is the truth preserved uniquely by a single member of
HMBOV:[1] 242 νεῶν] νεώς O, [H]; 265 εἰc] ἐc B, [H]; 693
προcήκομεν] προήκ- V (~V³), [H]; 710 cώζειν] cώιζ- M, [H]; 995
ἠϊόcιν] αἰόcιν O (~O¹ˢ), [H]; 1531 εἴcω] ἔcω V, [H].

And rarely is the truth preserved uniquely by two members: 667
χρή] δεῖ B¹ˢV, [H]; 1127 ἐκκλείcομεν] -κλήϊc- MB, [H]; 1491 ἔτεκε]
-κεν MB.

Occasionally the truth is preserved by two members of
HMBOV in combination with only one other manuscript, or
uniquely or nearly uniquely in a majority of HMBOV (but never
uniquely in all): 128 ἀπέθριcε] -cεν MBO; 238 ἐριννύεc] ἐριννέc
M⟨B⟩OC (~B²), [H]; 602 καθεcτᾶcι] -cιν BOG; 970 cτρατηλατῶν]
-τᾶν MOVC, [H]; 1264 εἶτ᾽ ἐπ᾽ ἄλλην] εἶτα πάλιν MBOC (~B²B³),
[H]; 1468 χρυcεοcάνδαλον] -cάμβαλον fere HM²⟨B⟩CK (~ fere
M¹ᶜB²).

(ii) *HMBOV as a group*

The true readings just quoted, unique or nearly unique to members of HMBOV, show that a connection exists among these
manuscripts. This connection may be further illustrated by several
unique, or nearly unique, errors shared by a majority of HMBOV:
2 cυμφορὰ θεήλατοc] -ὰν -ον M⟨B⟩O¹ᵞᵖVC (~M²BᶜV¹ˢ), [H]; 140
λεπτὸν] λευκὸν ⟨HB⟩OV (~HᶜB²O¹ᵞᵖV³ᵞᵖ) et ᵞᵖK¹R¹ξ¹Tᵗ¹/²; 349
πολλῇ(ι) δ᾽] πολλὴ δ᾽ M¹ᶜC, πολῆ δ᾽ V (~V¹ᶜ), πολὺ δ᾽ HMBOK¹ᶜ
(~B²O¹ᶜ) et ¹Σᵛ et Σᵛ; 757 κρινεῖ] κρίνει ⟨H⟩MBOC (~B³); 919 κά-
γορᾶc] -αῖc HOVC (~OᶜV²/³) et Abᶜ; 990 πελάγεcι] -εccι
MBOP¹ᶜ(T¹³), [H];[2] 1051 πάρα] ἄρα MBV (~M²B³V²/³), [H]; 1534
cώζειν θέλει (-ηι)] cώcη(ι) θανεῖν M¹ᵞᵖB¹ᵞᵖV, cώζη θανεῖν Cᵞᵖ;[3] 1644
ὑπερβαλ(λ)όνθ᾽ ὄρουc] -λόντ᾽ ὄρουc MOVMtᵘᵛ (~V²Mtᶜ²), -λλόντ᾽
ὄ- C, [H].

---

[1] I am concerned only with the readings of the first hand.

[2] πελάγεccι may, however, be right: see pp. 138–9.

[3] Again, cώcηι θανεῖν may be right.

In addition there are numerous errors unique, or nearly unique, to two of HMBOV: 58 ὑπ᾽] ὑφ᾽ MOCr, [H]; 68 τά γ᾽] τάχ᾽ OVC (~O¹ˢV¹ᶜ), [H]; 204 στοναχαῖcι] -άχεcι HM (-έcι M²); 208 παροῦσα παρθέν᾽ Ἠλέκτρα] παροῦc᾽ ἠλ- π- HM (~M¹ᶜ); 314 νοcῆ(ι)c] νοcήcη(ι)c HMC; 372 χερcὶ] -cὶν MO; 577 δοίη] δοίηι MO; 769 μενέλεω] -εωι MO, [H]; 785 ταῦτ᾽] ταῦθ᾽ MOC, [H]; 861 ἐν ἀργείοιc M+: ἀργείοιc V+: ἐν ἀργείων ⟨B²⟩O: ἀργείων Bᶜ+, [H];[4] 876 ἀνεπτέρωκε] -κεν BO, [H]; 940 δή] δεῖ OV (~V²ᐟ³ˢ); 954 δεῖ λιπεῖν cε] οὔ c᾽ ὁρᾶν δεῖ ʸᵖM¹B¹C, [H]; 1001 τό (τε) πτερωτὸν] τὸ τέτρωρον M¹ʸᵖBAaC (~ʸᵖB¹Aaʳ); 1062 πόλει] πατρόc ʸᵖM¹B¹, [H]; 1112 οἴουc] οἴουc MOAb, [H]; 1245 ὀφείλεται] -ετε M²O (~M¹ᶜ²O¹ˢ), [H]; 1335 (ἐπαξίοι)cí τ᾽ἄρ᾽O+: -cιν ἄρ᾽Va+: -cιν γὰρ MB, [H]; 1401 διδύμω] -μωι MOMt;[5] 1518 cίδηροc] cίδαροc HVP; 1537 ἰὼ ἰὼ τύχα] ἰὼ τύχα ἰὼ τύχα OV; 1620 τειχέων] τεκτόνων M¹ʸᵖO, [H]; 1621 κτίται] κτίcται BO (~Bᶜ ᵘᵛ), [H]; 1632 πρὸc cέθεν] προcέθεν MVC, [H].

(iii) *The relative value of HMBOV*

In an attempt to assess the value of HMBOV, relative to each other, I have tabulated all the readings in which one or more of HMBOV (or Va, where V is missing) disagree with the others. The number of readings is 781; H is present for 300 of these.[6] In classifying readings as right or wrong, I use my own judgement. Since the number of readings at issue is sufficiently large, a few disputable judgements ought not to distort the overall picture.

(iii *a*) I begin by ignoring H and examine the relationships among themselves of MBOV in these 781 readings. Each of MBOV may share the truth with other manuscripts when the remaining three are in error (O × 29, V × 28, M × 22, B × 16). MBOV have the following numbers of unique errors: B 4, M 26, O 65, V 69. They share the following numbers of errors with other manuscripts: B 35, O 79, M 92, V 163. From these figures, B emerges as much the least prone to error, V as much the most prone. M and O occupy an intermediate position: M is much less prone to unique errors than O, but exceeds O in shared errors. By

---

[4] Here, and in what follows, the symbol + indicates that a reading is found in other manuscripts.

[5] The transmitted text is doubtful both as language and as metre, and διδύμωι could be right, if a word such as ⟨ῥυθμῶι⟩ has been lost after it: see *CQ* n.s. 40 (1990) 120 n. 98.

[6] I have excluded the second hypothesis (which is absent from O) and a few *minutiae*.

far the most prone to shared errors is V. We shall see later that V is associated with a group of manuscripts (to be called Θ), which have no such close association with M or B or O.

The frequency of agreements between two of MBOV is: MB 56 (right 39, wrong 17), BV 51 (right 31, wrong 20), MO 50 (right 24, wrong 26), BO 46 (right 35, wrong 11), OV 44 (right 17, wrong 27), MV 44 (right 12, wrong 32).[7] No one of the six possible combinations of MBOV is significantly more common or less common than any other. But of these six combinations three are more often right than wrong (MB 39~17, BO 35~11, BV 31~20), one has an almost equal proportion of right and wrong (MO 24~26), and two are much less often right than wrong (OV 17~27, MV 12~32). The common factor in the combinations where right predominates is B, in the combinations where wrong predominates the common factor is V.

The numbers of right as opposed to wrong readings in each manuscript in these 781 readings are: B 613~168, M 512~269, O 504~277, V 399~382. The percentage of right is: B 78·5%, M 65·5%, O 64·5%, V 51·1%.

A consistent picture has emerged: B is the most reliable of these manuscripts, V the least reliable. Between M and O there is little to choose. The relationships between MBOV are too complex to be represented by stemmatic means.[8]

(iii *b*) In the 300 readings where one or more of HMBOV disagree with the remainder, H has the truth twice, when MBOV are in error: 204 γόοιϲ] γόοιϲι H[uv]Π[5]; 1540 cίγ'] cίγ' H+. H opposes MBOV in 14 shared errors and 25 unique errors.

No very clear picture of affiliation between H and members of MBOV is discernible in these 300 readings. H agrees with M against BOV (whether or not BOV share the same reading) in 17 readings (2 right), with V in 14 (1 right), with O in 5 (1 right), with B in 2 (both wrong). H agrees with each of MBOV (however many of these four share the same reading as H) in the following numbers of readings: with M in 179, with B in 178, with O in 152, with V in 123.

In these 300 readings the proportion of right to wrong is: B 254~46 (84·7%), O 213~87 (71%), M 206~94 (68·7%), H 170~130

---

[7] For agreements between these pairs in *Hec.* see Matthiessen 62–3, in *Ph.* Mastronarde 35–6.   [8] Mastronarde 36 offers a tentative stemma in *Ph.*

(56·7%), V 151~149 (50·3%). These percentages should be compared with those obtained for MBOV in the whole play. There, as
here, B and V occupy the ends of the scale, and M and O occupy
the middle. On the evidence of these 300 readings H, although our
oldest manuscript, is less reliable than M or B or O.[9]

The following histogram (Figure 1) shows the results which
have been achieved. The shaded area shows the numbers of true
readings achieved by each manuscript in the 300 readings for
which H is present. The additional unshaded area advances the
numbers to those achieved by MBOV in the 781 readings for
which they are present.

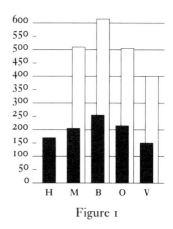

Figure 1

(iv) *Associates of HMBOV: C, Cr, gV*

(*a*) The manuscript which is most closely associated with
HMBOV is C. Several unique, or nearly unique, agreements between C and two or more of HMBOV were quoted above (under
(ii) and (iii)). C is very closely linked to M: 168 ἐλάcαcα super θωύξαc (sic) M¹ʸᵖ, super θωύξαc' ἔβαλεc Cʸᵖ;[10] 224 κόραιc] νόcω(ι)
Π⁶M¹ʸᵖCʸᵖ; 238 ἑῶcι(ν) c'] ἑῶcιν MCR; 303 λουτρά τ'] λούτρ' M,
λουτρ'C; 362 μαλέα(ι)] μαλέαν M (~Mᶜ), μελέαν C; 429 νόμουc] νόμον MCZmZu; 485 ἐν βαρβάροιc] ἀφ' Ἑλλάδοc ʸᵖM¹CV³; 585 τοι
om. MC (~C²ˢ ᵘᵛ); 629 πρόcπολοι] -οc MC (~M²ᐟ³C²); 704 δὲ τυν-

---

[9] For H in *Hec.* and *Ph.*, in both of which it is available for fewer lines than in *Or.*, see
Matthiessen 61, Mastronarde 38.
[10] ἔλαcαc (Willink, prompted by Longman) is likely to be right.

δάρεών τέ cοι] δ' ἐγώ cοι τ- ᵞᵖM¹C;¹¹ 709 ἀcτοί] αὐτοί MC
(~M²C²); 724 cωτηρίαc] cυμφορὰc M¹ᵞᵖ, τῆc cυμφορᾶc Cᵞᵖ (cυμφορᾶc V³ˢ); 787 ἦ] ἤ MC; 823 μεγάλη] ποικίλα M¹ᵞᵖ, ποικίλλα Cᵞᵖ
(ποικίλη T¹³); 955 c' ἐπωφέληcεν] cε ὠφ- ᵞᵖM¹C; 959 εἰc] εἰ MC;
964 καλλίπαιc] καλὴ παῖc M¹ᵞᵖC¹ˢ; 1031 μοι uel μὴ uel om.] μου
MC; 1050 τάδ'] τί δ' MC (~M²), τ✻δ' B (~B³); 1272 ἐχθροῖc εἶ]
-οῖcι MCAa; 1302 καίνετε] καίνυτε MC; 1302–3 θείνετε super πέμπετε M¹ᵞᵖ, in marg. post ὄλλυτε Cᵞᵖ (in textu post καίνετε
AbMnRwS, post φονεύετε R);¹² 1358 καθαιμακτὸν] καθαίμακτον
MᵘᵛCRw (καθ' αἱμακτὸν M²ᐟ³ᵘᵛO).

C does not descend in a direct line from M. Probably it descends
from an ancestor related to HMBOV, but related most closely to
M.¹³ For it shares with one or more of HBOV a few unique, or
nearly unique, readings absent from M: 68 τά γ'] τάχ' OVC
(~O¹ˢV¹ᶜ); 131 θ' om. HC (~H²); 132 αἴδ'] αἴδ' H²C, ✻✻δ' H; 338 ὅ
c'] ὅc HC (ὅc c' O¹ᶜV²³GL et ᵞᵖΣᵐᶜ); 681 οἶοc] ὅcοc CᵞᵖΣᵛᵞᵖ; 919
κἀγορᾶc] -αῖc HOVC (~OᶜV²ᐟ³) et Abᶜ; 989 cτόλωι] πώλω(ι)
B¹ᵞᵖC; 1005 δρόμημα] δράμημα BCA, δραμήματα M+; 1118 λέγειc]
-η(ι)c OC; 1198 κρατῶν] -τῆ HC.

(*b*) Cr shows a connection with O:¹⁴ 34 νοεῖ] ante νόcωι O, om.
Cr;¹⁵ 47 τινὰ] τινὰc OCr; 96 φέρουc'] βαλοῦc' O, βάλλουc' Cr; 170
οὐκ (alterum)] οὐδ' OCrAa³²; 233 γαίαc uel γαίηc] γαῖαν OCr; 320
δάκρυcι] δακρύοιcι OCr; 396 cύνοιδα] ξύν- OCr; 709 λέγω] λέγειν
OCr (-ει S); 795 ποδόc] ποδῶν OCr; 812 ἔριc] post ἀρνόc O, om. Cr;
934 οὐδὲν om. OCr; 942 cπάνιc] post γενήcεται OCr (post τόλμηc
C); 1286 εἰcακούουc(ιν)] εἰcακούετ' M²²OCr.¹⁶

---

¹¹ δ' (not γάρ, as Schwartz reports) is the reading of M¹ᵞᵖ. To Willink's argument in
favour of the variant may be added the observation that the name Τυνδάρεωc elsewhere in
Euripides occupies the position after the penthemimeral caesura (249, 457, *El.* 1018, *Hel.*
17, 568, [*IA* 67, 78], *IA* 1031, 1155) or after the hepthemimeral (459, 915, [*IA* 55]).
¹² C actually has γρ. καὶ θείνετε τὰ δύο, and Di Benedetto ought not to have emended
τὰ to τά‹c›, for τὰ δύο is a gloss (appearing as such in MBO) on δίπτυχα δίcτομα.
¹³ Turyn's claim (318–19) that MOC form a group derived from a common source in
Or. and *Ph.* (C is absent in *Hec.*) is rightly rejected by Matthiessen 62. See also Mastronarde
48.   ¹⁴ Similarly in *Hec.* (Matthiessen 73–4) and *Ph.* (Mastronarde 49).
¹⁵ Omission and transposition often go hand in hand in related manuscripts. I have illustrated this phenomenon in *CQ* n.s. 33 (1983) 352–3, and I shall often have occasion to
draw attention to it again (see pp. 37 n. 3, 37 n. 4, 38 n. 6, 39 n. 8, 70 n. 9, 74 n. 19, 113
n. 7, 117 n. 8, 127 n. 20). For the present let it be illustrated by two manuscripts which can
be shown to be very closely related, FSa (see p. 23): 1030 c'] ante ἐχρῆν F, om. Sa; 1063 cέ
δ'] δέ c' F, δ' Sa; 1065 Πυλάδη] post φόνου Sa, om. F (super τοῦ F²).
¹⁶ For a much smaller number of agreements between Cr and M or B or V see below,
p. 39.

(*c*) The early date of gV (the gnomologium Vatopedianum) associates it with HMBOV. But evidence for a special connection
between gV and any one member of HMBOV is lacking.[17]

In the 56 lines for which gV is present, the number of readings
in which one or more of (H)MBOV disagree with the remainder is
29; H is present for 17 of these. The numbers of agreements between gV and individual members of HMBOV (however many
other members have the same reading) are: (out of 29) MgV 21,
OgV 21, BgV 18, VgV 15; (out of 17) HgV 10. gV is right in 21 of
these readings, wrong in 8.

There are few agreements between gV and single members of
HMBOV: two with O, one with M, one with V. These agreements
are: 2 συμφορὰ θεήλατος OgV (et M²BᶜV¹ˢ+): -ὰν -ον M‹B›O¹ʸᵖVC;
388 μ' om. MgV+; 1182 μέλλειν] λέγειν OgV+ (et Vᵍˡ); 1523 ὁρῶν]
ὁρᾶν VgV+.

Twice gV agrees with other manuscripts against (H)MBOV:
794 φίλοις] φίλοισι gVgBAdAtLRwZZc et (postea del.) P¹ˢ; 1161
κοὐκ] οὐκ gVAdCr. The (unmetrical) reading in 794 is probably an
old error and not a corruption which has arisen independently in
the later manuscripts. The error at 1161 should not be taken as
evidence that any connection exists between gV and AdCr:
gnomologia commonly omit or alter connecting particles (thus 823
δ' αὖ] γὰρ gV; 824 τ' om. gV).[18]

(*d*) I postpone until later consideration of the claim which might
be made that a connection exists between Ad and MO.[19]

[17] Mastronarde 38 reaches a similar conclusion for *Ph*.
[18] See also Mastronarde 71–2. For the same fault in gBgE see below, p. 113 n. 2.
[19] See pp. 66–9.

CHAPTER IV

Θ

There exists a class, which I shall call Θ, consisting of AbFMnPrR SSa. This class may be subdivided into three pairs: FSa; AbR; MnS. Pr is a twin of Sa for about 400 lines; for the rest of the play it adheres now to FSa, now to AbR, now to MnS.[1]

(i) *FSa*

FSa share about 40 unique errors (they are particularly prone to omission and transposition). Here is a selection: hyp. 2.10 καταστροφήν] κατασκευήν FSa; 44 ὧν post ἔμφρων add. FSa; 83 ἄυπνος πάρεδρος] π- ἄ- FSa; 527 μαcτὸν] -οὐc FSa; 694 ἔλοι τιc] τίc ἔλοιτ' FSa; 784 ἄν γε] δέ FSa; 845 λύccηι] νόcω FSa (~Sa^{γρ}); 917 ἔλεγε τῶιδ'] τῶδ' εἶπ' FSa; 1049 φίλον] φίλτατον FSa; 1131 βουλεύ(c)ομαι] βεβούλευμαι FSa; 1593 ἤν] εἴ FSa.

(ii) *AbR*

AbR share about 25 unique errors. Here is a selection: 63 ὅτ'] ὅταν AbR; 252 καὶ (prius) om. AbR; 563 ἀνόcια] -ιον AbR; 797 ἱκετεύcω με] ἱκετεύω AbR; 919 ἄcτυ] ἄcτει AbR; 1413 κεῖθεν] ἔνθεν AbR (~R^{γρ}); 1477 πέτρουc uel -αc] -αν AbR (-ουc Ab^{IS}); 1514 δειλίαι] -λῆ(ι) AbR.

(iii) *MnS*

MnS share more than 80 unique errors.[2] Here is a selection: hyp. 1.14 ταύτην] τ- τὴν ἑρμιόνην MnS; 9–10 inuerso ordine MnS; 412 οἷc] οἷc γ' MnS; 802 coι post φίλοc add. MnS; 882 φίλωι om. MnS; 1338 μέγ' ὀλβίαι] μεγαλοβία MnS (~Mn^{γρ}); 1365 ἔφερεν post ἴλιον add. MnS; 1427 αὔραν (prius)] ἀόρον Mn, ἀόραν S; 1468 ποδὶ]

---

[1] Similar affiliations are found among these mansucripts in *Ph.*, where Pr is regularly linked to FSa (Mastronarde 38–44). In *Hec.* AbR and FSa are regularly paired, S is also associated with these manuscripts, Pr behaves rather differently, and Mn is present for only 16 lines (Matthiessen 67–77).

[2] I refer to errors which occur uniquely in the manuscripts which I have examined. Some of these errors will be shared by later manuscripts which have links with MnS. For example, Turyn (343 and 353) records that the reading at 9–10 is shared by HnPb (Matthiessen's symbols), the reading at 1512 by HnMs. I have not investigated HnPb; for Ms see below, pp. 75–6.

24   Θ

ποδιὸc MnS; 1501 ἀνόνητον] πολύπονον MnS (~Mnᵞᵖ); 1512 δι-
ώλετο] διοίχεται MnS (~Mnᵞᵖ); 1521 Γοργοῦc] -ᾱc MnS.

(iv) *AbR and MnS*

The following readings are unique or nearly unique to AbMnRS:
hyp. 2.17 καταδραθείc] κατα- cum gl. κοιμηθείc AbMnR, κοιμηθῇ
κατα- S; 468 δ᾽ post ποῖον add. AbMnRS (et ZZb); 486 ὁμόθεν]
ὁμόθετον AbMnRS (~Sᵞᵖ); 512 ταῦτα πατέρεc οἱ] π- τ- οἱ Ab
MnˢR, π- τ- MnS; 785 ἀcχάλ(λ)ων] ἀcχαλῶν AbMnRS (et J, ~Jʳ);
793 γενέcθω post ἴτω add. AbMnRS;³ 923 τὸν om. AbMnRS; 1318
περὶ] ὑπέρ AbMnRS (~Mnˢ) et Aaʳᵞᵖ; 1421 δ᾽ἐc] δὲ AbMnR²ᵘᵛS,
om. R.

And MnRS have the following unique agreements, when Ab is
missing: 1187 ὑπέρ] ὑπὸ MnRS; 1193 cε post χρή add. MnRS; 1212
εἴπερ] εἰ τάδ᾽ MnRS (~Mnᶜ); 1216 νῦν] δή MnRS; 1220 δ᾽ post
ἐλθών add. MnRS; 1243 τῇιδέ τε] καὶ τῇδέ τε MnS, καὶ τῇδέ τε
ἠλέκτρα R; 1252 εἰc] ἐc MnRS.

Sometimes three of AbMnRS share a unique agreement against
the fourth: for example hyp. 1.10 ἐπαγγειλάμενοc . . . προίεcθαι
om. MnRS; 1.13–14 Ἠλέκτρα . . . ἐπιφανεῖcαν] τὴν δὲ ἑρμιόνην
δείξαc ὁ ἀπόλλων MnRS (~Rᵞᵖ); 51 φάcγανον] -να AbRS; 787
ταῦτ᾽] τοῦτ᾽ MnRS (~ˢMnS¹); 1398 γᾶν] γαῖαν MnRS; 1407 κακ-
οῦργοc] δόλιοc AbMnᵞᵖR (~Abᵞᵖ); 1495 δωμάτων] δόμων MnRS.

(v) *Pr*

Pr is a twin of Sa between lines 1161 and 1557. In these lines they
share about 25 unique errors: for example 1161 ἐκποδών] ποδῶν
PrSa; 1233 ἐμοῦ om. PrSa; 1278 τά γ᾽] τάδ᾽ PrSa; 1341 ἡμᾶc om.
PrSa; 1459 ὄμμα] ὄμματα PrSa; 1474 τὰ post καὶ add. PrSa; 1493
ξυνήρπαcαν] ἐξ- PrSa; 1499 ἐκ δόμων] ἀν δωμάτων PrSa; 1556–7
om. PrSa (~ᵐPrSa²). They cease to be twins at some point before
1585.

It follows, as a consequence of the close association of FSa, that
FPrSa are frequently associated in 1161–1557. In these lines FPrSa
share about 20 unique errors: for example 1226 παῖc om. FPrSa;
1238 τάδε om. FPrSa (~Pr²); 1329 γε] τε FPrSa; 1368 ὅπωc] πῶc
FPrSa; 1426 ἔτυχον] ἐτύγχανον FPrSa (~Prᵍˡ).

---

³ γενέcθω is also a gloss in MB²ᐟ³JPr; cf. Hesych. I 1101 ἴτω· ἔcτω γενέcθω.

In the earlier part of the play PrSa share only one unique error (362 Μαλέαι] μελ- PrSa) and scarcely ever share a reading which is absent from all other members of Θ (hyp. 1.19 τὸν φόνον PrSa+: τοῦ φόνου AbFMnPrⁱˢRS+: τῶν φόνων Rⁱˢ+; 511 δὴ PrSa+: δὲ AbFMnRS+).

There are a few unique agreements in the earlier part of the play between Pr and FSa: 779 μολόντι] μολοῦντι F<Pr>Sa (~Prᶜ); 942 τῆς γε] τῆςδε FPrSa (et Rw); 1057 Μενέλαος] -λεως FPrSa; 1138 κάμοὶ om. FPrSa (~ˢPr²Sa²).

Pr has only one unique agreement with F (1685 ἄστρων] ἀστέρων FPrʸᵖ),[4] but it does share with F about 25 readings which are absent from the other members of Θ.

Outside of 1161–1557 Pr has several unique or nearly unique agreements with one or both of MnS, fewer with one or both of AbR:

Agreements with MnS: 390 ὄνομ'] ὄμμ' AnMnʸᵖPrʸᵖ; 400 θ'] δ' MnPr (~Prⁱˢ); 535 ὠφελεῖν τοῦτον] τ- ὠ- MnPrS; 592 στόμα νέμει] ν- cτ- MnPr; 618 -ουςα τάγ-] -ους'ἀγ- AdMnPrS;[5] 655 οὖν]μοι οὖν MnPr; 710 cε om. MnPr (~ˢMnPr¹); 724 γὰρ] μὲν MnPrS; 732 πράccειc] δράc(c)ειc ʸᵖMnPrS; 738 ἀπέδωκε] ἀπέδοτο ʸᵖMnPrS; 744 δὴ] δεῖ PrS (~Prⁱˢ); 788 ὁ θρῆνος post οὗτος add. MnS, s.l. Prᵍˡ; 1000 Ἀτρέως] ἀτρέος PrⁱˢS; 1044 χέρας] χέρα MnPrS; 1126 καὶ ante πρόcθεν add. MnPrS. In addition to these agreements, Pr shares with one or both of MnS about 20 readings which are absent from the other members of Θ.

Agreements with AbR: 133 μεταcτήcουc'] μεταναcτ- AbPr; 517 ὁ ante λαμβάνων add. Ab, s.l. PrᵍˡR¹; 527 ἐξέβαλ(λ)ε] ἐξέτεινε ʸᵖPrR¹ (et G²ˢ); 785 πατρῷον] πατρὸς AbPrʸᵖR¹ʸᵖ (et Cr). In addition to these agreements, Pr shares with one or both of AbR about 15 readings which are absent from the other members of Θ.

Pr sometimes shares a unique or nearly unique reading with all of AbMnRS or with at least one of each of the pairs AbR and MnS: 393 λέγειν κακά] κ- λ- AbMnPrRS; 622 τε] δὲ AbMnPrRS (et C²);

---

[4] Not strictly unique, for ἀστέρων is found also in the 'Moschopoulean' manuscripts Th and Xd (on which see pp. 76–8).

[5] In this line Willink appears to me to have demonstrated (as against West) that ὀνείρατ' is not acceptable; and his ὄνειδος appeals. But ὄνειδος ἀγγέλλουσα τὰ Ἀγαμέμνονος, 'publishing as a scandal/reproach τὰ Ἀγαμέμνονος', is not a fully convincing expression (in the parallel which he quotes, Andr. 1241, the attachment of Δελφοῖc to ὄνειδος makes a difference). I should take τἀγαμέμνονος (the manuscripts have τἀγ-, τ'ἀγ-, τὰ 'γ-) as τὸ Ἀγαμέμνονος, like A. ScT 539 πόλεως ὄνειδος, S. Ai. 1191 ὄνειδος Ἑλλάνων, OC 984 αὐτῆς ὄνειδος.

26   Θ

634 cυννοούμενος] ἐννο- AbMnPrRS; 638 εἶπας] εἶπες MnPrRS
(et K¹ᶜ); 731 cύγγονόν τε τὴν cὴν] τὴν cὴν cύγγονον AbMnPrRS
(~ʸᵖMnPrR²S); 760 φυλαccόμε(c)θα φρουρίοιc(ι)] φρουρίοιc φ- Ab
MnPrRS; 763 αὐτὸc] καὐτὸc MnPrRS; 894 ἐδίδου] ἐδείκνυ AbMn
PrʸᵖS (~ᵍˡMnS); 927 ἐκλιπόντα] -τας Ab¹ˢPr¹ˢR¹ˢSʸᵖ, -τες Prʸᵖ;
1031 περιβάληιc] πρὸc βάλληc R, προc(βάληιc) ʸᵖMnPrS, [Ab]; 1152
καλῶc (alterum)] κακῶc AbMnPrRS; 1573 ἐπικείμενον post cέλας
add. AbMnS, s.l. Prᵍˡ.

(vi) *MnS and FSa*

Although MnS have a much closer association with AbR than with
FSa, nevertheless MnS and FSa, or at least one member of each
pair, share a few unique or nearly unique errors (in which they may
be joined by Pr): hyp. 1.9 καθαρθέντι] -τος FS; 2.8 τῆc om. MnSSa;
2.10 τέλος ante τὸ add. SSa; 8 ὅτι om. FS; 213 ὡc εἶ coφή om.
MnSa (add. Mn¹ᶜ, ὡc λίαν εἶ c- add. Sa¹ᶜ); 368 δ'] τ'MnPrSSa; 488
πᾶν τοὐξ] πάντ'ἐξ SSa; 876 πόλιν] ὄχλον MnPrʸᵖSSa¹ʸᵖ (~Mnʸᵖ) et
M¹ʸᵖ; 1021 πανυcτάτην] πανύcτατον FMn, [AbS]; 1071 c' om.
FMnSSa (et Tᶻᵘᵛ, ~Tᶜ), [Ab]; 1117 γε] τε SSa (om. Pr); 1346
φίλοι] ἄνδρες FMnᵍˡPrSa; 1463 κακόc c'] κακόc' FS; 1678 προc-
τάccομεν] προcτάccομαι fere FMnSSa (~Sa¹ˢ), [Ab].

(vii) *AbR and FSa*

Similarly a few unique errors are shared by at least one of the pairs
AbR and FSa: hyp. 2.10 διαcκευὴ] καταcκευὴ FR²Sa, cκευὴ R; 121
τ'] δ'AbF; 882 ὥcτ'] ὡc AbFRSa; 1100 τοῦτο] -τον Ab²PrSa; 1463
ἀποκτείνει] -νη AbRSa et Pr uel Prᶜ, -κτενεῖ MʸᵖF.

(viii) *AbFMnPrRSSa*

Here is evidence that AbFMnPrRSSa form a unified group. In
these passages one or both members of all three pairs FSa, AbR,
MnS, with or without Pr, share a reading which is unique or nearly
unique: hyp. 1.5 τοῦ] τούτου MnRSSa (~Sᶜ ᵘᵛ); 2.19 ταύτην εἶναι]
εἶ- τ- Θ (et An); 73 τε om. AbFRSSa (et PZb¹ᶜ), [Mn]; post 108
add. ἠλ. (om. RSa) κἀγὼ γυναικῶν ἄφρον (-ων Pr) οὐχὶ παρθένος in
textu AbMnSSa (et CrRf), in margine PrR¹ (et G²);⁶ 128 παρ'] ἀπ'
AbMnPrRSa (~R¹ˢ) et Cr; 166 κινεῖ] κινεῖται Ab¹ʸᵖMnʸᵖRSa
(~ʸᵖR¹Sa¹), κινεῖτο S (~Sʸᵖ); 201 τε γὰρ ἐν] γάρ τ'ἐν AbMnRSa,

⁶ Cf. Matthiessen 85.

γὰρ τότε S; 204 ϲτοναχαῖϲι] -ῆ(ι)ϲι AbMnRSa (et Aaʳˢ), -οῖϲι S; 209 ϲε] γε AbMnSSa (~Abⁱˢ ᵘᵛ) et Xa; 212 μοι] με AbMnRSSa (~ᵞᵖMnSa¹); 223 πλευροῖϲ] -οῖϲι RSSa, -ῆ(ι)ϲι AbMnRⁱˢSaⁱˢ; 230 κτῆμ'] κτῆμα τ' AbMnRSSa; 249 τ' ante εἰϲ add. AbMnRSSa; 268 μοι] μου AbMnⁱˢRⁱˢSSaⁱˢ (~ᵞᵖAb²S); 271 χερί] χειρί AbFMnRSSa (et Rf); 281 ϲοι post μεταδιδούϲ (μεταδούϲ PrS) add. AbMnPr<R>SSa (~Rᶜ) et Aa; 282 παρθένωι] post ἐμαῖϲ AbMn PrRSSa; 302 βλέφαρον ἐκταθεῖϲα] ἐκ- β- AbMnRSSa; 421 δέ] ante χρόνοϲ AbFMnPrRS (et Mᵘᵛ<P²Xa²>, ~MⁱᶜPⁱᶜXaᶜ); 491 ἥκει] κεῖ-ται AbMnRSSaᵞᵖ (~ᵞᵖMnS); 509 χ' ὥ] χ' ὁ AbMnRSa (~Abᶜ) et M³; 771 προϲήκομεν] -ήκομαι (Mn)PrS (et Cr), -είκομαι AbRSa; 802 ὤν] ἂν Ab²ᵞᵖMnPrᵞᵖRSSa²ᵍˡ(~ᵞᵖMnR¹) et AdJXXaXb; 843 παθέων] πενθέων AbMnPrᵞᵖRSSaⁱᵞᵖ (~ᵞᵖAb²MnS); 928 εἰ τἄνδον] εἴ τ' ἔνδον (Ab)MnSSa; 1031 μοι om. MnRSSa (~Sa²); 1149 οὖν] αὖ AbFMnPrᵞᵖRSSa²ᵞᵖ (~Mnᵞᵖ) et Zu; 1330 ἄραρ'] -ρεν AbMn PrⁱˢRSSa; 1337 μετάϲχεϲ] -ϲχε MnPrRSSa, -ϲχεν Ab.

(ix) *A stemma for AbFMnPrRSSa*

The relationships which have been established among AbFMnPrR SSa may be represented by the following stemma (Figure 2).

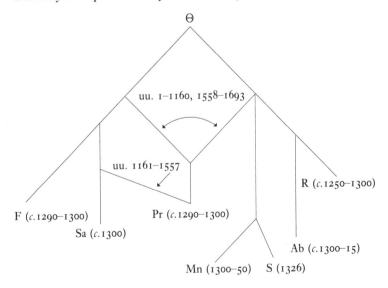

Figure 2

The stemma illustrates:

(*a*) the close relationships which exist between F and Sa, Mn and S, Ab and R;

(*b*) the closer relationship which exists between MnS and AbR than between FSa and either MnS or AbR;

(*c*) the derivation of PrSa from a common source in *c*.1161–1557;

(*d*) the hybrid nature of Pr in *c*.1–1160 and 1558–1693, in which Pr shows an affiliation now with FSa, now with MnS, and occasionally with AbR.

But while the stemma illustrates how Pr may have acquired its hybrid text, it reveals nothing of the cross-fertilization which has occurred among the other members of Θ. The lines which I have drawn between the manuscripts indicate their commonest, not their constant, affiliations. It can be seen from the evidence which I have presented that any individual member of one of the pairs FSa, AbR, MnS will occasionally desert its regular partner and side with one or more other members of Θ. The large number of variants (introduced by γρ(άφεται)) which has been seen to exist among these manuscripts suggests one explanation for this element of inconstancy.

From time to time one member deserts not only its regular partner but even the whole group, and shares a reading which is attested in earlier manuscripts (HMBOV), and very occasionally a reading which is attested not in them but in younger manuscripts. That such desertion is comparatively rare confirms that Θ is quite a tightly knit group. I shall now present the cases of desertion in individual members of Θ. I shall use the symbol θ to designate all members of Θ less one.[7]

(x) *F*

F is the least faithful member of Θ. It is also the member most liable, in its infidelity, to side with one or more of HMBOV in the truth or possible truth: hyp. 1.10 ἐκ τοῦ βίου FBV+: εἰc τὸν βίον AbMO+: ἐπὶ τὸν βίον Sa: βίον PrAd: [MnRS]; 2.5 μυθοποιία FBGP: μυθολογία θMV+: [O]; 108a non habet F;[8] 240 τὸ FM

---

[7] In the sections which follow I am concerned only with the readings of the first hands of members of Θ.

[8] For this additional verse see above, p. 26.

BV²/³ˢ+: τῷ VRf: τοῦ θO+; 281 coι post μετα(δι)δούς non habet F;⁹ 282 παρθένωι] post ἐμαῖς θ (~F); 291 μήποτε FB+: μήπω θMOV+; 360 μὲν FMBOV+: om. θ+; 462 cμικρὸν FB+: μι- θMOV+; 758 μῦθος FVP: μ- δ' θHMBO+; 771 προσήκομεν] -κομαι θCr (~F); 1271 κεκρυμ(μ)ένας ‹F²›M (-μμ- F, -μ- M): -ους F²θM¹ᶜBOVa+; 1337 μετάσχες] -σχε MnPrRSSa, -σχεν Ab (~F); 1364 ὀλόμενον bis FHMBO(Va)+: semel θ+; 1484 ἄρεως FM‹B›O+: -ος θHM²B² Va+; 1492 δραμόντε FHMBO+: -τες θVa+; 1567 κλή(ι)θρων FMB+: κλεί- θ(O)V+; 1571 κλῆ(ι)θρα FMB‹O›+: κλεῖ- θVO¹ᶜ+.

F, alone of Θ, has the following agreements in error with one or more of HMBOV: hyp. 1.5 περὶ] παρὰ FO; 1.7 μεθ' ἡμέραν δὲ αὐτός] αὐτὸς δὲ μεθ' ἡ- FBG; 1.7 ἦλθε(ν)] εἰσῆλθε FBGK (ἀνῆλθε V); 1.11 αὐτοῦ] -τῷ FV; 2.3 κατακριθεὶς θανάτωι om. FBG; 2.4 Ἑλένην καὶ Ἑρμιόνην] ἑρ- καὶ ἑλ- FBG; 2.10 δὲ post τὸ add. FBAG; 2.10–11 τοῦ δράματος] αὐτοῦ FB (-τῷ G); 2.21 κωμι- κωτέραν ἔχει τὴν καταστροφήν post δρᾶμα add. FB²ˢB³ˢ; 69 ὀχού- μεθ'] ὠχ- FM; 165 ὁ om. FOLPZm; 234 γὰρ post μεταβολὴ add. FVAaZc‹Zm›Zu‹T^z?› (~ZmᶜTᵗⁱ/²); 314 δοξάζη(ι) PrOA¹ˢG¹ˢ: -ζη(ι)ς FHM¹ᶜB+: -ζει ARw: -ζεις AbMnRSSa‹M›V+; 327 μανι- άδους] -ώδους FVAnP¹ᶜRw; 434 οὗ γ' οὐ LPZZbZcZmZuT^z: οὗ γ' οὐ PrMO: οὔκ οὐ fere FB²/³AC: οὔ*οὐ B: ὅ γ' οὐ M²: οὔκουν AbMnRSSaV+; 534 οὖν om. FO (~F²O¹ˢ); 556 μ' om. FM+; 805 cυντακῆι] -κεῖ FVZ (~Z²); 818 διccοῖcιν] -οῖς FB (~F²); 975 φονία] -εία FV (~F²); 990 διεδίφρευσε] -ευε FOCr (~O¹ˢ); 1030 οὐκέτ' εἶ] οὐκέτι fere FM¹ʸᵖOK (~F¹ᶜK¹ᶜ); 1253 τόδε MnRSMV+: τάδε FBOK: om. PrSaAa: [Ab]; 1307 παρὰ] περὶ FOZu; 1407 ἔρροι] -ει FB²ˢ; 1448 ἄλλοσε AbMnRSO+: ἄλλος' ἐν FHMB(Va)+: ἄλλο δ' ἐν PrSa; 1463 ἀποκτείνει MnSHMBOV+: -κτείνη AbPr²RSa: -κτενεῖ FM¹ʸᵖ; 1531 Μενέλεων] -λαον FO, -λεον H; 1596 ἔχηις] -εις ‹V?›+ (~V¹ᶜ), -οις FBP; 1679 νείκους] νείκας M, νεῖκος FBO+.

The above lists show a few unique agreements between F and each of MBOV. They also show that F, when it deserts Θ, agrees nearly twice as often with B (or B² or B³) than with any other member of MBOV.

(xi) *Sa*

Sa, alone of Θ, shares the truth four times: hyp. 1.19 cυνοικίcαι

SaRf (coni. Brunck): -ῇcαι θ+ (om. R); 303 cίτων SaMBC: cῖτον AbFMnPrSa¹ˢOV+: cίτον RB²B³ˢAd: cῖτα SRfRw; 406 γ'SaZcZm (coni. Kirchhoff): om. θ+; 421 δὲ] ante χρόνον θMᵘᵛ+ (~SaM¹ᶜ).

    Sa, alone of Θ, has the following agreements in error with one or more of HMBOV: hyp. 1.4 κοινὴν Ἀργεῖοι] ἀ- κ- SaVACr; 1.15 Μενέλαοc] ὁ μ- SaV; 1.19 καθαρθέντι δὲ] καὶ καθ- Sa, καὶ καθ- δὲ V; 2.17 τῶν] τῷ(ι) SaM; 13 τ'post πόλεμον add. SaV¹ᐟ²ᶜZZbZcZm ZuTᶻ (~Tᵗ³); 44 δὲ om. SaBCr (~B²Crˢ); 100 δέ μοι] δ'ἐμοὶ SaV, [Mn]; 345 τὸν] τῶν SaM+ (~SaʳM³); 361 ὤλετο] ὤλεθ'ἑᾶc SaV; 397 τοι AbMn¹ᶜPrRSHBO¹ᶜV+: τι FMnR²ˢSa¹ˢM+: om. SaORf Zb; 445 Ἀργείαc] -ων SaʳˢVRf¹ˢ (~V¹ˢ); 637 τότε] τάδε SaO (~O¹ˢ); 849 δ'om. SaOACrJ (~Aʳ); 1031 περιβάληιc] -βάλειc SaV (~Sa²), -βαλεῖc F, πρὸc βάλληc R; 1454 ὀβρίμα bis] ὀμβ- bis SaH+; 1587 πράccει] -ειc SaB²+.

    These lists provide clear evidence for a connection between Sa and V.

(xii) *Ab*

Ab, alone of Θ, shares the truth six times: hyp. 1.18 ὀρέcτη(ι) AbBO+: -ην θMV+; 147 ὑπόροφον AbAaAnAtCrJZZbZcZmTᵗ³ Tp: ὑπώρ- θAa³+; 292 ἔμελλε AbAdGJPRfRwZTᶜ et Ry aut Ryᶜ: ἤμ- uel ἔτ'ἤμ- θ+; 365 καταcταθεὶc AbHMBO+: παρα- Ab¹ˢθV+; 789 γε AbV (coni. Lenting): δὲ MnPrRM+: γὰρ FSaBOV²ˢ+; 1437 ὀρέcταc AbHMBO+: -ηc θVa+.

    The only member of HMBOV with which Ab shows any connection is V: 115 ἄχνην] -ηc AbV (~Ab¹ˢAb²V¹ᐟ²ˢ); 388 οὐχ ἥ] οὐχὶ AbVCRfʳZmᵘᵛ (~Zm¹ᶜ); 784 cου] coι Ab¹ˢV; 789 γε AbV (see above); 922 ἤcκηκὼc] ἐcκηκὼc Ab, ἐcχηκὼc V; 1517 ἄν om. AbVZb.

(xiii) *R*

R, alone of Θ, shares the truth eight times: 97 φίλων R¹ˢM²ᐟ³BV+: φίλον θMB³ˢOV²ᐟ³+, [Mn]; 212¹⁰ τε RΠ⁵XXaXb+: γε AbMnPrS SaHMBOV+: μοι F; 967 ἀτρειδᾶν RMVA: -ῶν θBOV²ˢ+, [Ab];[11] 1131 βουλεύομαι RMOV+: -coμαι AbMnPrSB+: βεβούλευμαι FSa; 1446 cυνεργὸc RHMO+: ξυν- θBVa+; 1475 ἐκβαλόντεc ROVa+: ἐμ-θHMB+; 1551 κλῇ(ι)θρα RH²MB+: κλεῖ-θOV+ (om. Pr); 1633 καὶ ὑπὸ RM, κ'ὑπὸ BO+: κἀπὸ FMnPrSB³V+: κἀπὶ Sa: [Ab].

¹⁰ See p. 52.
¹¹ Ἀτρειδᾶν is not the truth, since it is part of an interpolation. But it is presumably the older reading.

R, alone of Θ, agrees with one or more of HMBOV in the following errors: hyp. 1.7 τοῦ post ὑπὸ add. RVAt; 1.19 τὸν φόνον PrSaMO+: τοῦ φόνου AbFMnPr¹ˢRSV+: τῶν φόνων R¹ˢBG; 94 κασιγνήτηc] -ac RB+ (~ˢR¹B¹), -ου Ab (~Ab¹ˢ); 140 λεπτὸν] λευκὸν R¹ʸᵖ⟨HB⟩OV+ (~H^cB²O¹ʸᵖV³ʸᵖ); 238 ἐῶσι(ν) c'] ἐῶσιν RMC, ἐῶc' R¹ʸᵖ; 687 τὸ] τοῦ RO+; 929 εὐνίδαc (εὐμενίδαc MnPrSAa)] εὐνῖδαc RM (~M¹ᶜ); 1090 νῦν om. RVAt (~V²ᐟ³); 1101 ἀνάμεινον] ἄμεινον RM (~ˢR¹M¹), ἄμμ- M³; 1383 c' om. ROVa+ (~R¹ˢ); 1621 τ' om. RM+, [Ab]; 1684 πελάcω] -άccω RBC (aut C²).

These passages provide no clear evidence for a connection between R and any member of HMBOV.

(xiv) *Mn*

Mn has few noteworthy readings which are absent from the rest of Θ. The most noteworthy is 143 κοίταc] λέχουc MnRyZcT¹³, which I shall later give reasons for believing to be an early conjecture by Triclinius.[12] It may be significant that Mn offers two readings which are found only in manuscripts associated with the scriptorium of Thomas Magister and Triclinius: 526 ὦ τάλαc] post ψυχὴν MnZbZmZu, post τίν' Z; 1149 ἦν] εἰ Mn^ʸᵖP. The only notable reading shared by Mn, alone of Θ, with a member of MBOV is: 1076 οὐκ ἔcτι] οὐκ ἔcται MnV (οὐκέτ' ἔcται PrRSAa^ʸᵖ).

(xv) *S*

S, alone of Θ, shares the truth (or possible truth) eight times: 61¹³ cυμφοράc SΠ³AdGJKRyXXaXb (-âc S): -άν θ+: [Mn]; 119 πρευμενῆ S^ʸᵖM¹ʸᵖV³ʸᵖC^ʸᵖP: εὐμ- θHMBOV+; 147 ἀτρεμαίαν uel -αῖαν] -αῖον MBOV^cCGK¹ˢ, -αῖον S; 365 τόδ' SHMOV+: τάδ' θB+; 439¹⁴ ἔχειc εἰπεῖν SGJKLPXXaXbT^c: εἰ- ἔ- θ+; 475 χρόνιοc SMBCGK: -ον θB²OVG¹ᶜ+; 515 ὁcιοῦν SMK: ὁcίουν ⟨B⟩VCJ: ὡcίουν θM²B²ᐟ³OV²+ (u. om. Mn, add. Mn²); 1366 κλῆ(ι)θρα SH^s M¹ᶜ²B: κλεῖ- θ⟨M²⟩M²OVa+ (om. F).

S has two unique agreements with V (Va): 974 νιν om. SV (~ˢS¹V²); 1350 τόδε] τότε SVa, [V]. And it has acquired one further old reading unknown to the rest of Θ: 364 Γλαῦκοc] μάντιc S^ʸᵖHM⟨B⟩CCrGKRf (~B²).

---

[12] See pp. 99–100.   [13] See p. 52.   [14] See pp. 59–60.

(xvi) *Pr*

Pr, alone of Θ, shares the truth (or an approximation to the truth)
as many as 16 times: hyp. 2.15 πλ(ησιαίτερον προσκαθεζο)μένη PrA
XXaXbZu: πλ- οὕτω(c) -μένη FSaMBV+: οὕτω -μένη πλ- AbMn
RS+; 271 χερὶ] χειρὶ θRf (~Pr); 298 ἴσχναινε M¹ʸᵖCʸᵖLP: ἴσχαινε
Pr¹ˢBRf: ἴσχανε ΘMOV+; 314 νοῇ PrB³ʸᵖARf¹ˢ: -ήσῃ(ι)c HMC:
-ῇ(ι)c θBOV+; 314 δοξάζῃ(ι) PrOA¹ˢG¹ˢ: -ῇ(ι)c FHM¹ᶜB+: -ει
ARw: -εις AbMnRSSa⟨M⟩V+; 433 φόνου ⟨Pr⟩MBV+: -ος Pr¹ˢθO
V¹ˢ+; 434 οὗ γ' οὐ LPZZbZcZmZuTᶻ: οὗ γ' οὐ PrMO: οὔκ οὐ fere
FB²/³AC: οὔ⁎οὐ B: ὅ γ' οὐ M²: οὔκουν AbMnRSSaV+; 465
διοσκόρω(ι) PrB³OV+: -κούρω AbFRSSaMᶜ+: -κούρων Mn²⟨M⟩+:
-κόρ⁎ B, -κόρους B²ˢ (u. om. Mn, add. Mn²); 493 ἐγένετ' PrB²/³O+:
ʼγένετ' PZcZm⟨Tᶻ'⟩: γένετ' AbMnᶜRSSaMBV+: γένοιτ' Ab²ˢF:
γένητ' MnᵘᵛS¹ˢᵘᵛ; 514 κυροῖ PrMBOV+: -εῖ θ+: -ῇ Ab¹ʸᵖ; 787 λέ-
γωμεν Pr¹ˢBOV+: -ομεν ΘM+; 838 ἀγαμεμνόνιος Pr¹ˢMBᵘᵛOV+:
-ειος ΘB¹ᶜᵘᵛ+; 960 στεναγμὸν Pr¹ˢ⟨K²⟩Tᵗ³: -μῶν Θ+; 966 κάρα
PrMO+: κρᾶτα fere θBV+: [Ab]; 1645 παρράσιον PrMBOV+:
παρά- θ+: παρνά- M²+: [Ab]; 1653 ἧς PrᵍˡCrGᵗᶜJXXaXbZcTa²ˢ et
Mt aut Mtᶜ: ἧ(ι) Θ+.

Pr has one unique agreement with V: 747 θέλω] ποθῶ V, πόθω
Prʸᵖ (cf. 103 Ἄργει] -ους PrᵍˡV³ˢ; 1148 σπάσω μέλαν] σπασώμεθα
ʸᵖPrC [coni. Kirchhoff],¹⁵ -σόμεθα VZuʸᵖ).

(xvii) *Θ and V*

Θ is more closely connected to V than to any of HMBO. Several
unique agreements between V and individual members of Θ have
been recorded in the preceding sections (notably VF [section (x)]
hyp. 1.11, 975; VSa [section (xi)] hyp. 1.15, 1.19. 100, 361, 1031;
VAb [section (xii)] 115, 784, 789; VR [section (xiii)] hyp. 1.7, 1090;
VMn [section (xiv)] 1076; VS [section (xv)] 974, 1350; VPr [section
(xvi)] 747). Here is a series of unique or nearly unique agreements
between V and two or more members of Θ: hyp. 2.15 προ(σ)καθε-
ζομένη] παρακαθ- VMnSSa; 2.17 πλησιαίτερον] ἐγγὺς VMnRS;
2.19 ταύτην εἶναι] εἶ- τ- Θ (et An), εἶ- φασὶ τ- V; 179 δόμον] γόνον
ʸᵖV³Ab¹MnPrR¹SSa (et Cr); 255 μοι] μου VAbMnRSSa (~V²); 378
εἰς] ἐς VAbMnPrRS (et J); 430 ἐκκλείομαι] ἐκβάλ(λ)ομαι
V²/³AbMnRSSaʳˢ; 500 δ' post χρῆν add. VAbMnRS; 752 τοῦδε]
τούτου AbPrʸᵖR²ʸᵖ (et Cr), τούτου δὲ V; 762 ὡσπερεὶ] ὥσπερ VMnS;

---

¹⁵ This could be right: see p. 162.

791 κατάσχωσιν] -ωσι VAbF; 797 τό γε] τὸ δὲ VMnS, τόδε PrR, τὸ δε Ab, το∗ε F (~F¹ᶜ); 798 μηδ'] μήτ' VAbF¹ᶜMnRS, μὴ Sa; 856 ἔοικεν] -κας VAb¹ˢMnPr¹ˢSa¹ˢ; 864 δεῖ] χρὴ VFMnPr¹ˢSSa; 931 δ' post κοὐδείς add. VAbR; 941 φθάνοι] -ει VAbMnRSSa (et AdZcᵘᵛ); 953 φάσγαν'] -νον VAbMnRS (et O¹ᵍˡAaʳᵍˡZ); 1011 γενέτην] -ταν VMnS (et Tᵗ³); 1064 τολμήμασι(ν)] βουλεύμασι(ν) VMnPrʸᵖRSa¹ʸᵖ (~V²/³ˢMn¹ʸᵖR¹ᵐ) et Π¹⁵Aaʳˢ, [Ab]; 1081 οὐκέτ' ἔστι] οὐκέτ' ἔσται VMnPrS¹ᶜSa (οὐκ ἔστι F, οὐκ ἔσται S), [Ab]; 1122 γ' om. VAbMnRS; 1135 δ'] τ' VAbMnS; 1154 γένος] λέχος VAbMnPrʸᵖSSa²ʸᵖ (~Ab¹ʸᵖ); 1174 μὴ] οὐ VMnPr¹ˢSSa²ˢ (et L²Aa³ˢ Tᵗˡˢ); 1277 πρόσθε] -εν VaFPrSa, [Ab]; 1284 οἱ] ὦ Va²ʸᵖMnS; 1363 Ἑλλάδ' ἅπασαν] ἑλλάδα πᾶσαν VaMnS; 1516 κτανῶ] κτενῶ VMnS (et ⟨Zb²⟩, ~Zb³).

(xviii) Θ and C

A small number of readings is shared by members of Θ uniquely or almost uniquely with C: 4 κοὐκ] οὐκ CPrS, [Mn]; 464 θ'] δ' CPr; 697 λάβρον] μέγα CFSa; 736 καὶ om. CF; 1130 σύμβολον] -βουλον CMnS; 1148 σπάσω μέλαν] σπασώμεθα ʸᵖCPr (σπασόμεθα VZuʸᵖ); 1544 φόνου] πόνου CʸᵖPrSa (et Aa³ˢZʳʸᵖZbZm¹ʸᵖ⟨Zu⟩, ~Zb¹ʸᵖZuᶜ); 1647 ʳ' om. CFPrSa (et Zu), [Ab].

CHAPTER V

Associates of Θ (Rf Rw; Aa; Cr)

Four manuscripts which are often associated with Θ are AaCr RfRw.

(i) *RfRw*

RfRw are closely connected:[1] 312 c' om. RfRw; 441 πόλιν om.
RfRw (~Rf¹ˢ); 472 χεόμενος] χεάμ- RfRw (~Rf¹ˢ) et G; 487 τὸ
post καὶ add. RfRw; 698 ἐντείνοντι] -τα ˢRf¹Rw¹ (et gE); 756 ἀμφ᾽
uel ἀφ᾽ uel καθ᾽] ὑφ᾽ RfRw; 893 καλοὺς] -ῶς RfRw (~Rf¹ˢ); 977
πολύπονα] πολύςτονα Rf¹ᶜRw; 1076 οὐκ ἔςτι] οὐκ ἔτ᾽ ἐςτὶ RfRw
(οὐκ ἔςται VMn, οὐκέτ᾽ ἔςται AaᴿᵞᴾPrRS, οὐκέτι AAaAt, [Ab]);
1094 καὶ ante Φωκέων add. RfRw; 1111 γὰρ] δ᾽RfRw; 1169 οὐ om.
RfRw (~Rf¹ˢRw²); 1178 τ᾽] δ᾽ RfRw; 1233 ἐμας λιτας (diuersis
acc.)] ἐμῆς λιτῆς RfRw (et Mnˢ); 1287 εἰς] ἐς RfRw (et Tp); 1503
καινῶν] -οῦ ˢRf²Rw; 1548 Μυρτίλου] -ίλος RfᵘᵛRwᵘᵛ (~Rf¹ᶜ).

Here is a list of readings which are unique or nearly unique to
members of Θ and one or both of RfRw: hyp. 1.11–12 Μενελάου
τιμωρίαν λαβεῖν Ἑλένην] τ- μ- λ- ἐ- RfSa (τ- λ- μ- ἐ- Pr); 1.19
cυνοικῆcαι] -ίcαι RfSa; 2.8 ὑπέρ] ὑπὸ RfSSa (et An); 51 βαλεῖν]
λαβεῖν RwAbMnR (~Ab²ˢMnᶜ); 108a habent in textu RfAbMn
SSa (et Cr), in marg. G²PrR¹;[2] 134 δ᾽] τ᾽ RwAbF; 162 ἆ ἆ (uel
sim.)] ὦ RfMnRSa (~Rᴵᵞᴾ); 237 δή] δέ RfF (~F²); 271 χερί] χειρί
RfAbFMnRSSa; 276 πτεροῖς om. RwF; 294 ὄμμ᾽ ante ὦ add. RwF²
(et s.l. V³ᵍˡAaʳ); 303 cίτων uel cῖτον uel cίτον] cῖτα RfRwS; 391 μοι
om. RfSa; 396 εἰργαςμένος] ἐργαςάμενος RwAb; 397 τοι uel τι] τι
Rf¹ᶜSa¹ˢ, om. RfSa (et OZb, τοι O¹ᶜ); 445 Ἀργείας] -ων Rf¹ˢVSaʳˢ
(~V¹ˢ); 476 ὁμόλεκτρον] -λεκτον RwMn; 479 ὅδε] ὧδε RfPr¹ˢ; 487
μὴ om. RfMn (~Rf¹ˢ); 601 δὲ om. RwAb; 691 ἂν om. RfRwR (et
An); 757 ἢ (ἤ, ἦ)] ἢ δὴ RfFSa, ἢ δὴ Rw (δὴ etiam B²/³ˢ); 764
προcείη] προcήει RwMnS (et X); 783 τῆιδε] τόδε RfMnS; 793
γενέcθαι post ἴτω add. AbMnRS, καὶ γ- add. Rf (καὶ etiam Mnᵍˡ);
836 φόνωι] -ου RfMn¹ˢPrSSa¹ˢ (ἕνεκα φόνου ᵍˡVZu); 869 ἔφερβε]

---

[1] Also in *Hec.* (Matthiessen 68–9) and *Ph.* (Mastronarde 44–7).
[2] For this additional verse see p. 26.

ἔφερβ' ὁ RfPr; 890 ἐκπαγλούμενος] εὐλαβούμενος RfPr (~(Rf¹ˢ)Pr^γρ); 916 κατακτείναντι] -οντι Rf¹ᶜR²ˢFSa+, κατατείνοντι RfSa¹ʸρ, κατείνοντι Pr; 923 γ' post ὅς add. RfMnS; 933 Δαναίδαι] δαναοίδε RfPr (δαναοὶ δὲ FSa+); 934 οὐδὲν ἧσσον ἢ] μᾶλλον (μᾶλλον ἢ Rfᶜ) τοὔμῶ RfPr (~Pr^γρ) (μᾶλλον etiam ᵍˡSa+); 939 γὰρ om. RfPr; 942 τῆς γε] τῆςδε RwFPrSa; 958 còν om. RfRwPr (et At); 960 αἲ αἲ ante uel supra κατάρχομαι add. RfMnPrRSSa (et Zm); 976 ἐ-φαμέρων] ἐφημ- RfPr; 999 ὀλοόν] ὀλοὸν ὀλοὸν RwMnPrRS; 1004 ἀῶ] ἠῶ RfPr (ἠὼ Aa), [Ab]; 1023 φέρειν post μὲν add. RfMnPrS, [Ab]; 1263 διάφερ'] -φορ' RwPr, [Ab]; 1271 ἄρ' om. RfRwMn, [Ab]; 1302-3 θείνετε post καίνετε add. RwAbMnS, post φονεύετε R (nouit ʸᵖM¹C); 1358 δόμοις] -οισι RwAbMnRS (et ZTp); 1431 ἠλακάται] ἠλεκ- RwMnS (~S¹ˢ) (et Tp); 1473 δῆτ'] δ' ἦτ' Rf‹Rw²›F² (~Rw²); 1536 τε om. RfR (~R¹ˢ); 1541 προκηρύσσει] -ειν RfᵘᵛMn (~Rf¹ᶜ); 1545 ἐν ante βροτοῖσι add. RwR; 1551 φθάνοιτε] -ητε RfRwR (~ˢRwR¹) (et Aa¹ˢZv); 1601 τῶι om. RwPr (et AtXaXb), [Ab]; 1665 ἐξηνάγκασα] -έγκασα RfF (et Ad), [Ab]; 1667 ἄρ' om. RfRwR, [Ab].

The closest connections which exist between Rf and Rw and individual members of Θ are between Rf and Pr (eight unique agreements on the above list) and Rf and Sa (three unique agreements).

Just as V was the member of HMBOV with which Θ showed the closest association, so also Rf and Rw share a few unique readings with V: 91 ἀπείρηκεν (Π²)MBK, -κε C: -κ' ἐν BᶜO+: -κα ἐν Rf, -κα VRw; 349 πολλῆ(ι) δ'] πολλὴ δ' M¹ᶜC, πολῆ δ' V (~V¹ᶜ), πολὺ δ' HMBOK¹ᶜ (~B²O¹ᶜ) et ᶦΣᵛ et Σᵛ, (πολ)ὺς super πολλῆ(ι) V²/³Rw¹, πολὺς δ'ᶦΣRw; 721 ἄρ' om. VRfRw (~V²); 1326 ἡμῖν] ὑμῖν VaRw; 1352 πράσσειν] πράξειν VaRw (~Rw¹ᶜ). The only other unique agreements between Rf or Rw and members of HMBO are: 79 δ' om. B¹ᶜRw; 1418 προσεῖπε δ'] -πεν ORw.

(ii) *Aa*

The connection between Aa and Θ can be seen most clearly in these five readings: hyp. 1.1 μεταπορευόμενος] ἐκδικησάμενος AaAbMnRSSa; 1.5 τί δεῖ post τοῦ add. AaAbMnRSSa et G¹ˢ; 281 coι post μετα(δι)δούς add. AaAbMnPr‹R›SSa (~Rᶜ); 543 ἐκτήσατο] ἐδέξατο AaAbMnPrRS (~Aa³ˢPr^γρ); 593 πειθόμε(σ)θα πάνθ'] -θ' ἄπανθ' AaAbMnPrRS.

There are numerous other unique or nearly unique agreements

between Aa and one or more members of Θ: hyp. 1.9 τῶν ante
λόγων add. AaAb; 1.16 στερούμενον] ἐστερημένον AaAbR (-ω
MnS); 2.5 διεκωλύθη] ἐκωλ- AaAbR, ἐκολ- MnS; 2.7 Ἠλέκτρας om.
AaMnS; 2.15 προ(c)καθεζομένη] κατθημένη Aa, καθημένη Ab
(προκαθημένη Rw); 2.15 ὁ ποιητὴς] ante διὰ τὸν χορὸν AaAb et
Xa (~Xaᶦᶜ); 2.16 καὶ om. AaAb; 2.19 ταύτην] post εἶναι
AbFMnPrRSSa (et An), om. Aa;[3] 407 τάδε] post νοσεῖς AaFSa;
530 ὁμορροθεῖ] ὁμορρωθεῖ AaAbᵞᵖ, ὀμμορωθεῖ Ab (ὀμμοροθεῖ R);
569 ἄν om. AaSa; 579 μέν om. AaMn; 614 cῆι] τῆ AaFSa (τῆ Mnᵍˡ,
καὶ τῆ ᵍˡAb²PrR²), om. Ab; 735 cυγκατασκάπτοις] -εις AaAb (-ης
Abᶦˢ) et At; 738 ἀπέδωκε(ν)] ἐπ- AaAbR; 848 ζῆν ἢ θανεῖν] θ- ἢ ζ-
AaAbR; 929 εὐνίδας] εὐμενίδας AaMnPrS; 955 οὐδ'] οὔθ' AaFSa;
1041 cοῦ uel cου] coὶ Aa (~Aa³), coι FSa (~F²ˢ), [Ab]; 1076 οὐκ
ἔστι] οὐκέτ' ἔσται AaᵞᵖPrRS, οὐκέτι AaAAt (οὐκ ἔσται VMn, οὐκ
ἔτ' ἐστὶ RfRw), [Ab]; 1076 δή om. AaFSa, [Ab]; 1150 κατθανού-
μεθα] κτανούμεθα AaMnS (κατ Aaʳˢ); 1207 ἁμαρτήcη(ι)] -cεις
AaPrSa (~PrᶦˢSa²ˢ) et AtZcᶦᶜZu, -cης Aa³F, [Ab]; 1226 παῖς] post
còc Aa (~Aaʳ), om. FPrSa , [Ab];[4] 1243 τε (prius) om. AaFPrSa (et
At), [Ab]; 1247 Πελασγὸν] -ῶν AaʳˢFPrSa (~F²), [Ab]; 1253 με] μοι
AaF²MnRS (~Aaʳˢ) et ˢAtᶦKᵍˡRfᶠXXaXb, [Ab]; 1253 τόδε uel
τάδε] om. AaPrSa, [Ab]; 1259 ἐκφυλάξω] ἐμφ- AaF, [Ab]; 1263
ἐκεῖθεν] ἐκεῖθ' AaF (et At), ἐκεῖ Aa², ἐκεῖ δ'PrSa, [Ab]; 1273 γὰρ
post κενὸς add. AaMnRS, [Ab]; 1278 ἔνθεν] ἐνθάδ' AaʳˢMnS, ἐνθένδ' R, [Ab]; 1318 πέρι] ὕπερ AaᵞᵖAbMnRS; 1332 γόνασι] γού-
νασι AaFPrSa (et At); 1342 δ'] c'AaFPrSa (et Va); 1353 φίλαι] post
ἐγείρετε AaʳMnS, post κτύπον R; 1378 ὁ ante ταυρόκρανος add.
AaAbMnS; 1400 εἰς] ἐς AaʳˢMnS; 1405 δέ om. AaAb (et At); 1465
ὤμοι] ἰώ μοι AaFPrSa (et AtZb); 1494 πάλιν post πάλιν δὲ add. AaF
(et At), πάλιν δὲ add. PrSa; 1494 κόραν] κούραν AaPrSa (et Zm);
1497 ἤτοι φαρμάκοισιν om. AaPrSa (~Aaᶦᵐ) et At; 1537 δόμος] -οις
AaAbᵘᵛ (~Aa³Abᶜ).

Just as Θ is closely associated with V, so Aa shares three readings
unique or nearly unique to V: 286 ἐπάρας] ἐπ' ἄρας AaV²ᐟ³ˢR²ᵞᵖ;
926 χέρα] -ας AaʳˢV; 1122 ἐκδακρῦσαι V²ᐟ³ˢMnS+: ἐνδακρῦσαι
AaFPrSa+: ἐκδακρύειν AaʳˢV (ἐνδακρύειν Prᶦˢ, δακρύειν Ab(R)).
Note also 1342 δ'] c'AaVaFPrSa.

Aa has several unique agreements with one or both of RfRw: 33

---

[3] For the significance of this coincidence of omission and transposition see p. 21 n. 15.
[4] See n. 3 above.

θ'] δ' AaRf; 398 διαφθείρουςα] φθείρουςα AaRfRw; 450 coῖcι] coῖc AaRw; 861 (ἐν) Ἀργείοιc uel (ἐν) Ἀργείων] ἀργεῖοι AaRw; 1194 παρθένου] -ον AaRf (~AaʳˢRfᵗᶜ); 1563 ῥυcώμεθ'] -cόμεθ' AaRf; 1575 ἐπίφρουρον] -φρούριον AaRf; 1618 εἶ' uel εἴ'] εἶα AaRf.

Aa and one or both of RfRw have the following unique or nearly unique agreements with members of Θ: hyp. 1.17 ἠπείληςαν] ἠπείλουν AaRwAbMnRS; 2.15 πλ(ηςιαίτερον προςκαθεζο)μένη] οὕτω -μένη πλ- AaRwAbMnRS (πλ- οὕτω(c) -μένη RfSa+); 92 γ' ante ἄν add. AaRfAbRS, [Mn]; 347 τὸν] τῶν AaRwAbMnPrˢRSSa (~Aaʳˢ) et L; 1471 ἀριστεροῖcιν] -οῖc AaRwAbMnRS et Tᵗ³; 1477 πέτρουc] -ac AaRwFMn¹ˢ et Zm (-αν AbR); 1628 ὀρέcθ' uel -cτ'] -cτα AaRfFPrSa, [Ab]; 1689 Tυνδαρίδαιc] -είδαιc AaRf‹F›Pr (~F²) et Zb (~Zbᶦᶜ).

(iii) Cr

Here is the main evidence for the association of Cr with members of Θ: hyp. 1.1 μεταπορευόμενος] ἐκδικηcάμενος AaAbMnRSSa, μ-καὶ ἐκδικῶν CrFPr (et G; ἐκδικῶν B²ˢ); 22 μὲν om. CrFS (~F²) et J; 63 ἔλιφ'] ἔλειφ' CrF, [Mn]; 111 τοι] cὺ CrAb²ˢ; 114 ἐλθοῦcα δ'] ἐλθοῦc' fere CrAbSa; 128 παρ'] ἀπ' CrAbMnPrRSa (~R¹ˢ); 138 ἐμοί] ὅμως CrAbᶦʸᵖ et ut uid. Π⁴;⁵ 312 κἀκφοβοῦν] καὶ φ-CrMnRSSa (~ʸᵖMnR²Sa¹); 357 Tροίαθεν] -ηθεν CrAbᵘᵛMnPrR (-οθεν S); 394 κακῶν] -οῖc CrMnPr (~Pr¹ˢ) et ˢAdAt¹; 489 cὺ] ante νῦν Cr, om. Pr (~Pr¹ᶜ);⁶ 518 μὲν om. CrFSa; 570 τύχοι] -η CrMn; 681 δ'om. CrSa; 686 θνῄςκοντα καὶ κτείνοντα τοὺc ἐναντίουc] κτ-καὶ θν- τοὺc ἐ- Cr, κτ- τοὺc ἐ- καὶ θν- Sa; 739 ὥc om. CrSa; 749 τοῦτο] ταῦτα CrMnPr et Atᵘᵛ; 752 τοῦδε] τούτου CrAbPrʸᵖR²ʸᵖ (τούτου δὲ V); 752 μᾶλλον] om. CrFSa, post πατρὸc AaZ; 757 χρῆμα] πρᾶγμα CrAbFᶠᵍˡMnPrRS (et C¹ˢ); 762 πυργηρούμεθα] -μεθ' ἔcωθεν Cr, -μεθα cῶμα Sa; 771 προcήκομεν] -ομαι CrAbMn PrRSSa; 777 κατθάνω] θάνω CrFSa; 778 ἄν om. CrFSa; 780 κρεῖccον] κρεῖττον CrFSa; 781 γοῦν uel οὖν] γὰρ CrFSa (οὖν Sa²ᵍˡ); 784 ἄν om. CrFSa; 785 πατρῷον] πατρὸc CrAbPrʸᵖR¹ʸᵖ; 808 καὶ om. CrAb; 978 βαίνει] βαίνειν τῶν ἀνθρώπων Cr, βαίνειν Pr; 1057 ὁ (alterum) om. CrFPrSa (et Xa); 1073 cὴν] cὺ CrMnʸᵖPr (τὴν AdKPrʸᵖSSa¹ʸᵖ, ~Sʸᵖ), [Ab]; 1093 καλόν ποτε] ποτὲ κ- CrMnS (et Zb); 1131 δ'] post ἔγνωc CrMnS; 1143 μὲν om. CrAbMnS; 1643 Ἑλένην] ἑλλήνων CrF, [Ab].

⁵ See p. 118.   ⁶ See n. 3 above

The following are unique or nearly unique agreements between Cr and members of Θ and one or more of the other common associates of Θ, VAaRfRw: 62 δή om. CrRfSSa, [Mn]; 108a habent in textu CrAbMnRfSSa, in margine PrR͘¹ (et G²);[7] 179 δόμον] γόνον ᵞᵖCrV³Ab¹MnPrR¹SSa¹; 206 ἐπί] ἐπεί CrᶜAbMnPrRRfSa (~Rf¹ˢ); 254 ταχύc] ταχὺ CrVAaAbF²MnPrRRwSSa (ταχ∗F) et Mᶜ; 385 δέδορκα] δέρκομαι CrAaʳˢᐸAbᴵᵞᴾᐳMnPrRS (~ᵞᵖMnPrR²S); 731 κτε- νοῦντας] κταν- CrVFRfRwSa (~V¹ˢ); 960 αἴ αἴ ante uel supra κατάρχομαι MnPrRRfSa (et An²J²Zm), post Πελαcγία ᐸCr²ᐳAn (ras. iv litt.); 1550 τύχην] ψυχὴν CrAaMnS (~Aa³ˢ).

Cr has one striking agreement with V: 779 ἐcτι cωθῆναι] ἐcτιν ἐκβῆναι CrV. Other possible points of contact with V are: 757 λέ- ξον] om. Cr (~Crᵍˡ), ante χρῆμα V;[8] 1038 γόνον] δόμον Cr et ᵞᵖΣᵐᵇᵛᶜ. Solitary agreements with each of M and B are less striking: 1618 εἴ᾽ om. CrM; 1631 ἤν uel ὡc] om. CrB (ἤν B², ὡc B³ˢ), [C]. Several unique agreements between Cr and O have already been recorded.[9]

⁷ See p. 26.   ⁸ See n. 3 above.   ⁹ See p. 21.

CHAPTER VI

GK

G and K have links both with the older tradition (as represented by HMBOV) and with the younger tradition (as represented by Θ and associates) and have one further feature which links them with Palaeologan scholarship.

The close relationship between G and K is proved by a series of unique agreements:[1] 188 γ’εἴπω post ἄλλο add. GK¹ᶜ (εἴπ* K, εἶπες Gʳˢ) (γ’εἶπας, -ον, -οις, -ης add. alii); 386 γ’om. GK; 439 δρῶντες] δρῶσιν GK; 483 ὅδε] post πέφυκεν GK; 528 γὰρ post μὲν add. GK; 782 πρᾶγμ’] πρᾶγμα δ’GK (πρᾶγμα γ’XXaXb); 850 ἔοικε δ’] ἔοικεν GK (~G²) (ἔοικεν δ’A); 921 ὁμόσε] post λόγοις GK; 973 ὤν] post ποτ’GK; 999 ὀλοὸν semel uel bis] ὀλοὸν μέγα GK; 1064 πράσσειν] πάσχειν GK; 1169 ἔσχεν] ἔσχ’GK¹ᶜ;[2] 1187 τάφωι uel -ον uel -ου] -ων GK; 1326 τί δ’] τάδ’ GK (et Z²); 1357 ἴδω] ἴδωμεν GK; 1360 σαφῶς post συμφορὰς add. GK; 1367 notam ἡμ. add. GK (χο. O, ~O¹ᶜ; ἡλ. H); 1449 ἐν] ἐνὶ GK; 1607 (μ’) ἀνδάνουσιν] ἀνδάνουσί μ’ G, -ουσί K (-σιν μ’ M²); 1637 σωτήριος] -ρία GK (~G²ˢ); 1673 χαῖρε] χαῖρ’ ὦ GK.

One or both of GK are witnesses to readings (some of them true) attested by one or more of HMBOV which are absent, or all but absent, from the younger manuscripts: 91 ἀπείρηκ’ ἐν] -κεν K(Π³)MB (~Bᶜ), -κε C, -κα VRw, -κα ἐν Rf; 147 ἀτρεμαίαν uel -αῖαν] -αῖον GK¹ˢMBOVᶜC (~M²B²), -αῖον S; 242 Ναυπλίω(ι)] -ία(ι) GKΠ⁶MBOACRf (~B²ˢ); 364 Γλαῦκος] μάντις GKHM〈B〉C CrRfSʸᵖ (~B²); 458 τε om. GKOVACr; 475 χρόνιον] -ος GKM BCS (~G¹ᶜB²); 918 εὐωπός] εὔοπτος GKM¹ʸᵖO, εὔωπτος B¹ʸᵖ; 980 χρόνωι] post μακρῶι GKOCr; 1030 οὐκέτ’ εἶ] οὐκέτι fere KM¹ʸᵖOF (~F¹ᶜK¹ᶜ); 1061 ὡς ante ἀξιώτατα add. KO; 1094 ἀκρόπολιν] -πτολιν GKOAdXaXb; 1159 παρῆσθα] παρῆισθα KO; 1253 τόδε] τάδε KBOF; 1371 τέρεμνα] τέραμνα KMBSa²ZcZu; 1468 χρυ-

---

[1] GK are also linked in *Hec.* (Matthiessen 73). K is absent in *Ph.*

[2] In case any future collator should suppose, as I originally did, that ἔσχ’ is also the reading of F, I must warn him that what appears in photographs of F as an apostrophe is revealed by autopsy to be the compendium for εν almost obliterated by a blob of (extraneous) white paste.

ceocάνδαλον] -cάμβαλον fere K aut K¹ᶜ, HM²⟨B⟩C (~ fere M¹ᶜB²);
1507 προcπίπτων] -πιτνῶν GKOJZvT³, -πεcών XXaXb.

For agreements between G and BF in the hypotheses (1.7 bis, 2.3, 2.4, 2.5, 2.10, 2.10–11) see pp. 28–9, to which add a further agreement between G and B (1.19 τὸν φόνον uel τοῦ φόνου] τῶν φόνων GBR¹ˢ).

One or both of GK share several unique or nearly unique readings with members of Θ: hyp. 1.18 Ἑρμιόνην] post ἐπέταξεν KSa (~K¹ˢ); 2.12 κλινιδίου] -ίω(ι) GF; 314 γὰρ om. GF (~F²); 410 δ' om. GK¹ᶜF; 518 δὲ μιcῶ μέν] μὲν μιcῶ GAbᶜ (μὲν μιcῶ μὲν ⟨Ab⟩, δὲ μιcῶ CrFSa); 527 ἐξέβαλ(λ)ε] ἐξέτεινε G²ˢPrᵧᵖR¹ᵧᵖ; 558 -cι κούχί] -cιν οὐχὶ GKFSa (et AtZb); 586 κείνηc uel 'κείνηc] ἐκείνηc GAb²ˢF (et Zm, ~Zmᶜ); 638 εἶπαc] εἶπεc K¹ᶜMnPrRS; 718 ῷ] ὧν GKCr² ⟨Mn²⟩ (~Mnᶜ); 753 cῶν om. GFSa; 1002 μετέβαλεν] -βαλλεν GKF², [Ab]; 1073 cὴν] τὴν KPrᵧᵖSSa¹ᵧᵖ (~Sᵧᵖ) et Ad (cὺ CrMnᵧᵖPr), [Ab]; 1129 τείνειν] τίνειν ⟨G⟩KFPrSa (~G²); 1218 τελευτηθῆι] τελευτῆ KS (~K¹ᶜ), [Ab]; 1281 ἐν om. KMnS (~K¹ᶜ), [Ab].

One or both of GK share occasional unique readings with the common associates of Θ: (i) with V, 110 ὀρθῶc] καλῶc GKV; 141 τιθεῖτε] ψοφεῖτε KV (~K¹ᵧᵖV¹ˢ); 1004 προcαρμόcαc] -caca GV² (et Tp) (-αν O²ˢ); (ii) with Aa, 890 μέν om. GAa; 1231 ἵκου] ἱκοῦ KAa; 1242 γῆc ante πρόγονε add. GAa (et At); 1619–20 om. GAa (~G¹ᵐAa³ᵐ); 1620 μοι] ἐμοὶ G¹ᵐAa³ᵐ; 1644 γαίαc] γαίηc GKAa; (iii) with Cr, 912 γίνεται] γίγν- GCr; 1167 τοι om. GKCr; 1592 λέγων] λέγειν GCr; 1633 κἀπὸ] ἀπὸ GCr; (iv) with RfRw, hyp. 1.11 ὧν post αὐτοῦ add. G¹ˢRw; 2.18 παριcταμένων] ἱcταμένων KRw (~Rwˢ); 64 ἐμῆι] ἐμοί GRfRwᶜᵘᵛ (~Rf¹ˢ) et Z (~Z¹ᶜ); 70 γὰρ post ἄπορον add. GᵍˡRw (et P²ˢ); 71 κἀγ-] καὶ ἀγ- GRfRw; 377 τότ'] ποτ' GRf; 472 χεόμενοc] χεάμ- GRfRw (~Rf¹ˢ); 1005 Πλειάδοc] πελ- KRw¹ᶜᵘᵛ; 1013 κατακυρωθεὶc] κυρ- GRw; 1493 ὀρείαν] οὐρ- GRwᶜ (nisi Rw); 1594 φευξόμε(c)θα] -ούμεθα GRw (et Zd) (-ούμεcθα Aa³ˢ).

And one or both of GK share readings which are confined to members of Θ and one or more of the associates of Θ: hyp. 1.1 καὶ ἐκδικῶν post μεταπορευόμενοc add. GCrFPr (ἐκδικῶν etiam B²ˢ); 1.5 τί δεῖ post τοῦ add. G¹ˢAaAbMnRSSa; 1.16 τέκνον] -ων GKAa AbRfRw (-ω MnS); 13 ἔριν] ἔριc GV¹/²ˢFPrRf¹ᶜ (~F²Pr¹ˢ); 108a habent in textu AbCrMnRfSSa, in margine G²PrR¹;³ 111 γε om. GK⟨V⟩AbMnRRfS (~V³ˢ); 127 κεκτημένοιc] κεχρημένοιc GᵍˡAaᵧᵖ

³ See p. 26.

(Ab²ᵞᵖ)R¹ᵞᵖ; 137 ψοφεῖτε] κτυπεῖτε GKVAaʳᵞᵖAbMnRRfSSa (~Gᵍˡ (Mnᵞᵖ)Rf²) et ᵍˡPr+; 172 κτύπου] -ον GKAaAb²ˢMnᵍˡSSᵞᵖ (~GᶜS¹ˢ); 195 ἔκανες] ἔκτανες GMnPr²RfS (~Prᶜ²Rfʳ); 242 δέ om. GFMnRwSSa (~F²); 588 οὐ κατέκτανε] οὐκ ἀπέκτανε GAaAb; 694 μέν om. KCrSSa; 1078 γάμων] -ου GKVMnˢPr¹ˢRSa¹ˢ (~K¹ᶜR¹ˢ), [Ab]; 1333 μή] μοι KAbRf² (~K¹ᶜRf¹ᶜ²) et At.

The feature which links G and K to Palaeologan scholarship is conjectural activity in the non-lyric metres. I shall discuss this feature of GK later.[4]

---

[4] See p. 57 and Chapter XVII (especially pp. 157–8).

CHAPTER VII

AMt

Mt, which is available for only lines 1277–1693, is a very close relative of A.[1] It has few agreements with other manuscripts, against A, and none of moment. Here are its most telling agreements with A: 1328 κἄμ'] καί μ' AMt; 1585 ὅπως χώcω] ὡc θάψω AMtPr (ὅπως θάψω At, θάψω Mᵍˡ, χώcω Prʸᵖ); 1600 τῆcδε ante γῆc add. AMt (τῆcδε τῆc add. Pr); 1611 κτανεῖν] θανεῖν AMt; 1631 ἦν] ὡc AMt B³ˢAtZb²ʸᵖZmᴵʸᵖTᶜ (ἦν B², om. B). A final passage requires longer exposition: 1455 ἔδρακον ἔδρακον ἐν δόμοιc τυράννων] ἔδρακον | ⟨ἔδρακον ἐν δόμοιc(ι) τυράννων⟩ | ἔδρακον ἐν δόμοιcι τυράννων A;[2] ἔδρακον | Mt, (ἔδρακον?) ἐν δόμοιcι τυράννων Mtᵐ. Editors have reported only that there is a vacant line in A. But the line was not originally vacant, and ἔδρακον ἐν δόμοιc(ι) at least was written and then erased. I cannot tell whether Mt wrote ἔδρακον at the head of its marginal addition. The duplication of the line in A and its omission in Mt are presumably related phenomena. The anadiplosis ἔδρακον ἔδρακον may be at the root of the problem (AaAtFZb have single ἔδρακον). At all events, A and Mt coincide in the unique error δόμοιcι.

Apart from its link with Mt, A has no clear affiliation to any individual manuscript or group of manuscripts. It preserves the truth uniquely once, and once with Mt: 159 χαράν] χάριν Aᴵˢ; 1611 κτανεῖν] θανεῖν AMt. A third possible instance is 1447 ἀλλ' αἰεί (ἀλλ' ἀεί BOVaCrTᵗ³Tp)] ἄλλαι Aᵘᵛ (εἰ super αι A¹), coni. Scaliger. The merits of Scaliger's conjecture are discussed by Willink and West, and I pass no judgement on it here. How we should interpret A's reading (which earlier collators have not reported) is uncertain. The first hand probably wrote ἄλλαι rather than ἀλλαι (there is a vestige of what appears to be an accent, which has perhaps been partly erased); the same hand wrote εἰ above αι. Whether ἄλλαι was intended to be the transmitted reading (the scribe adding the suprascript letters through knowledge of the common reading),[3] or

---

[1] And so it is in *Ph.* (Mastronarde 47–8). It is absent for *Hec.*

[2] There is nothing unusual in A's colometry here: see p. 145.

[3] A does not use adscript iotas: so that ἄλλαι, if intended at all, was not intended to represent the adverb.

whether ἄλλαι was a mere slip which the scribe instantly, though incompletely, corrected, we cannot tell. MnRSTp write ἀλλ' for ἀλλ', and the glossator of Mn, at any rate, took this seriously, for he glossed it with ἀλλαχοῦ.

The credit for one further true reading is shared by A only with a corrector of V: 1165 ἀνταναλώσωμεν] -αλώσω μὲν AV²ᐟ³, -αλώ-coμεν V. There is little other solid evidence for a connection between A and V:[4] 99 γε om. AVZ (~A¹ˢV²ˢ); 244 τε ante καὶ add. AV. In the following passages A agrees with V alone of HMBOV in a reading which is otherwise weakly attested: hyp. 1.4 κοινήν] post Ἀργεῖοι AVCrSa; 443 ὑπερβαλών] -βάλλων AVAbMnRSa, -βάλων S; 1582 γε] δὲ AMtVCCrZu.

A is occasionally associated with members of HMBOV in readings which are unique or nearly unique to them: 269 ἐξαμύνασθαι] -ecθαι A(M)BMnZm¹ᶜ; 967 Ἀτρειδῶν] -δᾶν AMVR (~V²ˢ); 1005 δρόμημα uel δρομήματα] δράμημα ABC (δραμήματα M+); 1116 οὐ χάζομαι] οὐχ ἄζομαι ABOAt (~B³); 1258 ἐπειγώμεσθ' om. AMC KP (~K¹ᶜ); 1263 εἶτ'ἐπ'ἄλλην] εἶτα πάλιν MBOC (~B²B³), εἶτ'ἀπ' ἄλλην A (~A¹ˢ); 1381 ὤμοι] ὤιμοι AH²MBOAtJ; 1458 ἐν] ἐκ AMtHMBOVaCᵘᵛ<Zu²> (~M²Zuᶜ); 1545 θέλει] -η(ι) AHMVAtC (-ειν Mtᵘᵛ); 1632 κἀπὸ] κ'ὑπὸ AMt²BOC<Tᶻ²>, καὶ ὑπὸ MR (~Aʳʸᵖ Mtᶜ B³Tᶜ).

A has a few unique or nearly unique agreements with members of Θ: 201 τ'] δ'APr; 218 κἀνακουφίcω] -ίζω A¹ˢAbAdᶜ; 638 cιγῇ λόγου] cιγῆc λόγος AJ²R (~R¹ᶜ); 759 νῦν om. A(F)Sa (~A¹ˢ); 761 ἀγυιὰc] ἀγυὰc ASa; 781 θανῇ(ι) MBOVPr+: θάνῃ AAbᵘᵛ: θανεῖν FMnRSSa+; 894 φαιδρωπὸν] φαιδρὸν A et ᵍˡAb²MnPrR²S; 1585 ὅπωc χώcω] ὡc θάψω AMtPr (χώcω Prʸᵖ); 1600 τῆcδε (τῆcδε τῆc Pr) ante γῆc add. AMtPr.

A has a few agreements with the common associates of Θ (AaCrRfRw) and a few with members of Θ plus these associates: 92 τι] om. ARfS (et Ad), ante μοι Rw, [Mn]; 97 οὐχὶ] οὐ AAaRw (et RyZm); 238 ἑῶcι c'] ἑῶcιν c' AAa (ἑῶcιν MCR); 314 νοcῆιc] -ῇ APrRf¹ˢ (et B³ʸᵖ) (-ήcη(ι)c HMC); 314 δοξάζη(ι)c uel -ειc] -ει ARw (-ηc et -ειc Rwˢ), -η(ι) A¹ˢOG¹ˢPr; 368 τε om. AMnRw; 497 πλη-γεὶc] -ῆc ACrMn (~CrᶜMn¹ᶜ); 756 ἐπὶ φόνωι] περὶ φόνου AAa (et Zc, ~Zc²ʸᵖ); 760 πανταχῆ(ι) uel -οῦ] ἀπανταχῆ AAa (et AtZc); 816 ὅθεν om. ACr; 1018 c'om. AAa (et At); 1076 οὐκ ἔcτι] οὐκέτι AAa

(et At) (οὐκ ἔτ᾽ ἐcτὶ RfRw, οὐκέτ᾽ ἔcται AaᵞᵖPrRS), [Ab]; 1137 δ᾽
post ὀλολυγμὸc add. ARfRw (et J); 1272 ἐχθροῖc εἶ] -οῖc ἦν
AAaʳˢMnRS (et AdZcZu) (-οῖcι MAaC), [Ab]; 1421 δ᾽ ἐc] δ᾽ ACr
(δὲ AbMnR²ᵘᵛS, om. R); 1609 κτανεῖc] κτενεῖc AAa³ᵐFMnˢPrR
RwSᴵˢ (et AtJ) (u. om. Aa, add. Aa³ᵐ), [Ab].

A has a few unique agreements with one or both of GK: 47
μήτε] μὴ δὲ AGK (μηδὲ coni. Elmsley); 284 δ᾽ ἐμοί] δέ μοι AG; 622
δὲ om. AG; 1330 δ᾽om. AMtGK (et At); 1448 fere ἄλλον ἄλλοc᾽ ἐν
uel ἄλλον ἄλλοcε] ἄλλοc᾽ ἄλλον ἐν AMt²GK (et At) (ἄλλον ἄλλοcε
Mtᶜ²).

ξ (XXaXb)

I give the collective symbol ξ to three closely related manuscripts XXaXb. They have two especial features in common: (i) they have scholia composed by Moschopoulos, and (ii) they have some readings which appear to be conjectural. Turyn claimed that these manuscripts reflect a 'recension' by Moschopoulos himself.[1]

Before examining the evidence by which Turyn supported this claim, I shall examine the extent to which XXaXb disagree among themselves. Isolated errors by one of the three aside,[2] X rarely disagrees with XaXb (20 disagreements), Xb even more rarely disagrees with XXa (7 disagreements), but Xa not uncommonly disagrees with XXb (63 disagreements). While it is clear that XXaXb descend from a common source, it is equally clear that the lines of descent are not pure, but have been contaminated by the infiltration of readings from other sources. The proof of such contamination is that members of ξ may be witnesses, in a single place, to two readings which are attested in earlier manuscripts. Examples are: hyp. 1.19 λαβεῖν MBOVXXb+: γυναῖκα λαβεῖν Xa, λαβεῖν γυναῖκα (Π¹)Ad; 1.19 πυλάδη(ι) (Π¹)MBOXXb+: -ην VXa+; 101 δή BOVXXb+: om. MXa+; 279 αὖ BOVXXa²Xb+: om. MXa+; 390 μοι MOVgVX+: με HBO¹ˢXaXb+; 417 γ' MBOX+: om. VXaXb+; 455 ταῖcι MBVgVX+: ταῖc OXaXb+; 465 διοcκόρ-BOVXXb+: διοcκούρ- MXa+; 882 φίλω(ι) BOVXXb+: φίλον MXAʳˢ; 940 κατακτενεῖτε OVX+: -κτανεῖτε HMBXaXb+; 954 cε MBO¹ˢVXXa¹ˢXb+: om. OXa; 1085 πολύ M²OVXXb+: που MBVᶜXa+; 1414 ἔβαλον bis BOXXb+: ἔβαλλον bis HMVaXa+;

---

[1] Turyn 118 dates the 'Moschopoulean recension' c.1290. But the date of Moschopoulos' work on Euripides cannot be established with any precision. It may have been as late as c.1300. See J. J. Keaney, BZ 64 (1971) 303–21, Wilson 244, Mastronarde 24. All that we can say with reasonable certainty is that Moschopoulos preceded Thomas, the date of whose activities is equally uncertain (see p. 81 n. 2), and that the activities of Thomas preceded and probably overlapped those of Triclinius, which may have begun c.1305 and ended c.1330 (see p. 93). For a full bibliography on Moschopoulos see E. Trapp et al., Prosopographisches Lexicon der Palaiologenzeit, 8 (1986) 37.

[2] For the present purpose I class as isolated errors even those which may be shared by one or more of AdAnAtDrJMsThXcXdXeXfXgXh, which, as I shall later show (Chapter IX), belong, in varying degrees, to the branch of the tradition represented by ξ.

1537 αὖ MBOVXXb+: om. HXa+; 1655 γαμεῖν BOVXXa²Xb+: γαμεῖ MXa+.

Next I list disagreements between one of XXaXb and the other two, where the divergent member attests a reading found not in pre-Moschopoulean manuscripts but in manuscripts which are contemporary with Moschopoulos. By 'contemporary' I refer to manuscripts which were certainly or probably written c.1290–1300 (AFKPrRfRwSa) or may have been written even earlier (R).[3]

X possibly agrees once with R (398 με] μοι ⟨X²⟩R (~X²R¹ᶜ)) and once with K (1043 κενὴν] καινὴν⟨XK²⟩ (~X²K¹ᶜ), καὶ νῦν F (~F²)). More significant are two better attested errors: 756 ἀμφ'] ἀφ' XPrᵞᵖR (~R²) et AbGMnS; 1000 ἱπποβότα] -βάτα XF⟨Pr⟩Sa (~Prᶜ) et AaLMnZb (~Aa³). Xb agrees once with Rw: hyp. 2.17 τῶν ante γυναικῶν add. XbRw. Xa, which is the odd man out of the trio, provides richer material: it agrees with A (1345 γε om. XaA), F (939 μέν om. XaF (~F²) et Ab), Rf (1077–81 om. XaRf (~Rf¹ᵐ); 1498 ὕστερ'] ὕστερον XaRf et MnSZbZvTp), Sa (hyp. 2.15 and 2.17 πλησιαίτερον (XXb+) uel -έστερον] -αίστερον XaSa; 209 cε] γε XaSa et AbMnS (~Ab¹ˢᵘᵛ)), and it has several agreements with two or more of the contemporary manuscripts: 52 δέ om. XaAFRf (~F²Rf¹ᶜ) et CGZbZmZu; 278 ἠλάμεσθα (XXb+) uel -εθα] -άσμεθα XaPrRw et Ab, -άσμεσθα Xa²; 593 κεῖνος (XXb+) uel ᵏκεῖνος] ἐκεῖνος XaFSa et AaCLPZbZu (~L²); 872 Δαναόν] -ῶν XaPr¹ˢRfᵘᵛ (~Rf¹ᶜ); 877 κεῖνον] ἐκεῖνον XaFSa et Cr; 1057 ὁ (alterum) om. XaFPrSa et Cr.

It is important to recognize that XXaXb are not the uncontaminated descendants of their common ancestor. Once this is recognized, Turyn's treatment of them invites two questions: (i) If the descendants of the 'Moschopoulean recension' attest alternative readings, how are we to determine which of them was the reading

---

[3] Matthiessen 91 (see also *GRBS* 10 [1969] 299–300, and his review of Mastronarde in *BZ* 79 [1986] 344–6) treats these (with the exception of K) as pre-Moschopoulean. K (on which see his remarks, 93 n. 12) he would have treated as pre-Moschopoulean if he had by that time established its date as c.1291 (he did so later in *Scriptorium* 36 [1982] 255–8). Mastronarde 34 objects that 'The weakest aspect of Matthiessen's critique of Turyn is, I believe, the ease with which he assumes that mss *possibly* dating to the decade 1290–1300 are free of Moschopoulean and Thoman influence'. The outcome of the present inquiry will show that Matthiessen was, in effect, right (and that these manuscripts, while not demonstrably pre-Moschopoulean in date, are pre-Moschopoulean in content). But I offer the evidence in a way which does not prejudge the outcome.

In relation to the Sophoclean tradition, where similar issues arise, an approach similar to Matthiessen's is adopted by Dawe, *Studies* i. 55–6, and Wilson 246 and *JHS* 96 (1976) 172.

of that recension?[4] (ii) Since, in some cases, both of the alternative readings are pre-Moschopoulean, is there any good reason to suppose that an alternative reading, merely because it is not known to be pre-Moschopoulean, is unlikely to be pre-Moschopoulean? Turyn assumes that, in such cases, an agreement between the divergent member of XXaXb and a contemporary, or later, manuscript indicates the influence of the former on the latter. But the proof that the divergent member of XXaXb may attest a reading which is pre-Moschopoulean opens up the possibility that a divergent reading which is not demonstrably pre-Moschopoulean may be pre-Moschopoulean none the less. And once this possibility has been seen to be open, a further and more important possibility is opened, that any reading which is attested by the unanimity of XXaXb and is shared by contemporary manuscripts or is even shared only by later manuscripts may be pre-Moschopoulean too.

I pass from theory to an examination of the 58 readings[5] which Turyn (109–13) believed owe their origins to the 'Moschopoulean recension'. They show, he claims, the 'remarkable metrical alertness of Moschopulus in diagnosing corruptions and his skilful handling of corrupt passages in iambic trimeters and trochaic tetrameters' (117). To be sure, 'the best textual critic of that time' occasionally nods, for 'he himself made, either intentionally or by inadvertence, some changes conflicting with rules of versification or prosody' (117–18).

I divide these readings into three classes: (i) readings attested before Moschopoulos; (ii) readings attested in contemporary manuscripts; (iii) readings not attested before c. 1300. I cite first the pre-Moschopoulean attestation, then XXaXb, then contemporary manuscripts, then (separated from what precedes by an interposed 'et') the later manuscripts.[6] I mark with an asterisk readings which are certainly or possibly right. I do not generally mention which parts of the evidence recorded by me are not recorded by Turyn; the reader is invited to compare our two lists.

[4] Turyn has an answer to this question, and I shall later (p. 65) show how inadequate it is. Another answer is theoretically possible: that the 'Moschopoulean recension' was liberally equipped with variants. Since Turyn does not contemplate this possibility, I say no more of it.

[5] I have separated the reading at 1449 into two parts, one of which appears in list (i), the other in list (ii).

[6] I normally ignore the other 'Moschopoulean' manuscripts mentioned above, p. 49 n. 2.

(i) *Readings attested before Moschopoulos*

61* συμφοράν] -άς (Π³)ξK et GRyS. 'The coincidence of Moschopulus with the papyrus reading is certainly fortuitous', says Turyn, who does not cite GK (Ry was not available to him). The plural is right; and ξ gained it by inheritance, not by conjecture.[7]

212* γε] τε Π⁵, Stob. 4. 36. 1, pars codd. Plut. mor. 165e, ξR et Ry² (~Theoph. Achr.); μοι F. Turyn ascribes τε to 'Rᵖᶜ'; but it is in fact the original and only reading of R. The papyrus was not available to him.[8]

606 δυστυχέστερον] δυστυχέστατον Stob. 4. 22. 196, XXa; δυσχερέστατον Xb; δυσχερέστερον Z^γρ Zd^1ᶜ Zm^1ˢ Zu (~Zu^γρ); δυστχερέστερον Zd (~Zd^γρ). Turyn's assertion that the reading of XXa was 'taken over from the Stobaeus quotation' is as likely to be wrong as right.[9] The coincidence may be fortuitous, since comparative and superlative endings are regularly confused. Not fortuitous, however we choose to explain it, is the partial coincidence of Xb with the true reading preserved by the Thoman manuscripts.[10]

1048* χερῶν] χειρῶν OξA^1ˢ et PT^z (uel T^c). Turyn does not cite O (believing it to be post-Moschopoulean) either here or for the next two readings.

1094* ἀκρόπολιν] -πτολιν OXaXbK et G; τὴν ἀκρόπολιν T^t3, [T^z].

1449* ἄλλον ἄλλος' ἐν HMB+: ἄλλον ἄλλος ἐν Va+: ἄλλος' ἄλλον ἐν AGK+: ἄλλον ἄλλοσε OξRRw et AbCrMnPST^t3Tp.

(ii) *Readings attested in contemporary manuscripts*

69 ὀχούμεθ'] -μεσθ'ξRw.

169 νιν post οὖν add. ξB²ᵐB³⟨K²⟩ (~K^c). For all we know, the hand which I label B² may be pre-Moschopoulean.

228 μέλη] δέμας ξRw et G^1γρ T^t1/2γρ.

---

[7] See Zuntz, *Inquiry* 155, *Bulletin* 506, Willink ad loc. In what follows I shall normally not refer to the commentaries of Willink and West, except when I disagree.

[8] For the merits of τε (rejected by both Willink and West) see R. Kassel, *ZPE* 64 (1986) 39–40, Diggle, *Papyrologica Florentina* 19 (1990) 147–8. I am not persuaded by the counter-arguments of Di Benedetto, *ZPE* 70 (1987) 11–18. For Theophylactus Achridensis see p. 121 n. 1.

[9] A similar issue arises at S. *Ai.* 330: see Dawe, *Studies* i. 139, Wilson, *JHS* 96 (1976) 175.

[10] For this reading see below, p. 86. And for a more complete picture of the dissemination of δυστυχέστατον and δυσχερέστατον among the 'Moschopoulean' manuscripts see p. 79.

281* *cε*] *coι* ξA^IS Pr^IS RRw^IS et ZZcZmZu^cT^zs (~Zu^uv Zu^s). I discuss this below.[11]

327 μόχθων] κακῶν μόχθων ξ; ἐν ἄλλω μόχθων κακῶν A^rs; ἕνεκα τῶν κακῶν G^gl. I discuss this below.[12]

345 ἕτερον HMO+: ἄλλον ἕτερον BV+: ἄλλον (post γάρ) . . . ἕτερον Rw: ἄλλον ξA.

439* εἰπεῖν ἔχεις] ἔχεις εἰπεῖν ξK et GLPST^c. I discuss this below.[13]

609* ἀνάξεις] ἀνάψεις ξSa et F²Mn^cPR²s ZZbZuT^c (~Z^γρ). I discuss this below.[14]

782* τὸ] τῷ(ι) ξK^1c et Aa^rs GLZu^γρ; καὶ τὸ T^t3.

786* τὸ om. ξRf et LT^t3.

798* μητρὸς uel π̅ρ̅ς̅] μητέρος ξK et G; τῆς μητρὸς T^t3.

922 ἀνεπίπληκτον] ἀνεπίληπτον ⟨H?⟩ξK^1c Rf^IS Rw et CrGZ^γρ Zb²γρ Zb³ZcZd^γρ Zm^1γρ T^z (uel T^c) (~H^cG^1γρ Zc²γρ) et Georg. Pachym. decl. 9 (p. 165. 6 Boissonade).[15] ἀνεπίληπτον is in origin a gloss on ἀνεπίπληκτον (see Σ^mbvc, Schwartz 188. 20). If it really was written by H^ac, this passage should be promoted to list (i). A further possible pre-Moschopoulean testimony to ἀνεπίληπτον is found in Hesychius. In one entry he attests ἀνεπίπληκτον (A 2331 ἀκέραιον ἀνεπίπληκτον· καθαρόν, ἄκακον), but a later entry (A 4919) reads ἀνεπίληπτον· ἄμεμπτον, ἀκατάγνωστον. Turyn's statement that this entry 'cannot refer to the old Euripides text which did not contain the word' will be untrue, if H^ac did have that reading; even if it did not, the statement may still be untrue, since the reading is widely disseminated.

1066 κατθανόντοιν] -όντων ξB³s Rf^IS Rw^IS et GMn^uv (~Mn^1c); -όντας Aa (~Aa^rs); -όντι γ' ZdZu^1c; -όντ**ν L (~L^1c); -όντ*** T^z (~T^c).

1125 τοῖσιδ'] τοῖσιν ξAPr et ZmT^c; τοῖσδ' CrL; τοῖσι MnZb (~Mn^1c); δ' FSa.

1216 νῦν] δὴ MnRS; om. ξF et CrZ.

1387 σκύμνον] σκύμνου ξR (~R^1s).[16]

1600* τε] γε ξAFPrSa et MtZZbZcZmT^z.[17]

1602 δὴ om. ξFPrSa et P.

1622 οὐχί] οὔκουν ξK et GT^c.

[11] See pp. 58–9.   [12] See pp. 57–8.   [13] See pp. 59–60.   [14] See p. 60.
[15] George Pachymeres is dated 1242–c.1310 (Wilson 241).
[16] Matthiessen 106 n. 51 is mistaken in attributing this also to Sa.
[17] Cf. Zuntz, *Inquiry* 155–6.

There are several other readings, not listed by Turyn, which have an equal claim to be included in this list:[18]

hyp. 2.15* οὕτω(c) om. ξAPr et Zu.

hyp. 2.15 χορὸν] χρόνον XXbRf.

hyp. 2.18* cίγα cίγα] cῖγα cῖγα ξ et G; utroque accentu A¹.

340 βροτοῖc] -cιν ξPr et Cr.

523* ἀμύνω] ἀμυνῶ ξK¹ᶜ et Aa³GTᶜ.

538 δ' om. ξK et G.

594* πειθόμενοc] πιθ- XXaᶜXbK et Aa¹ˢGᶜTᵗ¹/².

608 φρένα] φρένας ξPrRRf et AbMnSTᶻ.

635* ὅπη(ι)] ὅποι ξRfRw et Cr<L>PZZbZm (~L²Zʳ); [K].

753* ἐτόλμηcε] -cεν ξK et Tᶻ (uel Tᶜ).

791* κατάcχωcι(ν)] -ωc' ξK et Tᵗ².

802 ὤν] ἄν ξPrʸᵖR et Ab²ʸᵖMnSSa²ᵍˡ (~ʸᵖMnR¹; ὤν post φίλοc ξᵍˡ).

832 γᾶν] γῆν ξFSa et Tp.

1005 δράμημα uel δρόμημα] δραμήματα MMnSTp (~Sʸᵖ), δρομήματα ξPrʸᵖ et G¹ᶜ.

1024 c' om. ξRf et CrS.

1254* ἔννεπε] ἔνεπε ξRw² (~Rw aut Rwᶜ) et Tᵗ³.

1294 cκοποῦca πάντα (uel πάντη)] cκοποῦc' ἅπαντα ξF et ZZcTᵗ³Tp.

1299* ἀένναον] ἀέναον ξA et LTᵗ³; [Mt].

1323 μοι] με ξRf et B³ˢRw²ZcZm¹ˢTᵗ³ (~Tᵗ³ˢ).

1341 κἀπικούφιcον] κἀπο- ξFRw et Aa³ˢZb.

1364 ὀλόμενον bis] semel ξPrRSa et Ab(Mn)MtSZm.

1372 τριγλύφουc] -αc ξRf et Tᵗ³Tp et Mt aut Mtᶜ.

1448 ἐκλήιcε] ἐκκλήιcε ξA et ZcZd (ἔκλησεν Zd²ʸᵖ).

1601 τῶι om. XaXbPrRw.

1607* γε] γ' ξK et ZTᵗ².

1609* θυγατέρα] θυγατέρ' ξK et PZTᶻ.

1626* c' post Φοῖβος X(Xa)XbB¹/²ᶜAK et GMtZbZmTᶜ. If c' was added by the first hand of B, then the reading is pre-Moschopoulean and should be promoted to list (i). The hand B² might also be pre-Moschopoulean.

1653* ἤ(ι)] ἦc ξPrᵍˡ et CrG¹ᶜZcTa²ˢ et Mt aut Mtᶜ.

---

[18] Turyn's criterion (106) for deciding what to include and what to exclude is arbitrary. It is necessary to consider these additional readings, since we cannot form a proper judgement on what he has included unless we know what he has excluded.

(iii) *Readings not attested before* c.*1300*

116 ϲτᾶϲ´] ϲτᾶϲα γ´ξ.[19]

162 ἄρ᾿ om. ξ.

286 ἔργον] ἔργον ἐϲ ξ; εἰϲ ἔργον ZZbZcZmZu<T²> (~T^tc); εἰϲ super ἔργον ^glB²OAa²GKT^t.[20]

326 ἐάϲατ᾿] ἐᾶτ᾿ ξ.

373* ἁλικτύπων] ἁλιτύπων ξ.

378* ἐξέλιπον] ἐξέλειπον ξ et T^c pot. qu. T^z.

403 πότερα] πότερον ξ.

407* ἐκ φαϲμάτων] φανταϲμάτων ξ et R²gl et ^iΣg; φαϲμάτων An^cAtMs; ἐκφαϲμάτων B³ et interpretatur V^glΣAa. I discuss this below.[21]

424 ἔφυϲ κακόϲ] εἰπὼν κακῶϲ ξ (εἰπών etiam T^t2γρ).

447 εἰϲ] πρὸϲ ξ.

535 τοῦτον] αὐτὸν ξ et T^t2γρ.

592 νέμει] ante ϲτόμα MnPr, post ϲαφέϲτατον ξ et Aa.

698 αὐτὸν uel αὑτὸν uel αὐτῷ(ι)] αὐτὸϲ ξ et T^c (αὐτ** T^z), αὐτὸϲ Aa³.

747 τόδε (uel τάδε) γὰρ] τοῦτο γὰρ V; τοῦτο γ´ξ et T^t3; [T^z].

750 ϲπείραϲ] ϲπείρων ξ.

779 μολόντι] μολόντα ξ et T^t1s.

782* τὸ πρᾶγμ᾿] τὸ πρᾶγμα γ´ξ; τὸ πρᾶγμα δ᾿GK; μὴν τὸ πρᾶγμ᾿ T^t3.

790 αὖ λέγειϲ] ἀγγελεῖϲ ξγρ.

963 ἔλαχ᾿ ἁ (uel ἥ)] ἔλαχε ἁ S; ἔλαχε CrKRfZb³ (ἔλα** Zb); ἔλαχεν ξ.

982 καὶ post μέϲον add. ξ et Tp et ΣPi. Ol. 1. 91a cod. E, ante μέϲον T^t3. Turyn's claim that Pindar cod. E gained its reading from ξ is controversial, as he acknowledges.[22]

985 γέροντι πατρὶ (uel πατέρι)] πατρὶ γέροντι ξ.

1029 μέλεοϲ] τλῆμον ξγρ.[23]

1039* ἔχω· ϲὲ δ᾿] ἐγὼ ϲὲ δ᾿ξ. I discuss this below.[24]

1115 δοῦλον (alterum)] δούλων XXa^1cXb et T^ts.

1135 ἔκτειν᾿] ἀπέκτειν᾿ξ.

1160 τ᾿ uel δ᾿] om. ξ.

---

[19] I assume that the motive for the interpolation was not syntactical (Zuntz, *Inquiry* 161 n. †) but prosodic.　　　[20] Cf. Zuntz, *Inquiry* 163.　　　[21] See pp. 61–2.
[22] Cod. E (Laur. 32. 37) is dated by Turyn (*De codicibus Pindaricis* [1932] 21–2) to the 14th century, by Irigoin (*Histoire du Texte de Pindare* [1952] 308) to c.1300.
[23] Cf. Zuntz, *Inquiry* 160 n. †.　　　[24] See p. 62.

1180 γ' om. ξ.

1254 μοι om. ξ.

1357 ἄν post πρὶν add. ξ et G¹ᶜZdTᵗ³.²⁵

1399 Ἀίδα] κατ' ἀίδου ξ; (ἀίδ)ου ˢB²VaAaʳZm¹Tᵗ³.

1449* ϲτέγαιϲ] ϲτέγηϲ ξ et AaMnMtᶜ˙ˀSTᵗ³Tp, -αϲ Cr.

1465 ἀνίαχεν ἴαχεν] ἀνίαχεν ἀνίαχεν HAMt+; ἀνίαχεν fere
MRw; ἴαχεν ἴαχεν ξ et MtᶜZcZv; ἴαχεν γ' ἴαχεν γ' Tp.²⁶

1507 προϲπίπτων] -πιτνῶν OGKZvTᵗ³; -πεϲών ξ.

Here are some further readings which Turyn might have
included:

hyp. 1.6 αὐτῶν] -τοῦ XXb.

hyp. 2.14 καθέζεται om. ξ.

101* εἰϲ] ἐϲ ξ.

186* ὦ om. ξ et Tᵗ³.

350 ὁρᾶϲθαι] ὁρᾶται ξ et Aa³.

355 ηὔχου] εὔχου ξ.

736 ἐμέ] ᾽μέ M; με ξ.

821 μελάνδετον] μελάνδευτον ξ et Zd.

822 ἀελίοιο] ἠελ- ξ; ἠελ- AaSa²ˢZm¹ˢ (~Aa¹ˢ); ἀελ- CrK.

899 οὔτε (prius)] οὐδέ ξ.

933 Δαναΐδαι] δαναΐδαι XXaᶜˀXb.

1004 οὐρανοῦ προϲαρμόϲαϲ (-ϲαϲα V²GTp, ~V²ᐟ³; -ϲαϲαν O²ˢ)]
προϲαρμόϲαϲ' οὐρανοῦ ξ.

1010 δολίοιϲι] -οιϲ ξ.

1027* ἀπ'] ὑπ' ξ et AaMnSZbZc.

1278 τἀπίϲω uel sim.] τοὐπίϲω ξ et Gᴵᶜᵘᵛ.

1465 ἀ (ἄ)] ἤ ξ et Tp.

1488 δ' ἐφεύγομεν uel δὲ φ-] δ' ἐκφ- ξ.

1491 τλάμων] τλήμων ξ et Tp.

1525* με] μ' ξ et Tᵗ³.

1596 μή γ'] μὴ δ' PrSa; μήτ' ξ et Tᵗˢ.

1598* τάδε] τάδ' ξ et Tᵗ².

1605* ϲε] ϲ' ξ et Tᵗ².

1606* μητέρα] μητέρ' ξ et Tᵗ²ᐟ³.

1684* Διὸϲ] ζηνὸϲ ξ. I discuss this below.²⁷

²⁵ Cf. Zuntz, *Inquiry* 158 n. ††.
²⁶ I have discussed these readings in *CQ* n.s. 40 (1990) 115–22.
²⁷ See p. 62.

Turyn's assertion that, whenever any one of AFKPrRRfRwSa (and the fourteenth-century manuscripts) agrees with ξ in a reading which is not attested earlier, it has probably taken that reading from the 'Moschopoulean recension', is beyond proof and beyond probability. Several of the readings on list (ii) are metrical adjustments which also appear in K (439, 523, 594, 753, 782, 791, 798, 1607, 1609, 1622; note also 1094 on list (i)), a manuscript which has many metrical adjustments absent from ξ,[28] and which has no claim to be considered as a witness to the 'Moschopoulean recension'. This suggests that there were scholars contemporary with, or earlier than, Moschopoulos, who had an understanding of metre, and that their handiwork finds expression sometimes in K, sometimes in ξ, sometimes in both. Another metrical adjustment is shared by ξ not with K but with Rf (786), and another with Pr (1005). Two readings actually destroy the metre (1601, 1602) and so are presumably slips, not conjectures. The uneven distribution of these 'Moschopoulean' readings (some in K [in addition to those listed above note also 61, 169, 538, 922], some in one or both of RfRw [hyp. 2.15, 69, 228, 281, 635, 786, 922, 1024, 1066, 1254, 1323, 1341, 1372, 1449, 1601], some in A [hyp. 2.15, 2.18, 281, 327, 345, 1048, 1125, 1299, 1448, 1600], some in one or more of the related manuscripts FPrRSa [hyp. 2.15, 212, 281, 340, 608, 609, 802, 832, 1005, 1125, 1216, 1294, 1341, 1364, 1387, 1449, 1600, 1601, 1602]) suggests that we are dealing not with the influence of a single source, such as is presupposed by the hypothesis of a 'Moschopoulean recension', but rather with a common fount of corrections and corruptions, as well as a trickle of older readings, which emerged in the second half of the thirteenth century and spread through several different channels.[29]

A particularly interesting case is 327 (κακῶν μόχθων ξ; ἐν ἄλλῳ μόχθων κακῶν A^r), which Turyn regards as 'proof that A had at his disposal a Moschopulean ms.; he recorded here the Moschopulean reading only reversing the sequence of words'. On the contrary, the most natural inference is that there existed, in some pre-Moschopoulean manuscript, a gloss κακῶν written over μόχ-θων, and that the source of ξ incorporated it in one place, the source of A^r in another. As it happens, I have found μόχθων κακῶν in Xg.[30]

---

[28] See p. 157.

[29] Much the same view is expressed very well by Zuntz, *Inquiry* 158–9.

[30] On which see p. 78.

In other manuscripts κακῶν probably replaced μόχθων in the text. Possibly the gloss in G (ἕνεκα τῶν κακῶν) was designed to accompany a text with κακῶν, not with μόχθων, since glossators regularly explain a genitive which has no governing preposition by prefixing ἕνεκα.[31] This, then, is evidence for the independence of A from ξ, rather than for its dependence on ξ.[32]

Of the readings on lists (i) and (ii) which I have marked with an asterisk as being right or possibly right, some are universally accepted as right and need no discussion (hyp. 2.18, 523, 594, 753, 782, 786, 791, 798, 1048, 1094, 1600, 1609, 1626). In virtually all of them the fault was also recognized by Triclinius, although he sometimes adopted a different solution. These are all minor (mostly metrical) adjustments, presumably within the capacity of Byzantine scholars, although I should not exclude the possibility that a few (1094, 1600, 1626) are inherited readings. Two readings (1254, 1299), both involving single for double ν, could be lucky accidents, since in the former case metrical considerations would not have prompted the change (the syllable in question is the initial *anceps* of a dochmiac), and in the latter case recognition of the dactylic metre is less probable than casual substitution of the more common form for the rarer. One reading (1005) might have been included in list (i) rather than (ii), since it is a slight trivialization of the truth preserved in M. At 1653 the truth (for such I take it to be) may have been taken over by ξ from an existing gloss (such as we find in Pr).

Three other asterisked readings on list (ii) require fuller discussion:

281   αἰcχύνομαί cε μεταδιδοὺc πόνων ἐμῶν.

cε] coι ξA¹ˢPr¹ˢRRw¹ˢ et ZZcZmZuᶜTᶻˢ (~ZuᵘᵛZuˢ)   μεταδιδούc coι
AaAbMn‹R›Sa (~Rᶜ), μεταδούc coι PrS, μεταδοὺc K

coι appears in one place or other (in both places in Rᵃᶜ) in a substantial number of manuscripts: either as a substitute for cε or as an unmetrical interpolation after μετα(δι)δούc. There are two ways of accounting for this phenomenon: either (i) coι is a gloss which began life above the line (where it still stands in APrRwTᶻ), de-

[31] Cf. 1286, where FPrSa actually omit κακῶν, but PrSa add the gloss ἕνεκα τῶν κακῶν.
[32] On the issue of the relationship of A to ξ see Matthiessen 90 and *BZ* 79 (1986) 346, Mastronarde 113–14, and (for Sophocles) Dawe, *Studies* i. 57. It will be seen that I side with Matthiessen, rather than Mastronarde.

signed to clarify the construction of μεταδιδούς, and then became incorporated in the text in one place or the other; or (ii) it is right, and ce is a corruption, which ousted coι, which in turn first became a supralinear variant and then found its way back into the text in the wrong place in AaAbMnPr‹R›SSa. The former explanation is logical and more economical. But the latter, I believe, is right. First, coι is the choicer word, since αἰςχύνομαι requires no object, either expressed or unexpressed, while μεταδιδούς gains by the addition of a dative, which, if it is not expressed, must be understood (i.e. 'I feel ashamed to be giving you' is preferable to 'I feel shame before you, by giving ‹you›'). For the absolute use of αἰςχύνομαι see *El.* 900 αἰςχύνομαι μέν, βούλομαι δ' εἰπεῖν ὅμως. And it is possible that Dobree was right to delete the c' at *Ion* 934 αἰςχύνομαι μέν c', ὦ γέρον, λέξω δ' ὅμως. For αἰςχύνομαι with the participle see *IA* 981, fr. 452, [A.] *ScT* 1029–30, *PV* 642, S. *Ant.* 540–1, *Phil.* 1383. Second, coι is the less obvious reading, because the corruption of coι to ce after αἰςχύνομαι would be more natural than the reverse corruption. And, although the position of coι might appear unnatural (which itself would facilitate the change to the more obvious ce), its position is, in fact, a normal one, for the enclitic has exercised its natural tendency to move towards the beginning of the clause.[33] The reading coι is commended by Zuntz[34] and by Willink. It is certainly not conjectural. If right, it must be inherited.

439 εἰπεῖν ἔχεις] ἔχεις εἰπεῖν ξK et GLPST^c. Turyn calls this an 'excellent metrical correction'. Whether it is a 'correction', and whether it is right, are questions which are open to dispute. I do not believe that the text as usually punctuated is acceptable: τί δρῶντες ὅτι καὶ ϲαφὲς ἔχεις εἰπεῖν ἐμοί; The ὅτι καί is most unnatural and is not supported by the parallel (adduced by Willink) of *Ion* 232 πάντα θεᾶϲθ', ὅτι καὶ θέμις, ὄμμαϲι, where ὅτι is not, as here, the direct object of a verb. The parallel would support the punctuation τί δρῶντες; ὅτι καὶ ϲαφὲς (sc. ἐϲτίν) ἔχεις εἰπεῖν ἐμοί; This could be the right answer: Menelaus is asking for clarification of Orestes' enigmatic statement that the Argives do not allow him to live ('What are they doing? Can you give me a *clear* statement?').

[33] See J. Wackernagel, *Kl. Schr.* i (1953) 1–104, E. Fraenkel, *Beobachtungen zu Aristophanes* (1962) 45–6, Barrett on *Hi.* 10–11, Diggle, *CQ* n.s. 27 (1977) 236 and *Studies* 100, West, *BICS* 31 (1984) 182.   [34] *Inquiry* 156.

For the καί after ὅτι see Denniston, *Greek Particles* 295, and for the
ellipse of ἐcτί see *Hi.* 191, *Hel.* 1137, *Ba.* 881 (= 901), 894, *Hyps.*
fr. I. ii. 11 (p. 26 Bond). But the scholia imply a variant: Σᵐᵇᶜ ἐὰν
δὲ γράφηται ἢ τί, ὁ cτίχοc οὕτωc· τί δρῶντεc; ἢ τί καὶ cαφὲc εἰπεῖν
ἔχειc; This version can be made metrical by writing cαφῶc
(Reiske) for cαφέc, and we might then write either ἢ (Hermann) or
εἴ (Lenting) for the ἢ of the scholia: either τί δρῶντεc; ἢ τι καὶ
cαφῶc εἰπεῖν ἔχειc; (Nauck), or τί δρῶντεc, εἴ τι καὶ cαφῶc εἰπεῖν
ἔχειc; (Lenting). But the sense is hardly improved; and the omission of ἐμοί, though the word is not indeed needed, receives only
doubtful support from its omission by the scholia; and cαφῶc gains
little support from its appearance in the two other attempts by the
scholia to interpret the transmitted text (Σᵐᵇᶜ εἰπέ μοι cαφῶc ὃ
ἔχειc εἰπεῖν, Σᵐᵇᵛᶜ εἰπέ μοι cαφῶc [cαφὲc B] ὅτι δρῶντεc), for it is
natural that the scholia should use adverbial cαφῶc and not cαφέc
in a paraphrase which links the word with εἰπεῖν. And for cαφέc
see A. *Pe.* 705–6 cαφέc τί μοι | λέξον. A further possibility is
Hermann's τί δρῶντεc; ἢ τι [καὶ] cαφὲc ἔχειc εἰπεῖν ἐμοί; But I am
much attracted by a suggestion of H. C. Günther, τί δρῶντεc; ἢ
καὶ cαφὲc ἔχειc εἰπεῖν τί μοι;[35]
    At all events, if the order ἔχειc εἰπεῖν is right, the change (trans-
position of words) is different in kind from the types of metrical
conjecture found elsewhere in the play, and it could be inherited.

    609 ἀνάξειc] ἀνάψειc ξSa et F²MnᶜPR²ˢZZbZuTᶜ (~Zʳʸᵖ). This
is far too good and recherché to be a conjecture, and ἀνάξειc would
cause no offence to a Byzantine reader.[36] It could be a happy
chance, though the confusion usually goes the other way (*Med.*
107, 1382, A. *Ch.* 131).[37] And so I regard it as inherited truth. I see
no cause for preferring ἀναζεῖc (West). For the use of the future
tense see Kühner-Gerth 1. 172.

    I now turn to list (iii). Two of the readings marked as true or
possibly true are simple but creditable changes made at the
prompting of metre (378, 782). The former change was accepted
by Triclinius; the latter is an improvement on the change found in
GK (and here Triclinius disgraces himself). In four places (1525,

---

[35] *WS* 102 (1989) 117–18. For τί μοι occupying the last foot of the trimeter see *Studies* 84.
[36] Cf. Zuntz, *Inquiry* 155 (though I am not sure that he is right in supposing that ἀνάψειc
is implied by Σᵐᵇᵛᶜ [Schwartz 160. 6]).   [37] See *CQ* n.s. 34 (1984) 52–3.

1598, 1605, 1606) elision is restored for *scriptio plena* at change of speaker; in all of these Triclinius also made the change. At 373 ἀλιτύπων appears, at first sight, to be another metrical conjecture. But I doubt if it is. No Byzantine reader would have baulked at a fourth-foot anapaest;[38] at any rate, Triclinius did not. There is a strong possibility that this is inherited truth.[39] Nor can the elimination of ὦ at 186 be conjectural, since no scholar before Triclinius understood the principle of strophic responsion. So either it is inherited,[40] or it is a lucky accident.[41] It is interesting that ξ cure the metrical fault at 1507 with προcπεcών and not with προcπιτνῶν, since the 'Moschopoulean' manuscripts cure a similar fault at S. *Ai.* 58 with -πιτνῶν, while the inferior remedy -πεcών is found only as a variant in L.[42] That προcπιτνῶν was in existence in the time of Moschopoulos is proved by its occurrence in the earlier O and the contemporary K. Turyn, who draws attention to the Sophoclean passage, registers no awareness that it does nothing to support his belief in the Moschopoulean authorship of προcπεcών. Over two other readings (1027 and 1449) editors will continue to differ. I believe that both readings are right (except that in 1449 we need Cr's Doric form).[43]

Three readings invite fuller discussion:

At 407 φαντάcματων solves the problem posed by the two prepositions ἐκ and ὕπο, one of which must go.[44] Whether it is inherited or conjectural, is not easily decided: The claim that 'the grammatical problem . . . was not of a kind likely to trouble a Byzantine scholar' (Willink, who favours inheritance) is controverted by ΣAa, which acknowledges the problem and resolves it by positing a noun ἐκφαcμάτων (τινὲc λέγουcι τοῦτ᾽ εἶναι δύο μέρη τοῦ λόγου· ἀλλ᾽ οὐχί· ἔcτι δὲ τὸ ἔκφαcμα ἕν μέροc λόγου), and this interpretation is reflected by V[gl], which writes ἕν μέροc λόγου over ἐκ φαcμάτων, and by B[3], which adds a subscript mark (ἐκφαcμάτων) and glosses the word with ἐκπλήξεων. Other manuscripts (An[c]AtMsXeXfXg) omit ἐκ. It is possible that φαντάcματων is implied by Σ[g]: ὑπὸ φοβημάτων ποίων πανθάνη (sic, ut uid.) ταῦτα καὶ

---

[38] Even modern scholars happily embrace fourth-foot anapaests (C. Prato, *Maia* 9 [1957] 49–67, W. J. Verdenius, *Mnem.* 41 [1988] 405 n. 2, S.G. Daitz at *Hec.* 1159). See my remarks in *JHS* 95 (1975) 199.
[39] Zuntz, *Inquiry* 161, takes a different view.   [40] So Barrett, *CQ* n.s. 15 (1965) 70.
[41] Cf. 153 ὦ (again before φίλα) om. XaZc (~Xa[1c]).   [42] Cf. Dawe, *Studies* i. 43, 83.
[43] At 1449 I agree with Willink. Zuntz, *Inquiry* 167 n. ‡, takes a different view.
[44] So Willink. West's defence is unconvincing.

φαντασμάτων; If φαντασμάτων is a conjecture, it is a remarkably good one. There is a strong possibility that it is inherited truth.[45]

At 1039, where most editors are content with αἷμ' ἔχω· cὲ δ', one part of the Moschopoulean manuscripts (ξAdThXcXdXeXh) has αἷμ'· ἐγὼ cὲ δ', the other (DrJMsXfXg) has αἷμ'· ἐγὼ δέ c'.[46] I believe that the latter is right, and that neither of the Moschopoulean readings is conjectural. I have given my reasons elsewhere.[47]

At 1684 one may doubt whether any Byzantine scholar before Triclinius would have conjectured Ζηνός for Διός in anapaests.[48] And here not even Triclinius shows awareness of the metrical fault, for he accepts Διός.[49] But he replaces Διός with Ζηνός (whether by conjecture or inheritance) at S. Tr. 956 in an iambic dimeter. And he applies the same remedy at S. El. 1097, but there he is preceded by L^γρ. These passages (and S. Ant. 1149, if Bothe is right) prove that Ζηνός may be corrupted to Διός.[50] And so, even if we suppose (what we cannot prove) that Ζηνός is conjectural rather than inherited here, it may still be right. It is far from certain that Nauck's Δίοιc is to be preferred.[51]

It is clear from the evidence presented above that scholars existed in the time of Moschopoulos who were capable of making simple corrections in iambics and trochaics. Whether Moschopoulos himself was responsible for any of these corrections we cannot say.[52] It is equally clear that ξ had access to sources now lost to us.[53] The proof of this is the coincidence in truth between ξ and the papyrus at 61 and 212 and between Xa and the papyrus at hyp. 1.19.[54] Other

---

[45] Cf. Zuntz, *Inquiry* 161 n. † (who, however, repeats the error derived by Murray from Wecklein that O too has φαντασμάτων).

[46] For these 'Moschopoulean' manuscripts (other than ξ) see Chapter IX, especially p. 79.   [47] *CQ* n.s. 40 (1990) 105–6.   [48] Cf. Zuntz, *Inquiry* 162 n. ‡.

[49] See p. 98.   [50] Cf. Dawe, *Studies* i, 193, iii. 43.   [51] Willink agrees.

[52] 'In such cases, a Moschopoulean correction should be credited to the name of Moschopulus in critical apparatuses of future editions' (Turyn 117). It should not. Even Zuntz (162), after so admirably demonstrating that the text offered by ξ does not add up to a 'Moschopoulean recension', comes to what seems to me a mistaken conclusion: 'the upshot is a set of readings not attested before Moschopulos and so definitely uniform in character that one is bound to regard him as their originator.'

[53] Cf. R. Browning, *BICS* 7 (1960) 11–21 (= *Studies on Byzantine History, Literature and Education* [1977] no. XII).

[54] See pp. 49, 52, 71, 117. In *Ph.* we have the more telling evidence of P. Oxy. 2455 and 2544, which proves that ξ have a text of the hypothesis much older than and superior to that of any other manuscript (Barrett, *CQ* n.s. 15 [1965] 58–71, Mastronarde 91–2), and possibly derived by Moschopoulos from Planudes (see Mastronarde's Teubner edition [1988] 2).

instances might be quoted of readings which have all but escaped the older manuscripts and first appear in ξ and contemporary manuscripts: such as (the correct) γόους for λόγους at 1022, recorded as a variant by M^{ιγρ}, but thereafter appearing only in ξPrRfZb^{ιc} and as a variant in MnR^{2}Sa. And as a further indication of access to lost sources I should appeal to the variants at 790 (ἀγγελεῖς ξ^{γρ}) and 1029 (τλῆμον ξ^{γρ}). To suppose that these are conjectures is perverse: they are variants, wrong indeed, but inherited from manuscripts now lost.

CHAPTER IX

Associates of ξ

So far I have conducted my discussion of the 'Moschopoulean recension' on the terms dictated by Turyn. It was he who chose
XXaXb as representative witnesses to that 'recension'. And it is
worthwhile to examine how he came to make that choice. He began
by taking X: 'a typical representative of a manuscript with pure
Moschopulean scholia . . . X is a representative of the Moschopulean recension, if we rely on the basic rule that the concomi-
tant scholia of a certain recension indicate likewise that the poetic
text of the ms. in question belongs to the same recension' (42–3).[1]
Later he added Xa: 'for the Moschopulean recension, I shall take
the concordant testimony of . . . X . . . and Xa' (98). When the testimony of X and Xa proves discordant, he adds the testimony of
Xb, 'in order to establish *the* Moschopulean reading' (98).

What Turyn has done is to choose three manuscripts which
generally agree with each other and to assume that the mere fact of
their agreement confers a special status on their common reading.
But why should it? The general affinity of XXaXb proves that they
are derived from a common source. And that is all that it proves.
It still remains to be proved that, if such a thing as the 'Moschopoulean recension' ever existed, the common source of XXaXb
is the source which gives us closest access to it. Turyn's own inves-
tigations showed that over a hundred other manuscripts agree and
disagree in varying measure with the 'concordant testimony' of
XXaXb. He assumed that these agreements and disagreements are
indications of the relative fidelity and infidelity of those
manuscripts to the 'Moschopoulean recension'. But, since it has
not been proved, and cannot be proved, that XXaXb most nearly
reflect that 'recension', these agreements and disagreements may
be taken only as an indication of relative fidelity and infidelity to
XXaXb. Suppose that five manuscripts which generally agree with
XXaXb share a reading among themselves but not with XXaXb:
by what right do we say that this reading is less 'Moschopoulean'
than the reading of XXaXb? In short, we must not be seduced by

---

[1] The 'basic rule' has no proven validity: see above, p. 2.

the 'concordant testimony' of XXaXb—at least, not until we have
investigated the behaviour of that large body of manuscripts whose
text, in varying measure, is akin to the text of XXaXb.[2]

To investigate all, or even a fair proportion, of the 'Moschopoulean' manuscripts listed by Turyn would be truly *in tenui
labor*, and the glory more tenuous still. But I have investigated, in
whole or part, thirteen. I have chosen four (AdAnAtMs) on the
recommendation of Matthiessen (122–3), who himself has investigated AdAnMs in *Hecuba*, even as Mastronarde has investigated
AdAnAt in *Phoenissae*. I have chosen two others (DrTh) because
(partial) reports of their readings are available.[3] I have chosen two
(J and Xc) because they were close at hand.[4] And at a late stage I
investigated as many as I had time for during a vacant day in the
Bibliothèque Nationale (XdXeXfXgXh).

The presentation of my results will be uneven. For example, Ad
requires much longer exposition than the rest, since claims have
been made about the nature of its text which require detailed
scrutiny. And since I have inspected XeXfXgXh only in part, they
will not occupy much space in my discussion.

(i) *Ad*

According to Turyn (121–2), 'The main bulk of the ms., compris-
ing *Hecuba* ca. 600–end, *Orestes*, *Phoenissae* ca. 600–end, is Moschopulean . . . The sections *Hec.* ca. 1–600 and *Phoen.* ca. 1–600
seem to have a predominantly old text.' Matthiessen (37–8) has expressed the view that in *Hecuba* Ad is essentially a *uetus*, showing
less Moschopoulean influence than Turyn alleged, and he surmises

---

[2] This point is appreciated by Mastronarde 89: 'even in the unlikely event that he
[Moschopoulos] paid deliberate attention to the constitution of the text of each line of the
play . . . we cannot be certain that his choices are all reflected in the readings of XXaXb,
the leading witnesses of the form of text which I term χ, for these mss are all about a gen-
eration later than Moschopoulos' work.' Similarly Matthiessen, *BZ* 79 (1986) 346: 'Diese
Hss. stimmen zwar in ihrem Text stark überein, so daß man von einer recht geschlossenen
Gruppe sprechen kann, wir haben aber keine Anhaltspunkt dafür, in welchem Umfang
diese Übereinstimmung auf das Wirken des Mosch. zurückzuführen ist.'

[3] Reports of Dr and Ms are taken from Beck (see above, p. 11), of Th from
Pappageorgiou (see p. 11), and so I cannot guarantee their accuracy or completeness. Where
I have inferred a reading from the silence of Beck or Pappageorgiou, I indicate it by the
symbols ⟨Dr⟩ or ⟨Ms⟩ or ⟨Th⟩.

[4] J is not, indeed, included by Turyn in his list of 'Moschopoulean' manuscripts, but is
treated separately by him as a representative of the so-called 'dyad' (*Hec.*, *Or.*). But the nature of its text shows that it belongs with the other manuscripts with which I deal in this
chapter.

(123 n. 2) that the same may also be true of *Orestes*. Mastronarde (37 and 119) has detected links between Ad and MO in *Phoenissae*. Although I should not accept as evidence for a link all of the agreements which Mastronarde adduces (for reasons which will soon become apparent), there are nevertheless several agreements which must be accepted as evidence, of which the most significant are: *Ph.* 198 γὰρ] δὲ MOAd; 301–2 Φοίνιccαν ὦ νεάνιδες βοὰν ἔcω | δόμων κλύουcα τῶνδε] φοίνιccαν βοὰν κλύουcα | ὦ νεάνιδες fere MOAdCr.

It is important to determine whether a link exists between Ad and any of HMBOV in *Orestes*. And at first sight it appears that evidence does exist for a link between Ad and MO. But on closer inspection most of that evidence evaporates. Ad is an extraordinarily careless manuscript. Addition of letters; omission of letters, syllables, words; confusion of vowels and diphthongs; confusion of case-endings and verb-inflexions—these are to be found on every page. Since Ad is so prone to errors of this kind, agreement in such errors is no proof of affiliation. Here are the agreements in unique or nearly unique errors between Ad and one or both of MO:

hyp. 1.7 ἦλθε] -εν MOAd, at sentence-end. But at 1.6 Ad has εἰcαπέcτειλεν (with BFGSZu) at the end of a clause, and at 1.11 it uniquely has cυνεβούλευcεν in mid-sentence, when the following word begins with a consonant.

hyp. 2.8 τῆc τοῦ Ὀρέcτου] τῆc ὀρ- MAd (et AnJThXd), τοῦ ὀρ- MnSSa, [O]. The manuscripts are erratic in their admission of the article before names in the hypotheses. For the most part they omit it; its widespread attestation here is unusual. But Ad is prone to omit the article in the poetical text: 646 τοῦ om., 1065 τοῦ om., 1149 τὸν om. Here the presence of two articles (τῆc τοῦ) may have facilitated the loss of one (note that MnSSa omit τῆc).

88 ὅδε] ὧδε MAd (~M³). Confusion of o and ω is the commonest of the errors of Ad: for example, 19 ὁ] ὤ, 91 οὕτωc] οὗτοc, 112 Ἑρμιώνη, 247 μόνοc] -ωc, 350 δῆλοc] δῆλωc. See also on 535, 852, 1541 below.

383 ἱκέτηc] -τιc M²/³AdMnᵘᵛ (~Mnˡᶜ). Other unique confusions in Ad of η and ι: hyp. 2.21 χείρηcτον, 47 πυρή, 511 προβίcεται, 576 ἴcθετ', 710 μί.

472 χεόμενοc] χεύμενοc M, χευμένοc Ad, χεάμενοc GRfRw (~Rfˡˢ). In the same line Ad has εὔκλυον for ἔκλυον. And it has a unique confusion of υ and o at 1563 μιαιφύνων.

535 τοῦτον] τούτων M (~M²/³), τοῦτων Ad. See on 88 above, 852 and 1541 below. Note also 217 ὕπνον] -ων, 302 ἄυπνον βλέφαρον] ἀύπνων βλεφάρων, 352 cτρατὸν] -ῶν, 384 καιρὸν] -ῶν, 416 φόνον] -ων.

751 θυγατέροc uel -τρὸc] -τέραc MAd. Other changes of case-endings unique to Ad: hyp. 1.18 Ἑλένην] -ηc, 2.7 αἵ] ἅc, 6 πέτραν] -αc, 25 ὑφάcματι] -τοc, 86 ὁ] οὐ, 376 ὅc] ὅν, 888 πατρὶ] -ὸc, 1115 τὸ δοῦλον] τοῦ δούλου, 1175 ὅ] ὅν, 1470 ἀρβύλαν uel -ην] -ηc, 1665 μητέρ᾽] μητρὸc.

852 τλῆμον] τλήμων MAb¹ˢ, τλῆμων AdXc (~Xc¹ᶜ). Ad uniquely has τλῆμον for τλήμων at 293 and 947. See also on 88 and 535 above, 1541 below.

865 κεκτημένην] -νη MCAdZb³ (-οc Zb). Ad commonly drops the letter ν, not only in final position (58 ὧν] ὦ, 166 and 344 ἐν] ἐ, 969 τῶν] τῶ, 1346 ἄγραν] ἄγρα) but also in initial or medial position (10 νόcον] ὅcον, 1569 cυνθραύcω] cυθραύcω, 1587 μητροφόντηc).⁵

1091 καὶ (prius) om. OAd (~O¹ˢ). Ad also omits καὶ uniquely in 1090. Other omissions of words: 1167 παῖc, 1375 πᾶι, 1458 ἄλλοc.

1102 τι om. OAdCL (haplography, before τιμωρήcομαι). Compare 450 φίλοιcι coῖcι] φίλοι coῖcι, 1065 φόνου γενοῦ] φόνοῦ, 1345 cώθηθ᾽ ὅcον] cώθηcον.

1243 τε] γε Ad et aut M (~M²) aut M² (~M). Ad uniquely has τε for γε at 1345.

1271 κεκρυμμένουc] -υμέναc M, -υμένουc MᶜAdCr (~Ad¹ᶜ). Similar errors: 583 cύμαχοι, 730 cύλογον, 953 ἀλ᾽(etiam Mn).

1310 τὰc Cκαμάνδρου] τὰ cκ- MAd, τὰcκ- S. Single for double c again at 535 πράc᾽. Ad sometimes omits final c even when a different consonant follows: 974 δυcμενὴ, 1112 οἴου, 1126 τί, 1160 δίδω, 1365 πάρι.

1541 δωμάτων] δομάτων MAd. See on 88, 535, 852 above. Note also 112 δόμων] δωμάτων RyTa, δομάτων Zm; 1506 δόμων] δωμάτων R, δομάτων Msʸᵖ.

1565 χερί] χειρί MᵘᵛOAdL (~M¹ᶜAdᶜ²). The two forms are constantly interchanged. An example, unique to Ad, of the reverse error: 1017 παράcειροc] -cεροc.

1650 βραβεῖc] -ῆc OᵘᵛAd (~Ad¹ᶜ). The right form, but the same

---

⁵ For this reason I should be reluctant to regard Ad's κατενάcθη at *Ph.* 207 as a 'gem' (Mastronarde 139). Equally, βοτρ- for βοcτρ- (*Ph.* 1485; Mastronarde ibid.) is unlikely to be a preservation of the truth (Ad commits exactly the same error, uniquely, at *Or.* 1267; cf. 1427 βότρυχον Lᵘᵛ, ~L²). See on 1310 below, and p. 71 (on 473 cεcωμένοc).

change as 43 κρυφθείς] -ῆς. Unique substitution of η for ει is especially common in Ad: hyp. 1.17 πορθήν, 1.17 ὑφάψην, 27 σκοπήν, 64 τρέφην, 97 στείχην, 1624 ἐξηργασμένος; conversely 848 ζεῖν, 1548 πέσειμ᾽.

1692 βίοτον] βίον OAd (~Ad^{1s}). The confusion is common enough, and so is omission of syllables by Ad. See on 1102 above.

I find only three agreements between Ad and MO for which community of source may be a more plausible explanation than independent corruption:

162 ἆ uel ἆ ἆ uel ὤ uel sim.] om. M^{c}OAdT^{t3}. This is far from conclusive. It may be significant that Xe also omits ἆ ἆ (together with the preceding *nota* ἠλ.; they were added by the scholiast). At 328 Ad omits ὤ (HMO+) or ὄ, in company with RyT^{t3} (Ad^{1s} adds ὄ), and it omits ὤ (with Th) at 1246. Omission of letters, syllables, and words is among the commonest faults of Ad.

1375 ξέναι] ξένα MAd, -ος M^{2s}Ad^{1s}; -οι O$^?$ (~O$^{1c?}$); -ος uel -οι Rw^{1s}; -ε GMt^2; -** H (~H^2). The agreement of MAd in ξένα for -αι could be dismissed as fortuitous, since Ad elsewhere uniquely confuses α and αι: 425 τιμωρία] -ίαι, 435 ἀπ᾽] αἰπ᾽, 557 αἰδοῦμαι] -μα. But the further agreement of M^{2s}Ad^{1s} enhances the possibility of a connection.

1679 νείκους] νεῖκος BOAaFRZb; νείκας M, νίκας Ad. Unless νείκας is right, which is most unlikely, M is probably to be regarded as having committed the same error (α for ο) which was common to MAd at 751. Ad would be capable of writing νίκας not only for νεῖκος but also for νείκους. I have no instance of this precise confusion (α and ου) in Ad, but a few further examples of confusion of vowels and diphthongs, different in kind from those which I have already illustrated, will show that νίκας for νείκους was not beyond the range of Ad: hyp. 2.12 κείμενος] κύμενος, 56 πολύστονον] -στηνον, 331 μεσόμφαλοι] μεσόφαυλοι (and again at 590), 404 ἀναίρεσιν] ἀνώρεσιν, 517 λαμβάνων] λαμβώνων, 1065 βραβεύς] βραβές, 1550 ὀξύπουν] -πην.

On pp. 52–6 I listed 110 readings which are either exclusive to or characteristic of ξ. Ad has 81 (73·6%) of these. And so Ad, in *Orestes* at least, is what Turyn claimed it to be. But the fact that it lacks 29 of those 110 readings suggests that it is not a descendant of any of the existing members of ξ. Rather, it is descended from a manuscript whose text was akin to that of the source of ξ. It is an easy and misleading assumption (it is Turyn's assumption) that any later 'Moschopoulean' manuscript which departs from the text of ξ is an impure and contaminated representative of the tradition represented by ξ. But if we abandon the notion that ξ have some canonical status, then we may also abandon the notion that the later 'Moschopoulean' manuscripts, such as Ad, are debased representatives of the text of ξ. The reason why Ad has fewer 'Moschopoulean' readings than ξ, and shares some readings which are absent from ξ, is not necessarily that 'Moschopoulean' readings have been deliberately eliminated and non-'Moschopoulean' readings introduced. The reason may be that Ad derives from a source which never had all of the readings which made their way into ξ.[6]

When Ad differs from ξ, we occasionally find agreements with a minority of other manuscripts which cannot be explained as independent errors. Ad has acquired three readings characteristic of the Thoman manuscripts: 348 ποδί post στείχει add. AdC²PZcZmZu (et DrMsXe); 741 ἦ ante καί add. AdZZbZcZdZmZu‹T²› (et An Ms) (~Zb³T^c); 775 εἰ] τί AdCrP^{ιc?}ZZbZcZdZmZuT^{τι} (~Zu^{γρ}), εἴ τι AaF²ˢ (~Aa³), τι ˢV¹Ab¹R²S¹. There are several agreements with members of Θ, of which the most significant are: 92 τι om. AdARf S;[7] 218 κἀνακουφίcω] -ίζω Ad^cA¹ˢAb; 394 κακῶν] -οῖc Ad¹ˢCrMnPr (~Pr¹ˢ) (et At¹ˢᵘᵛ); 613 οὐκ] κοὐκ AdFSa (cf. 1161 κοὐκ] οὐκ AdCr et gV);[8] 948 τὸν ante βίον add. AdAa (cf. 288 τὸν ante πατέρα add. Ad); 1272 εἰ] ἦν AdAa^{rs}MnRSZcZu (~Mn^{γρ}). In view of the agreement of Ad with FSa at 613, it may be relevant that in two places where FSa omit a word Ad transposes it: 870 δέ] post γενναῖον FSa, om. Ad, 1072 με] post ζῆν FSa, om. Ad.[9] One reading is attested in Θ (FPrSa) and is the sole reading of the Thoman manuscripts: 756 ἀμφ' Π¹¹HMBOXaXb+: ἀφ' X+: καθ' AdVAAa AnAtCrFPrSaZZbZcZd ZmZuT². A few other agreements (which may be fortuitous): 45 πῶλος om. AdRf (~Rf¹ˢ) (see on 1091 above), 519 κατέκτανεν] -έκτεινεν AdMVCMnPrSSa, 1333 cù μή] μή cù AdCrL (cf. 16 τὰc] ante Ἀτρέωc Ad).

[6] Ad lacks, for example, such readings as 373 ἀλιτύπων and 782 πρᾶγμα γ', both of which are widely disseminated in the other 'Moschopoulean' manuscripts (see pp. 78–9). It is, in theory, possible that these were eliminated by collation with non-'Moschopoulean' manuscripts. But this is not more likely than the explanation which I have given.

[7] The agreement may be fortuitous: the omission of τι before π is a kind of haplography (see *Studies* 18 n. 1; add 875 τι ante πολεμίων om. M).

[8] I ascribe no significance to the agreement with gV: see p. 22.   [9] See p. 21 n. 15.

In summary, the text of Ad is basically that of ξ, minus a few readings characteristic of ξ and plus a few readings absent from ξ but attested in other manuscripts. There is little evidence which would support the claim that Ad derives from a source which had independent access to an older tradition.

We are now in a position to consider the credibility of four unique readings of Ad which have a claim to be considered as true, and one reading in which Ad agrees with a papyrus:

473 ϲεϲωϲμένοϲ] ϲεϲωμ- Ad, coni. Wecklein. True,[10] but presumably an accident, since Ad is prone to omission of letters (cf. 68 ἀϲθενοῦϲ] ἀθ- Ad, and on 1310 above, and p. 68 n. 5). At 1152 Ad has ϲεϲοϲμένοι, at 1632 ϲεϲωϲμένη.

891 καλοῖϲ] -οὺϲ Ad (~Ad^ɪᶜ), coni. Hartung. True, but Ad has no reliability in case-endings. See on 751 above, and add these unique errors: 291 ξίφοϲ] -ουϲ, 555 γένουϲ] -οϲ, 633 ὁδούϲ] -όϲ, 737 κακῆϲ] -οῖϲ, 739 τοῦδ'] τήνδ', 757 φόβου] -ουϲ, 837 βλεφάροιϲ] -άριϲ, 972 μακαρίοιϲ] -άριοϲ.

Less straightforward to explain are three readings in the hypotheses:

hyp. 1.19 λαβεῖν] λαβεῖν γυναῖκα Ad, λαβει]ν γυνα̣[ικα Π¹, γυ- ναῖκα λαβεῖν Xa. It seeems likely that the papyrus had the same reading as Ad.[11] In view of the connection between Ad and ξ, and of the not uncommon isolation of Xa from XXb,[12] it is possible that Ad obtained γυναῖκα from a source akin to Xa. The fact that Ad has the word-order not of Xa but of the papyrus does not make this any the less probable. For the fact that γυναῖκα is attested in two different positions is an indication that at some stage it stood probably not in the text but in the margin or, perhaps more likely, above λαβεῖν. And there it may have stood in the source common to Ad and Xa. If we accept γυναῖκα (and its appearance in Π¹ is at least a guarantee of its antiquity), then it is better accepted in the place where Ad and the papyrus have it—the word-order is choicer and better accounts for the omission. I believe that λαβεῖν γυναῖκα is right, for reasons which I have given elsewhere.[13]

hyp. 2.14 δέ] γὰρ ἂν Wecklein (ἂν post μᾶλλον iam Nauck); γὰρ C, coni. Kirchhoff; δ' ἂν Ad; καὶ Aa; δὴ Xd. Wecklein's conjecture

[10] See Fraenkel on A. *Ag.* 618.   [11] See pp. 49, 62, and *ZPE* 77 (1989) 8–9.
[12] See p. 49.   [13] *ZPE* 77 (1989) 8–9.

(made without knowledge of C and Ad) is probably right: γὰρ is more appropriate than δέ, and ἄν is, at the very least, highly desirable. An exact parallel for the corruption of γὰρ ἄν to δέ is provided by V two lines below: 2.16 διηγέρθη γὰρ ἄν] -θη γὰρ AbFSXh; -θησαν γὰρ S; -θησαν ἄν XbXcXe, -θη ἄν A; -θη δέ V.

hyp. 2.16 οὕτω post διασκευάσαι habet Ad, e coni. add. Wecklein. A word like οὕτω certainly seems to be needed. That οὕτω is conjectural in Ad seems unlikely. Whether it is inherited truth must remain an open question. But a third possible explanation exists. In the preceding line a good many manuscripts have an unnecessary, and presumably interpolated,[14] οὕτω(c): 2.15 πλ(ησιαίτερον προσκαθεζο)μένη] πλ- οὕτω(c) -μένη MBVCFGKRfSaZc: οὕτω -μένη πλ- AaAbMnRRwS. It is possible that the οὕτω which Ad offers in 2.16 really belongs to 2.15: in other words, that in an ancestor of Ad it had been added in the margin, designed for a place in 2.15, and was then wrongly inserted by the next copyist in 2.16.

(ii) *An*

An is described by Turyn (149) simply as 'Moschopulean'. In *Hecuba* Matthiessen (129–30) has found it to be 'im Kern ein Vetus, bei dem man allenfalls von einem gewissen Moschopuloseinfluß sprechen kann'. In *Phoenissae*, where it is available for only lines 916–1073, Mastronarde (172) has found occasional divergences from ξ. In *Orestes* (1–771, 879–1026) An has 38 out of a possible 54 readings (73·7%) on my list of readings exclusive to or characteristic of ξ.

An shares a few unique errors with members or associates of Θ. Here is a selection: hyp. 1.6 εἰσαπέστειλε] ἀπ- AnV; 2.19 ταύτην] post εἶναι AnΘ; 390 ὄνομ'] ὄμμ' AnMn^γρ^Pr^γρ^ (~An^c^); 427 δέ om. AnCr; 691 ἄν om. AnRRfRw. An also shares a very small number of readings with Thoman manuscripts: 179 Ἀγαμεμνόνειον] -νιον AnZZb (~Zb³); 286 εἰς ante ἔργον add. AnZZbZcZdZmZu⟨T'⟩ (~T^c^) (et Th) (ἔργον ἐς fere ξAdAtMs); 352 χιλιόναυν] -ναυ AnZc (~An^c^); 927 μήτε] μὴ AnZc (~An²Zc^1c^).

An has unique orthographical truth at 64 (παρέδωκε] -κεν An, coni. Porson), 377 and 471 (Κλυταιμνήστραν] -μήστραν An, ~An^c^), and 992 (λευκοκύμοσι] -σιν An, ~An²).

An has been corrected for the use of the printer of the Aldine

---

[14] Unless οὕτω(c) is a mistake for αὐτῶι (Nauck) or τούτωι (Barnes).

edition[15] by collation with the text of MnS. Almost all of the corrections of An² restore the reading of MnS, and there are several unique agreements: 898 ἠγόρευε] ἀγ- An²MnS, 1002 ἀελίου] ἠ- An²MnS, 1012 còc om. An²MnS, 1020 ἰδοῦcá c' ἐν uel ἰδοῦc' ἐν] ἰ- δοῦcá c' AnM^{ιγρ}B^{ιγρ}VAdJξ, ἰδοῦc' An²Mn (et Th), [S].

(iii) *At*

According to Turyn (121; see also 325), 'Hecuba and Orestes ca. 1–400 are Moschopulean . . . The rest, Orestes ca. 400–end and *Phoenissae*, is old.' For *Orestes* Turyn is right.[16] Up to line 403 At has 22 out of a possible 25 'Moschopoulean' readings, thereafter only six.[17]

After 403 At has numerous unique or nearly unique agreements with members and associates of Θ. Here is a selection: 511 ποῖ] post κακῶν AtAb (et Π^{10}, ~⟨Π$^{10\text{c}}$⟩); 730 αὐτὸc om. AtF; 808 ἄν' om. AtCr; 839 ὅτε om. AtRw; 867 δεόμενοc] βουλόμενοc AtMnS; 927 μήτε cτρατεύειν] μήτ' ἐκcτρ- AtCr (et Th); 968 ὅδ'] ὧδ' AtFMnS; 1286 κακῶν om. AtFPrSa (~F²); 1468 δὲ om. AtCr (~Cr^{s}); 1590 οὐκ ἄν] οὐ AtRw.

From 1075 onwards At has numerous unique or nearly unique agreements with Aa. Here is a selection: 1158 τά τ'] ποτ' AtAa (ποτὲ etiam B³ᵐ; τά τε et ταῦτα Aa^{ryp}); 1227 cὲ γὰρ] γὰρ cὲ AtAa; 1242 δίκηc cέβαc] c- δ- AtAa; 1276 ἀγγελίαν ἀγαθάν] ἀγ- ἀγγ- AtAa (~Aa^{r}); 1288 ἀργείων] ἀργεῖοc AtAa; 1512 ἄρα (ἄρα)] post παῖc AtAa. There are also several agreements with A, sometimes in the company of Aa,[18] of which I cite about half: 581 ἔδραc'] -cεν AtA; 821 δὲ om. AtA; 1018 c' om. AtAAa; 1076 οὐκ ἔcτι] οὐκέτι AtAAa. Note also (A/Aa in conjunction with Θ): 894 φαιδρωπὸν] φαιδρῶν At, φαιδρὸν A et ^{gl}Ab²MnPrR²S; 1091 οὖν om. AtAAaPr (et P, ~P²); 1497 ἤτοι φαρμάκοιcιν om. AtAaPrSa (~Aa$^{\text{1m}}$); 1585 χώcω] θάψω AtAMtPr (et M^{gl}; ~Pr^{γρ}). There are also two unique agreements with P: 1251 ὑμῶν om. AtP; 1461 ἀντίοι] ἀντία AtP.

At has unique orthographical truth at 929: εὐνίδαc] εὔνιδαc At, coni. Hermann.

---

[15] See p. 11; also Matthiessen 19, 129–30, Mastronarde 20.
[16] For *Ph.* see Mastronarde 119, 136.
[17] At 594, 1323, 1364, 1465 (ἥ), 1601, 1602. Of these only 1465 is (virtually) unique to ξ.
[18] For agreements between A and Aa see pp. 46–7.

(iv) *Dr*

Dr, according to Turyn (124), is 'Moschopulean throughout'. In *Orestes* it has (at least, on the information which may be found in, or inferred from, Beck) 78 of the 105 'Moschopoulean' readings for which it is available (74·3%).

In the readings which Dr shares with manuscripts other than ξ no pattern of agreements emerges. There are a few unique agreements: 382 ἔρρεις] ἔρρη(ι) DrR²ᵞᵖ; 792 νοσοῦντος] post ἀνδρὸς DrgB; 795 φίλα γ'] φίλ'DrP; 867 τὰ om. DrA (~Aʳ). There are several agreements with Θ and associates: 407 τάδε] post νοσεῖς AaFSa, om. Dr;¹⁹ 732 πράσσεις] δράς(c)εις ᵞᵖDrMnPrS; 861 (ἐν) Ἀργείοις uel (ἐν) Ἀργείων] ἀργεῖοι DrAaRw (~Aaʳˢ); 916 κατα-κτείνοντι uel -αντι] κατατείνοντι DrRfSa¹ᵞᵖ (~Rfᶦᶜ); 1233 ἐμοῦ om. DrPrSa; 1233 ἐμας λιτας (diuersis acc.)] ἐμῆς λιτῆς DrMnˢ RfRw; 1421 δ'ἐς] δὲ DrAbMnR²ᵘᵛS (om. R). Here is a selection of other agreements: 233 πόδας] πόδα DrPZcZmZu; 236 δὲ] γὰρ DrF LZu (et Th); 489 κτήσομαι] κεκτήσομαι DrAb¹ˢCFPZZc⟨Zm⟩ (Zu)⟨T'⟩ (~ZmᶜTᶜ); 1141 βέλτιον] βέλτιστον DrCGZbZm; 1286 εἰσακούους(ιν)] -ούεθ' Dr, -ούετ' DrˢM²⁇OCr (~Oᶦᶜ); 1526 μετα-βουλευσόμε(c)θα] -σώμεθα DrAaZu.

(v) *J*

'Basically . . . Moschopulean', says Turyn (207), rightly.²⁰ J has 84 of the 109 'Moschopoulean' readings for which it is available (77%). But Turyn fails to report one distinctive feature of J. It has picked up 14 Triclinian emendations: 332 ἰώ] ὦ JʳTᵗ³Ry (~Ry³) et Aa³ˢ; 816 ὅθεν] ἔνθεν J²Tᵗ³; 861 καὶ ante τίνες add. J², τε καὶ add. Tᵗ³; 977 πολύπονα] πολύστονά τε δὴ καὶ πολύπονα (-ποινα Tᵗ³) J²Tᵗ³; 1248 αὐδάν] λόγον JTᵗ³; 1248 cὺ ante πότνια add. JTᵗ³; 1267 πάντα] ante διὰ JTᵗ³; 1276 μοι om. JTᵗ¹; 1284 ἐν] ὡς JTᵗ³; 1305 τὰν ante λ(ε)ιπόγαμον add. JTᵗ³; 1345 ἐμοί] ἔμ' fere JTᵗ³ et Vaᶦᶜ; 1358 καθαιμακτὸν] αἱμ- JTᵗ³; 1464 τὸν ante κασιγνήτου add. JTᵗ³; 1491 ἁ post ἔτεκε(ν) add. JTᵗ³ et (Zu) (ἡ add. MsS); note also 831 καὶ] ἢ JPTᵗ³.

No other pattern of agreements emerges. Here is a selection of agreements in weakly attested readings: 22 μὲν om. JᵃCrFS (~JᵝF²);²¹ 35 ὅδε uel ὁ δὲ] οὐδὲ JBᶜᵘᵛL²RyZZbZmZuᶜTᵗ¹ (~ᵞᵖJᵝʳ) (et

---

¹⁹ See p. 21 n. 15.   ²⁰ For *Hec.* (J lacks *Ph.*) see Matthiessen 95.
²¹ J writes 1–42 twice (= JᵃJᵝ).

Th); 234 γλυκύ] ἡδύ JPRy (et ThgBgE); 920 γῆν] πόλιν JAaZ^{γρ}Zb
⟨Zm⟩Zu (~Aa^{γρ}Zm^{ιc}); 1137 δ᾽ post ὀλολυγμὸc add. JARfRw; 1507
προσπίπτων] -πιτνῶν JOGKZvT^{t3}, -πεcών ξAd⟨Dr⟩Th.

(vi) *Ms*

Turyn (343) asserts that Ms is 'Moschopoulean' in *Or.* 1–*c.*1219
and *Hec. c.*786–end (it lacks *Phoenissae*). Matthiessen claims (123
n. 5) that Turyn has overestimated the extent of Moschopoulean
influence in *Hec.*, and denies (70 n. 43) that there is any qualitative
difference in the text between the two parts of the play.[22]

In *Orestes* Ms has 53 out of the 110 'Moschopoulean' readings.
Thus Ms, with 48·2%, has a much lower proportion than Ad
(73·6%), An (73·7%), At in lines 1–400 (90%), Dr (74·3%), and J
(77%). In lines 1–1219 it has 41 out of 76 (54%), in 1220–end it has
12 out of 34 (35·3%). Ms is less 'Moschopoulean' than those others,
but it is 'Moschopoulean' none the less, and it is only a little less so
in the later part than in the earlier.

Ms has several unique agreements in the later part of the play
with Mn or MnS: 1284 οἱ] ὦ MsMnS (et Va^{2γρ}); 1294 cκοποῦcα]
-cαι ^{γρ}MsMn; 1338 μέγ᾽ ὀλβίαι] μεγαλολβία MsMnS (~Ms^sMn^{γρ});
1353 φίλαι] post ἐγείρετε MsMnS (et Aa^r); 1363 Ἑλλάδ᾽ ἅπαcαν]
-δα πᾶcαν MsMnS (et Va); 1373 φροῦδα φροῦδα γᾶ γᾶ] φ- γᾶ φ-
MsMnS; 1485 ἐγενόμεθ᾽] -μεcθ᾽ MsMnS; 1497 τέχναιc] -αιcιν Ms
MnS; 1512 διώλετο] διοίχεται MsMnS (~Mn^{γρ}); 1567 δὲ post cὺ
add. MsMnS; 1677 καὶ (prius) om. MsMnS (~Mn^s).

Ms has numerous agreements, throughout the play, with Θ.
Most of these readings are shared by one or both of MnS. Here is
a selection: hyp. 1.5 τί δεῖ post τοῦ add. MsAaAbMnRSSa (et G^{1s});
271 χερί] χειρί MsAbFMnRRfSSa; 303 χροΐ] χρωτί ^{γρ}Ms(Mn)Sa¹;
430 ἐκκλείομαι] ἐκβάλλομαι ⟨Ms⟩V^cAbMnRSSa^{rs}; 535 ὠφελεῖν]
post τοῦτον MsMnPrS; 545 λυπήcειν] λυπῆcαι Ms^{γρ}VMnPr^{γρ}R^{2γρ}
S^{1s}Zu (~Mn^{γρ}); 853–4 ἠλέκτρα | λόγουc MsRwSSa; 1190 τριccοῖc]
τοῖc Ms^{γρ}, τοῖc coῖc ^{γρ}MnR¹; 1193 cε post χρή add. MsMnRS; 1273
γὰρ post κενὸc add. ⟨Ms⟩AaMnRS; 1302 θείνετ᾽ post καίνετε add.
MsAbMnRwS; 1378 ὁ ante ταυρόκρανοc add. MsAaAbMnS; 1398
γᾶν] γαῖαν MsMnRS; 1407 κακοῦργοc] δόλιοc Ms^{γρ}AbMn^{γρ}R
(~Ab^{1γρ}); 1529 δόμων] init. 1530 scr. MsAbMn, om. S.

[22] It should be remembered that Turyn's reports of Ms (like mine) are taken from Beck,
and that Matthiessen has collated Ms for himself from microfilm (the microfilm, in the
IRHT, lacks *Orestes*).

There appear to be few agreements exclusive to Ms and members of Θ which are not shared by MnS. The following, of those known to me, are the more notable: 298 θ' om. MsF (~F²); 521–2 ζηλῶ | κακῆc MsCrSa; 785 πατρῶιον] πατρὸc Ms^γρAbCrPr^γρR^ιγρ; 845 θεομανεῖ] -ῆ(ι) MsR; 1414 ἔβαλον (Mn) uel ἔβαλλον (S) bis] ἔβαλλον semel MsF², ἔβαλον semel FPrSa; 1506 δόμων] δομάτων Ms^γρ, δωμάτων R.

But Ms has also acquired readings absent from both ξ and Θ. The following are the more interesting: hyp. 1.7 δὲ] καὶ MsAa, δὲ καὶ Cr; 1.20 ἄρχειν] ἔχειν MsZc et (ante Ἄργουc) Sa; 2.16 διαcκευάcαι] -άcαcθαι MsZcZu, [ZZbZm], -άcθαι G; 2.19 ταύτην εἶναι uel εἶναι˙τ-] τ- εἶναί φαcι Ms, εἶναι φ- τ- V (εἶναι τ- φ- Va); 110 ὀρθῶc] καλῶc MsVGK et ᵍˡJTh; 273–4 τόξων | πτερωτὰc Ms Rw; 317 ὦ om. MsA; 348 ποδί post cτείχει add. MsC²AdDrPZc ZmZu (et Xe); 358 ἀθλίοιc] ἀθλίωc MsM²ᐟ³L⟨Zm⟩Zm¹ˢZu (~Ms^s Zm¹ᶜ), utrumque O¹, ἄθλιοc M; 418 εἰcί(ν)] εἰcìν οἱ MsAaPRfRw Zb; 429 νόμουc] νόμον MsMCDrZmZu; 483 ὅδε] post πέφυκεν GK, om. Ms; 522 ἐλθόνθ' οὔνεκ'] οὔνεκ' ἐλθ- MsL; 704 τέ coι] coì τὲ Ms L; 798 τῆc ante μητρὸc add. MsT^t3; 1068 δ'om. MsGJ; 1148 ἐκείνηι] -ηc MsAaGZu; 1275 μοι om. MsCrGL (~Ms^s); 1397 Ἀcιάδι] -δη MsZu.

(vii) Th

'Moschopulean . . . There were occasionally some interpolations from Thomas' (Turyn 152).[23] So far as I can judge from the published reports, Th has at least 70 of a possible 108 'Moschopoulean' readings. Agreements with the 'Thoman' manuscripts are very few: 35 ὅδε uel ὁ δὲ] οὐδὲ ThB^cuvJL²RyZZbZmZu^cT^t1; 282 παρθένωι] ante παρέχων ThZZu; 286 εἰc ante ἔργον add. ThZZbZcZm ZuAn⟨T²⟩ (~T^c). There are a few agreements with one or both of MnS: 229 om. ThS (~Th²); 303 cίτων uel cῖτον] cῖτα ThS (et Rf Rw); 925 κάθεον] ἄθεον ThMnS (et Zb); 1020 ἰδοῦcá c' (ἐν) uel ἰδοῦc' ἐν] ἰδοῦc'ThMn (et An²), [S]; 1156 τι (τοι MnS¹ˢ) om. ThS. And there are a few agreements with Cr: 756 ἐπὶ φόνωι om. ThCr; 927 μήτε cτρατεύειν] μήτ' ἐκcτρ- ThCr (et At); 1438–9 ὦ Διὸc παῖ om. ThCr (~ΣTh) (et Xd); 1529 cε om. ThCr (~Th^s) (et Zb). Few other readings are noteworthy: 85 δ'οὐκ] κοὐκ ThRf; 234 γλυκύ] ἡδύ ThJPRy et gBgE; 1659 μενεῖ] μένει ThΠ^19uvCrJL (~Π^19cuv), μενεί Ad.

---

[23] For Ph. see Mastronarde 172–3.

At 410 ἀποτρέπει ThJ² (~J²), if taken as second person middle (-ηι Musgrave), may be preferable to Hermann's ἀπετρέπου as a correction of ἀποτρέπου, for a reason given by West (whose defence of ἀποτρέπου will not do). But, if right, it is likely to be a lucky slip.[24]

(viii) *Xc*

Xc is a fifteenth-century manuscript, used by Barnes, King and Porson, but thereafter disregarded.[25] Turyn (123) rightly describes it as 'Moschopulean throughout'. It has no fewer than 102 of the possible 110 'Moschopoulean' readings. When XXaXb disagree among themselves, it generally sides with Xb: hyp. 2.16 διηγέρθη] -θησαν XcXbS; 2.16 γὰρ om. XcXbA; 2.17 τῶν ante γυναικῶν add. XcXbAtRwTh; 2 ξυμφορὰ XcXb+: ϲυμ- XXa+; 606 δυϲτυχέϲτερον] δυϲτυχέϲτατον XXa, δυϲτυχε Xc (del. Xc¹ᶜ), δυϲχερέϲτατον Xc¹ᶜ Xb (evidently the source of Xc had both 'Moschopoulean' readings). But there are a few agreements with X or Xa or both against Xb: 417 γ' XcX+: om. XaXb+; 1023 κρανθέντ' X¹ᶜXb+: κραθ- XcX Xa+. Xc has few readings unknown to ξ. The most interesting are: 54 Ναύπλιον] ναυπλίειον ξ+: ναυπλήιον XcZu; 142 ἀπόπρο] ἀπόπροθι XcOᵍˡAn²CrLMnRfᵍˡSSaZZbZmZu (~XcᶜMnᵞᵖ); 150 λόγον δ'] λόγον Xc+; 199 τε om. XcHACrLRf (et DrTh); 511 δή] δὲ Xc+; 1160 τ'] δ' Xc+, om. ξ; 1281 ἐν om. XcKMnS (~K¹ᶜ); 1605 δ' om. XcACCrLMtZuT². Turyn mentions that, in addition to Moschopoulean scholia, Xc has some scholia which are old. And the scholiast has added as variants several readings which are absent from ξ: 424 ἔφυϲ κακός, 612 ὄχλον] χοχόν (χορόν CGKLZʳᵞᵖZb²ZcZmZu, ~CᵞᵖZm¹ᵞᵖZuᵍˡ), 922 ἀνεπίπληκτον, 1062 πατρός (ᵞᵖM¹B¹), 1182 λέγειν.

Xc has one true reading not found in any manuscript which I have collated, 654 ἀπολάβοιϲ for -ης, a lucky slip. Biehl reports it from another 'Moschopoulean' manuscript, Mon. 500 (Turyn 134–5).

(ix) *Xd*

I have collated only the parts of *Orestes* which belong to the original manuscript (1–163, 898–1693), dated by Turyn (148) as early four-

---

[24] I have elsewhere argued that the answer is ἀπετράπου (*CQ* n.s. 40 [1990] 101).
[25] See Matthiessen 22 nn. 16–17.

teenth century. He describes the original manuscript as 'a good representative of the Moschopulean recension'. In *Phoenissae* Mastronarde (172) says that it has 'very few deviations' from XXaXb. In *Orestes* too it has few deviations, and none of significance, except perhaps 38 φόβωι] φόβον XdV^{3s}Va^{1s} (~Xd^{2}), coni. Willink (rightly, I believe). Of the 65 'Moschopoulean' readings for which it is available it has 64 (the exception being a trifle, χερῶν for χειρῶν at 1048). It appears to be related to Th: hyp. 1.11 πρῶτα XdTh; 1423 τὴν om. XdThAbAt; 1438–9 ὦ Διὸς παῖ om. XdThCr; 1448 ἄλλοθι XdTh (-εν Xd^{1s}); 1493 ξυνάρπασαν Xd ThTp; 1529 σε om. XdThCrZb (~Th^{s}); 1685 ἀστέρων XdThFPr^{γρ}.

(x) *XeXfXgXh*

Turyn (141–2) labels all these as simply 'Moschopulean'. Xe he dates to the fourteenth century, the others to the fifteenth.[26] I have examined them only in the 110 'Moschopoulean' readings on my list. The proportion of agreements is: Xe 53 out of 110 (48·2%); Xf 91 out of 110 (82·7%); Xg 80 out of 105 (76·2%); Xh 65 out of 77 (84·4%).[27]

Xe is the odd man out. A full investigation will be needed to establish its affinities. The following readings caught my eye: hyp. 2.12 ἐπὶ] ὑπὸ XeG; 2.19 πιθανὸν] -ὴν XeVAaAtGJMnZu; 2.19 ταύτην] post εἶναι XeAnΘ; 103 τ'] τῶ(ι)δ' XeRw^{uv}ZZcZmZu<T$^{z?}$> (~T^{t1}); 162 ἆ ἆ uel sim.] om. XeM^{c}OAdT^{t3} (~ΣXe);[28] 282 παρθένωι] post ἐμαῖς Xe^{γρ}AbMnPrRSSa; 1125 τοῖσιδ' ἕξομεν] τοῖσιν ἕξομεν ξ+, τοῖσδ' ἐφέξομεν XeL.

To illustrate in full the behaviour of each of these thirteen 'associates' of ξ in the 110 passages on my list would occupy much space and would duplicate in part information already presented. Instead I offer a small selection in order to show the kind of distribution which these readings enjoy.

61 συμφοράς ξAdDrJXcXdXfXg (~AnAt<MsTh>XeXh)
116 στᾶσα γ' ξAdAnAtDrJXcXdXfXh (~<MsTh>XeXg)
281 σοι ξAdAnAt<Dr>J^{rs}<Ms>XcXeXfXgXh (~J<Th$^{?}$>); [Xd]
286 ἔργον ἐς ξAdAtJ(Ms)XcXh, εἰς ἔργον ZZbZcZdZmZuAn ThXe; (~DrXfXg); [Xd]
373 ἀλιτύπων ξAtDrJ<Th>Xf (~AdAn<Ms>XcXeXgXh); [Xd]

[26] For Xf in *Ph.* see Mastronarde 171.

[27] I had time to examine only 77 passages in Xh.

[28] See p. 69.

378 ἐξέλειπον ξAdAtJ‹Th›Xc (~An‹DrMs›XeXfXgXh); [Xd]
424 εἰπὼν κακῶc ξAdDrJXcXfXg (~AnAt‹MsTh›Xc^γρXeXh); [Xd]
750 cπείρων ξAdJThXcXg (~AnAt‹DrMs›XeXfXh); [Xd]
782 πρᾶγμα γ’ ξ‹Th›XcXfXg, γε πρᾶγμ’ Dr^cXe; (~AdAtDrJMs Xh); [AnXd]
782 τῶι ξAdDrJMs‹Th›XcXfXg (~AtXeXh); [AnXd]
798 μητέρος ξAdJ‹Th›XcXeXfXh (~AtDrMsXg); [AnXd]
982 μέcον καὶ ξAdAnDrJMsThXcXdXeXfXgXh (~At)
1094 ἀκρόπτολιν XaXbAdXcXdXfXh (~XAtDrJMsThXeXg); [An]
1488 δ’ ἐκφεύγομεν ξThXcXdXfXg (~AdDrJ‹Ms›XeXg²); [An Xh]
1507 προcπεcών ξAd‹Dr›ThXcXdXfXg (~AtJMsXe); [AnXh]
1684 ζηνόc ξAd‹Dr›J‹Ms›ThXcXdXfXgXh (~AtXe); [An].

All of these readings were included in Turyn's list. For him they were typical features of the 'Moschopoulean recension'. But most of them are lacking in a substantial number (sometimes more than half) of the manuscripts which Turyn believed were influenced by that 'recension'.

I add a few readings[29] which are common to some of these thirteen 'associates' but are not shared with them by the 'concordant testimony' of ξ:

hyp. 1.8 τυνδάρεω AtThXdXe (~ξAdAn‹Ms›Xc); [JXfXgXh]
hyp. 1.16 αὐτῶν] αὐτοῦ XXbAnAtMsThXcXdXeXh, -ὸν Ad; (~XaXf); [DrJXg]
hyp. 2.8 τοῦ om. MAdAnJThXd (~ξAt‹Ms›Xc); [XeXfXgXh]
hyp. 2.17 τῶν γυναικῶν RwXbAtThXcXdXe (~XXaAdAnJ ‹Ms›); [XfXgXh]
39 δὴ om. RwAnAtDr (~ξAdJMs‹Th›XcXd); [XeXfXgXh]
407 φαντατcμάτων ξAdDrJXc, φαcμάτων An^cAtMsXeXfXg; (~An‹Th?›Xh); [Xd]
606 δυcτυχέcτατον XXaDr^s(Xc)XfXg, δυcχερέcτατον XbTh Xc^ιcXf^γρXh (~AdAnAtDrJ‹Ms›Xe); [Xd]
1039 ἐγὼ cὲ δ’ξAdThXcXdXeXh, ἐγὼ δέ c’DrJMsXfXg (~At); [An].

²⁹ This is a selection from a much longer list which I have compiled of unique agreements among these manuscripts. In many of these passages, however, I do not know the readings of XeXfXgXh.

Clearly the 'associates' of ξ enjoy relationships with each other which they do not share with ξ. But the patterns of these relationships cannot be traced, on the evidence at present available. And even if we did succeed in tracing relationships among these thirteen, the pattern would probably need modification with every further 'associate' of ξ that we collated.

I return briefly to the last two readings on the preceding list: 606 δυϲτυχέϲτατον /δυϲχερέϲτατον and 1039 ἐγὼ ϲὲ δ΄/ἐγὼ δέ ϲ΄. In both places I believe that the truth or (in the former) the closest approximation to it is to be found not in the 'concordant testimony' of ξ but among these 'associates'. At 606 the true reading δυϲχερέϲτερον, attested only in 'Thoman' manuscripts, is reflected by the δυϲχερέϲτατον of Xb and three 'associates'. Since the 'Thoman' manuscripts must have inherited the truth,[30] we are entitled to believe that δυϲχερέϲτατον may also be an inheritance. At 1039 the reading of the six 'associates' of ξ need not be regarded as a deliberate modification of the reading of ξ. It is just as likely to be an inheritance from a purer branch of the ξ-tradition.[31]

My purpose in this and the preceding chapter has been to establish: (*a*) that there never was such a thing as a 'Moschopoulean recension'; and (*b*) that, even if there was, it is idle to suppose that the evidence of XXaXb will tell us what was in it. The evidence of XXaXb, taken by itself, shows that by the beginning of the fourteenth century there had come into being a branch of the tradition which owes something to Palaeologan scholarship, but which, at the same time, is based on sources now lost to us. And just as K, which does not belong to that branch of the tradition, shows evidence both of Palaeologan scholarship and of access to older sources now lost, so it is reasonable to accept in principle the possibility that other manuscripts which do, in varying measure, belong to the branch to which XXaXb belong may bear occasional traces, unknown to XXaXb, of these same two features. In short, even if we were to accept that the 'Moschopoulean' manuscripts reflect a recension of the text by one or more Palaeologan scholars, it would be injudicious to suppose that, just as there is *nulla salus extra ecclesiam*, so there is no trace of that recension outside of XXaXb.[32]

---

[30] See pp. 52, 84, 86.   [31] See above, p. 62.

[32] Prof. Matthiessen will recognize that I have stolen this *mot* (which he applies to a different purpose) from *GRBS* 10 (1969) 304.

ζ (ZZbZcZdZmZuZv)

I designate by the collective symbol ζ the manuscripts ZZbZcZd ZmZu(Zv) (this last available for lines 1385–591 only). The link which connects them is their scholia, compiled by Thomas Magister. The number may immediately be reduced by one, for the youngest of them, Zd, is a descendant of Zu, as I shall show later; and for the present I shall ignore it, except where it differs from Zu.

Turyn believed that these manuscripts share a yet tighter link than their scholia. He claimed that Thomas edited the triad twice; that Z (and its twin Za)[1] represent the first edition, and that Zb is the purest representative of the second edition; and that the second edition was 'annotated with optional variants', with the result that its other representatives ZcZmZu often disagree with Zb and among themselves. He listed 51 readings which he believed were deliberately introduced by Thomas into one or other edition.

We do not know at what date Thomas compiled his scholia (and, on Turyn's hypothesis, edited the text). Let us assume that this work fell within the period 1290–1310.[2] I shall divide the non-Thoman manuscripts into three categories: (i) those which are certainly to be dated before 1290 (HMBOV); (ii) those which are probably to be dated c.1290–1300 (AFKPrRfRwSa) or even earlier (R),[3] and so possibly ante-date the work of Thomas; and (iii) those which are probably or certainly to be dated after 1300 (AaAbCCrG LMnMtPRySTTp), and so possibly (in some cases certainly) post-date the work of Thomas. I shall divide Turyn's 51 readings into three lists, according to whether they are first attested (i) before

---

[1] Turyn (99–100) was right to describe the younger Za as a twin and not a copy of Z. I have cited Za in places where the original reading of Z, obscured by a correction, may be inferred from the reading of Za (in such places I use the symbols ⟨Z⟩Za) or where Z and Za disagree.

[2] Schartau (II. 77 n. 7) suggests 1285–1300, Mastronarde (135) c.1290–5. But the first positive trace we find of Thomas is in 1301, and he lived until at least 1346 (Wilson 247; cf. JHS 96 [1976] 172–3, Schartau II. 84 n. 32). It is not certain that any of the Thoman manuscripts is to be dated before c.1315 (see pp. 11–13). For further biographical information see H. P. Dietz, *Thomas Magistros' Recension of the Sophoclean Plays Oedipus Coloneus, Trachiniae, Philoctetes* (diss. Illinois, 1965) 22–5. See also above, p. 49 n. 1.

[3] See p. 50 n. 3.

1290, (ii) *c.*1290–1300, (iii) after 1300. I shall cite all the evidence available for these readings,[4] but I shall not generally mention which parts of the evidence recorded by me are not recorded by Turyn (he normally cites only ZZbMBVACRST). In order to make the distinctions between the three categories clearer, I shall cite manuscripts in this order: first the manuscripts from category (i), second the manuscripts from category (ii), third the Thoman manuscripts, and fourth the manuscripts from category (iii). I include XXaXb in category (ii) in spite of their later date, because it would follow, from Turyn's belief that they reflect a recension by Moschopoulos, that their readings were in existence before the time of Thomas. I mark with an asterisk readings which are certainly or possibly right.

(i) *Readings attested before 1290*

13 τ' post πόλεμον add. V$^{1/2c}$SaζT^z (~T^{13}). The corrector of V was almost certainly pre-Thoman.[5]

326 γόνον] δόμον ⟨M⟩ZZa^{1γρ} (~M^{1c}Z^{γρ}Za). Turyn does not report M.

922* ἀκέραιος] -ον Hesych. A 2331, FζLPT^{z}gE (~Zb^{3}T^c) et Chr. Pat. 395.

938 om. OPrXZZbT^z (~O^{1m}Pr^{1c}Σ^{x}Z^{2}Zb^{2}T^{zc}), ante 936 habet S.

1445 παθεῖν post ἔμελλε(ν) add. ORwZZbZmZuCrL (παθεῖν ^{gl}H^{2}B^{2}Ab^{2}MnRfSa). 'The Thoman interpolation was prompted by a gloss.' But O proves that the interpolation was not first made by Thomas.[6]

(ii) *Readings first attested c.1290–1300*

Inscriptio Εὐριπίδου 'Ηλέκτρα ZLP. 'Thomas was so consistent in giving the *Orestes* the title *Electra* that in his own scholium on Aristoph. *Ran.* 303 . . . he referred to the line Eur. *Orest.* 279 in this way: ἐν Εὐριπίδου μὲν 'Ηλέκτρᾳ.'[7] If Thomas was so consistent, we may wonder why no other Thoman manuscript besides Z has this title, and why he never calls the play *Electra* in his *Eclogae.*[8] The

---

[4] But I shall generally cite only ξ and not the 'associates' of ξ (see Chapter IX).

[5] See p. 6.   [6] It should be remembered that Turyn dated O *c.*1320.

[7] Cf. Eberline 86.

[8] ZZa uniquely offer the title Οἰδίπους for *Phoenissae*, although the Thoman hypothesis has the title right (Mastronarde 131). On alternative titles in antiquity see E. Nachmanson, *Der griechische Buchtitel* (1941) 6–7, R. L. Hunter, *Eubulus: the fragments* (1983) 146–8, A. L. Brown, *CQ* n.s. 34 (1984) 268–9.

title *Electra* may well have been in existence before the time of Thomas, for it appears in two 'Moschopoulean' manuscripts (*Εὐρ-'Ηλέκτρα* Xc, *ὑπόθεσις τῆς 'Ηλέκτρας δράματος* Xa) and in the scholia to Aristides, iii. 603.6 Dindorf, cited by Turyn.[9] See also the *subscriptio* (list (iii)), where *Electra* appears in Xg as well as in PZ.

42 χλανιδίων] -ίδων PrZZaZmZuGP (~ZaᶦᶜZuᶜ), -ύδων Zc. Thomas has the truth in his *Eclogae* (p. 399. 14 Ritschl). Turyn attributes χλανίδων also to Tᶻ, and -ιδίων to Triclinius; but I can see no indication that -ιδίων was not the original reading of Tᶻ.

47 μὴ (prius)] μήτε RwZZmZuAa et Bᵍˡ.

142 ἀπόπρο μοι] ἀπόπρο Rf, ἀπόπροθι μοι ZZbZm, ἀπόπροθι SaZuCrLMnS (et ᵍˡORf) (~Mnᵞᵖ) et Dion. Hal. comp. 11. 63 (Usener–Radermacher) cod. V (saec. xvi).[10] Cf. 1452 ἀπόπρο] ἀπόπροθι PrSaᶦˢTp.

289 με χρή] μ' ἐχρῆν PrZZbZmZu (~Zuᶜ).

415 μὲν om. FKSaZZmZuᶜGP (~KᶦˢG²ˢ). 'A metrical interpolation prompted by the fact that the line has 13 syllables.' Several dozen lines in this play have 13 syllables, and many have more than 13.[11] Just as μέν and γάρ are regularly confused,[12] so μὲν γάρ is often curtailed to μέν or γάρ.[13]

489 κτήσομαι] κεκτήσομαι FZZc⟨Zm⟩AbᶦˢCP⟨Tᶻ⟩ (~ZmᶜTᶜ), κεκτήμαι Zu.

783 καὶ ante μᾶλλον add. APrRfζCrMnᶜP⟨Tᶦᶦ⟩ (~Tᵗᶜ).

787 οὖν om. FKSaZZbZmCrP (~F²Kᶦᶜ).[14]

1011 σὺν ante πολυπόνοις add. PrRfζCrLTᵗ³Tp (et ᵍˡM¹B²OV³ AaʳC).

1266 βλέφαρον] -ρα FZbZcZmZuAaGTᵗ³ (~F²Zcᶦˢ).

1274 οὐ] σὺ ARfᶦˢζCrLP, σὺ οὐ AaZmᶦᶜ.

1329 γε om. RwXaXbZZbZcZuAaL (~Lᶜ). Turyn wrongly reports that Xb has γε. Its omission is more markedly a 'Moschopoulean' feature than he was aware.

⁹ This scholion is found in an Oxford manuscript, New College 259, dated to the end of the fourteenth century (F. W. Lenz and C. A. Behr, *P. Ael. Aristidis opera* I [1976] xxi–xxii).
¹⁰ See p. 126. ¹¹ Cf. Zuntz, *Inquiry* 163, Matthiessen 98 n. 33, Mastronarde 130.
¹² 513 μὲν] μὲν γὰρ G; 528 μὲν] μὲν γὰρ GK; 552 μὲν] γὰρ AaZb; 724 γὰρ] μὲν MnPrS; 866 μὲν] γὰρ R (~Rᵞᵖ). For examples in Aeschylus see Dawe, *Coll.& Inv.* 56.
¹³ 360 μὲν om. AbCr+, γὰρ om. Rw; 415 μὲν om. FGK+ (~G²ˢKᶦˢ); 939 μὲν om. AbAtFXa (~F²), γὰρ om. PrRf; 1076 γὰρ om. Zu; 1132 γὰρ om. FSaZu (~F²Sa²).
¹⁴ Turyn's statement that οὖν is omitted by A is wrong.

1406 πολέμου] -ω(ι) Pr¹ˢSa¹ˢZZbZmZuAaL et (ἐν π-) Tᵗᵍˡ, -οιc MnSᵘᵛ.

1607 μ᾽post γάρ add. RfZZcZmAaCr¹ˢMnPSTᶻ (~Aa³) (μ᾽post ἀνδάνουcι(ν) M²G).

1631 ἦν] ὡc B³ˢAZb²ʸᵖZm¹ʸᵖMt et Tᶜ pot. qu. Tᶻ; om. BCr (~B²).

(iii) *Readings not attested before c.1300*

35 ὅδε uel ὁ δέ] οὐδὲ ZZbZmZuᶜBᶜᵘᵛL²RyT¹¹; [L].

97 cτείχειν] ἥξειν Z.

147* ὑπώροφον] ὑπόροφον ZZbZcZmAaAbCrTᵗ³Tp (~Aa³).

168 ἔβαλεc ἐξ] ἐξέβαλεc ZTp et ᵍˡMBVAb²(F)MnPrR¹ξZc; ἔβαλλεc F, ἔβαλεc Tᵗ³.

282 παρθένωι] ante παρέχων ZZu, post ἐμαῖc AbMnPrRSSa.

286 ἔργον] ἔργον ἐc ξ; εἰc ἔργον ζ‹Tᶻ› (~Tᶜ); εἰc super ἔργον ᵍˡB²OAa²GKTᵗ.

427 δράcαc] πράξαc ZCrᵍˡ.

482 ὅδ᾽ante ἐcτιν add. ZZc‹Zm˙›Zu‹Tᶻ› (~Tᶜ; ἐcτ᾽Zm¹ᶜ).

491 οὐ ante coφίαc add. ‹Z›ZaZbZc²Zm¹ʸᵖTᶻ (~Zᶜ) et Xa²ˢ; ante coφίαc duo litt. spat. uac. P; cf. Σᵐᵇᵛᶜ (Schwartz 154. 8–10) . . . οὐ δεῖται ἀγῶνοc coφίαc . . . οὐ coφιcμάτων γὰρ προcδεῖται . . . οὐ καιρὸc ἡμᾶc περὶ coφίαc ἀγωνίζεcθαι.

509 ἀνταποκτενεῖ] ἀποκτενεῖ ζ‹Tᶻ› (~Tᶜ).

577 δίκην δοίη] δοίη δίκην Z, δίοι δίκην Za.

606* δυcτυχέcτερον] δυcχερέcτερον ZʳʸᵖZm¹ˢZu (~Zuʸᵖ); δυc-χερέcτατον XbXc¹ᶜXfʳʸᵖXhTh; δυcτυχέcτατον XXa(Xc)XfXgDrˢ et Stob. 4. 22. 196.

632 κυκλεῖc uel -οῖc] κινεῖc ZʳʸᵖZmZuL (~ʸᵖZm¹Zu).

699 ὑπείκοι] -κει ZZbZcZuC˙LPTᶻgE (~C¹ᶜ˙P¹ᶜTᵗ¹/²ˢ).

741 ἤ ante καὶ add. ζ‹Tᶻ› (~Zb³Tᶜ).¹⁵

747 τόδε γὰρ] τάδε γὰρ ZZbZcZmAa; τοῦτο γὰρ V; τοῦτό γ᾽ ξTᵗ³; [Tᶻ].

775 εἰ] τί ζCrP¹ᶜ˙Tᵗ¹ (~Zuʸᵖ), εἴ τι AaF²ˢ (~Aa³); τι super λέγοιμ᾽Ab¹R²S¹, super ἀcτοῖcιν V¹.

778 μένηιc] μείνηc ζLTᵗ¹ᵘᵛ (~Tᵗ¹ᶜ); μένειc MZuʸᵖMnS (~M¹ᶜ); μείνειc Cr; μείνοιc Sa.

920 γῆν] πόλιν ZʳʸᵖZb‹Zm›ZuAa (~Zm¹ᶜAaʳʸᵖ).¹⁶

---

¹⁵ Cf. *Ph.* 724 εἰ] ἤ LSaζ (Mastronarde 133).
¹⁶ Cf. *Ph.* 571 γῆν] πόλιν B.

1081 οὐκέτ᾽ ἔςτι] οὐκ ἔςτ᾽ ἔτι ZZu; οὐκέτ᾽ ἔςται VMnPrS¹ᶜSa; οὐκ ἔςτι F; οὐκ ἔςται S.

1141 τοῦτ᾽] τόδ᾽ ZZbZm.

1143 δεῖ (prius)] δή Z.

1192 πᾶν] πᾶςι ZZbZcZmCrLPTᶜ.

1215 αὐτό] αὐτῷ ZZbZmTᵗˢ; -τῇ L; εἰς αὐτὸ G (εἰς ᵍˡB³VaXXa ZcTᵗ).

1267 τε post κόραιςι add. ZZbZmZuˢAa.

1493 ὡς ante ςκύμνον add. ZZcMnᶜTᵗ³ (ὡς ᵍˡAaʳ, ὥςπερ ᵍˡCrPr).

1506 τοὐμόν] ante ἐκ δόμων ZZdˢPTᵗ³.

1548 ἐκ] om. Z; ἐ S.

1680 καῖς post ςυμφοραῖς add. ZZm (init. 1681 Z).

Subscriptio Εὐριπίδου δράματος Ἠλέκτρας τέλος Z (et Xg), τέλος Εὐρ- Ἠλέκτρας P (τ- ὀρέςτου ZmZu, om. ZbZc).

Of the 51 readings listed by Turyn as 'Thoman interpolations', five are known to have been in existence before the time of Thomas (list (i)). Of the remainder, 16 are found in manuscripts roughly contemporary in date to Thomas (list (ii)), and the other 30 are either certainly or possibly not attested before the time of Thomas (list (iii)). Several of these readings are in origin glosses (47, 142, 168, 286, 427, 775, 1011, 1445, 1493),[17] and all but two of these glosses (427,[18] 1493) are known to have been in existence in the time of Thomas. Other additions, which are not found as glosses in any manuscript, may be assumed to be, in effect, glosses, added for clarity (482, 741, 1267, 1607, 1680). Many of the remaining readings are careless slips, ruining the metre (42, 282, 489, 509, 577, 1081, 1548), or thoughtless substitutions of a more or less synonymous or homophonous word (97, 289, 632, 699, 747, 778, 920, 1141, 1143, 1215). Two are trivializations (1266 the more obvious plural for singular, 1406 the more obvious dative for genitive). Evidence of rational thought is almost non-existent. The interpolation of οὐ at 491 is, indeed, evidence of thought; but the thought, prompted by the scholia, need not have been that of Thomas.[19]

[17] Cf. Zuntz, *Inquiry* 159, 163.

[18] πράξας for δράςας, although it appears as a gloss in Cr, should perhaps not be described as a gloss 'in origin', and might have been included in the following list of thoughtless substitutions of synonyms. These two verbs are commonly interchanged: 622 δράςω] πράςςω Rw; 732 πράςςειс] δράς(ς)ειс ʸᵖMnPrS; 775 ἔδραςας] ἔπραξας VAbᵍˡL MnPrʸᵖS (~Mnʸᵖ); 1318 δεδραμένων] πεπραγμένων B²ᵍˡAaFGMnʸᵖMtᶜPrSaξZbZmTᵗ³, δεδραγμ- PrᵍˡR¹ˢSSa¹ˢ; 1579 πράςςειс] δράςειс V; 1583 δρᾶςαι] πρᾶξαι V; 1598 δράςη(ι)ς uel -ειс] πράςςειс F.

[19] See p. 155.

There are only three correct readings on the list: 147 ὑπόροφον, 606 δυςχερέςτερον, 922 ἀκέραιον. The first, restoring dochmiac metre, is either inherited truth (it is shared by the earlier or contemporary Ab) or a lucky slip.[20] The second is less likely to be a lucky slip than inherited truth, since the corruption usually goes the other way.[21] For the third see below, p. 123. The more exquisite word-order at 1506, if it were offered by more respectable authority than ZZd^{s}PT^{t3}, we should gladly accept. But *non tali auxilio.*

Many of these readings are shared by members of Θ: F/Sa (13, 142, 415, 489, 787, 922, 1266, 1406), Pr (42, 289, 783, 938, 1011, 1406), Ab/R (147, 489, 775), Mn/S (142, 775, 1607). It is no coincidence that at 282 both ZZu and AbMnPrRSSa misplace παρ-θένωι, although in different places. There are also several agreements with two of the common associates of Θ, Rf/Rw (47, 783, 1011, 1274, 1329, 1445, 1607). There are also a few agreements with A (783, 1274, 1631) and K (415, 787). In all these cases of agreements between the Thoman manuscripts and manuscripts which may be contemporary in date with Thomas, Turyn's hypothesis invites us to believe that the readings originated in the Thoman manuscripts and were imported from them into the non-Thoman manuscripts. This is unbelievable. The diffusion of these readings suggests, rather, that the Thoman manuscripts have taken over readings which, by the time of Thomas, had gained wide currency.

Among the manuscripts which are possibly to be dated later than Thomas we find numerous agreements with Aa (47, 147, 747, 775, 920, 1266, 1267, 1274, 1329, 1406, 1493, 1607) and Cr (142, 147, 427, 775, 783, 787, 1011, 1192, 1274, 1445, 1607), both of which are commonly associated with Θ. There is no good reason to suppose that Aa and Cr gained these readings from the Thoman manuscripts rather than from a source common to them and the Thoman manuscripts. The same may be said of agreements with G (42, 415, 1266), which is related to K.

With LP and T the situation is different. T^z (that part of T which was written by the original scribe) is actually a 'Thoman' manuscript,[22] and so it is no surprise that T^z has many of the readings listed above (13, 286, 482, 489, 491, 509, 699, 741, 922, 938,

---

[20] Unless the truth is rather ὑπνοφόρον (Musgrave, commended by Willink).

[21] Cf. Zuntz, *Philologus* 104 (1960) 140–2, *Inquiry* 152–3. See also above, pp. 52, 80, below, p. 127.   [22] See pp. 95–6.

1607). L and P presumably had their origins in the scriptorium of Thomas and Triclinius at Thessalonike; and so, again, it is no surprise to find one or both of them in agreement with members of ζ (*inscriptio*, 35, 42, 142, 415, 489, 491, 632, 699, 775, 778, 783, 787, 922, 1011, 1192, 1274, 1329, 1406, 1445, 1506, 1607, *subscriptio*).[23]

In the numerous agreements between members of ζ and Triclinius, can we be sure that in all cases it is Triclinius who is the debtor? It has recently been suggested that the earliest of the Thoman manuscripts may owe something to the activities in the Thoman scriptorium of a young Triclinius.[24] I shall argue later that Ry bears witness to the earlier work of Triclinius, prior to that which finds its final form in T (by the hand which I call Tᵗ).[25] And it is at least possible that the Thoman manuscripts may bear occasional witness to Triclinian changes later found in Tᵗ or (what is much more speculative) to changes which are not found in Tᵗ because they had been abandoned by Triclinius in the interval. Here is a list of unique or nearly unique agreements between Triclinius and members of ζ, in which the possibility of direct Triclinian influence on ζ may be contemplated:[26]

104 νῦν] νυν ZbᶦᶜᵘᵛZdZuᵘᵛTᵗᶦ/² (~⟨Zb²⟩Zb³) and 1281 νυν Zc Tᵗ³;[27] 118 τε] γε ZbZcTᶜ; 143 κοίτας] λέχουc ZcTᵗ³MnRy, [Tᶻ]; 497 ὑπέρ] ὑπαὶ ZbTᵗ³ (~Zb³);[28] 973 ὧν om. ZbTᵗ³ (~Zbᶦᶜ); 1314 βοήν] βοῆς ZmZu²Tᵗ³ˢ (~Zuᶜ); 1330 ἄραρ'] ἄρηρ'ZbᶜZdTᵗ³ et Zu aut Zuᶜ (cf. 1571 ἄρηρε Tᵗ³);[29] 1402 ὁ om. ZmTᵗ³ (~Zmᶦ super πατήρ); 1470 ἀρβύλαν] -ύλλαν ZcTᵗ³; 1493 ὡς ante cκύμνον add. ZZcTᵗ³ Mnᶜ (ὡς ᵍˡAaʳ, ὥσπερ ᵍˡCrPr); 1506 τοὐμὸν] ante ἐκ δόμων ZZdˢᵗTᵗ³ P; 1611 τίνα] τίν'ZTᵗᶦ/²K; 1612 φονεύcετε (-cετ'ξ)] -cεθ'ZTᵗ²/³.

---

[23] See Zuntz, *Inquiry* 164–74, Matthiessen 99–100.

[24] See O. L. Smith, in the articles cited on pp. 11–12 (under Z and Zm), and Mastronarde esp. 121, 136, 149–50. Turyn (180–1) claimed that Zc was written by a young Triclinius. He is followed by Schartau II. 52–65, esp. 58–9 (I am bound to warn the reader that I have found many mistakes in Schartau's selective reports of Zc [I. 19–21]) and Smith, *Studies* 99 n. 80. For reservations see Zuntz, *Bulletin* 516 n. 3, Matthiessen 51. See also above, p. 12, for the suggestion that a correcting hand in Zb is that of Triclinius.

[25] See pp. 99–103.

[26] For other agreements between ζ and Triclinius see below, pp. 96–8.

[27] For this as a possibly Triclinian feature see Mastronarde 141–2. But the distribution of νυν in our manuscripts shows that Triclinius did not devise the form: 251 XZZuTᵗᶦ/², 759 XXbTᶻ, 795 Z, 1037 AdTᶜ, 1101 KLXXbZbZuTᶻ aut Tᶜ, 1103 KLXXbZZbTᶻ aut Tᶜ, 1181 Zd, 1216 Zb, 1599 KLXZZuᶜᵘᵛTᶻ.

[28] Triclinius introduces ὑπαί at A. *Ag.* 1164 and S. *OT* 476 (Zuntz, *Inquiry* 209).

[29] Triclinius consistently changes ἄραρε to ἄρηρε: *Med.* 322, 413, 745 (also 1192 ἀρηρότως), *Hcld.* 398, *Hi.* 1090, *Andr.* 255.

The most significant item on this list is 143, where λέχουc in Zc
may be considered (on the evidence of its appearance in Ry) to be
an early conjecture by Triclinius.[30] The other agreements are compatible with the hypothesis of Triclinian influence, but do not demand it.

One further piece of evidence may be brought into play. If (as it
has been claimed)[31] Tp reflects the earliest work of Triclinius on
the lyrics, we may consider whether there exist any agreements between Tp and ζ, such as might betray the handiwork of Triclinius.
A few exist, but their value as evidence is slight: 153 μ' post
μετάδοc ZTp (μοι Zc, ἐμοί ˢZʳZmᵍˡRfᵍˡ); 168 ἔβαλεc ἐξ] ἐξέβαλεc Z
Tp (et ᵍˡMBVξZc+); 319 ἐλάχετ᾽ ἐν] ἐλάχετε ZTpP (-ητε Ab; ἐν
ˢZʳᵍˡAb¹); 816 ἐξαμείβων] ἀμείβων ZmTpL; 1275 δέ] δαί ZZbZcZd
ZmTp; 1480 ὁ om. ZcTp. Of these the most interesting is 1275 δαί,
which is a metrical conjecture in Tp, designed to turn dochmiacs
into iambics (Tp adds δή after ἔτι, but ZZbZcZdZm do not), a recourse for which Tᵗ³, recognizing the antistrophic nature of the
lyrics, had no need. It is possible that δαί in ZZbZcZdZm is a
simple phonetic error (Z has δαί for δέ uniquely at 672). But it is
at least possible that these manuscripts reflect an early Triclinian
idea, later abandoned.[32]

I now offer evidence for the claim made above about the relationship of Zd and Zu. That Zd is a descendant of Zu or of the parent of Zu is proved by about 100 unique agreements.[33] Further,
their colometry and the location of their glosses are identical (Zd
has gained some extra marginal scholia). Divergences are few, and
yet there are enough to show that Zd is not a simple apograph of
Zu but has acquired readings from another source—either from
the common parent, which must then be assumed to have had variants, or (more probably) from an intermediate copy (whether of the
common parent or of Zu) into which had been introduced some
corrections and variants. These are the divergences (isolated errors
of Zd excluded): hyp. 1.11 φίλοc] ante ὁ Πυλάδηc ZdRf (post αὐτοῦ
Aa); 781 θανῇ(ι)] θανεῖν ZdZF+; 790 κεῖνο] κοῖνο ZuAaMnᵘᵛ

---

³⁰ See pp. 99–100.   ³¹ See pp. 103–10.
³² For δαί as a Triclinian remedy see El. 978, 1116, IA 1443.
³³ Zd does not have Ph. For Hec. my information is limited to the selection of readings
quoted by Matthiessen 97–8, which contains a few divergences between Zd and Zu but also
one unique agreement (1021 ῥέξαc for πράξαc). Turyn's statement that 'Zu is especially related to the ms. Zb' (186) is wide of the mark.

(~Mnᶜ); 821 μελάνδετον] -δευτον Zdξ; 914 πέτροις] -αις PZu (-ης Z); 1279 πελάζεται] πλάζ- ZcZu; 1303 πέμπετε post φάσγανα add. ZdMBOVaGKξ; 1339 εἰςιδεῖν] ἰδεῖν ZcZu; 1357 ἄν post πρίν add. ZdGⁱᶜξTᵗ³; 1448 ἐκλήιςε] ἐκκλήιςε ZdZcAξ, ἔκληςεν Zd²ʸᵖ (ἐκκλή-ιςεν [om. δ'] Th, ἐκλήιςεν δέ γ' Tp); 1477 ἀγκύλας] ἀγγ- ZdⁱʸᵖF; 1487 προςβολάν] προβ- ZdⁱʸᵖZv+; 1506 τοὐμὸν] ante ἐκ δόμων ZdⁱˢZPTᵗ³; 1508 τάδ'] τόδ' ZdⁱʸᵖAa³ˢ; 1510 που] πω ZdⁱʸᵖZCrGP Rw; 1567 χερὶ] -οῖν ZdⁱʸᵖF²PPrSa; 1585 τάφωι] -ον ZdO (~Zdⁱˢ); 1594 φευξόμε(ς)θα] -ούμεθα ZdGRw, -ούμεςθα Aa³ˢ; 1648 δέ τ'uel sim.] δέ γ' Zd²ʸᵖZcACrGKMtSa.

Several of these divergent readings of Zd could be explained as errors committed independently by Zd and by the manuscripts with which Zd is in agreement (914, 1448, 1585, 1594) or as conscious corrections by Zd of an easily remediable error committed by Zu (790, 1279, 1339). But at least one reading requires a different explanation: 821 μελάνδευτον, shared with ξ, is unlikely to be an independent error (note also the agreement of Zd and ξ at 1357). Whatever the cause of the few divergences between Zd and Zu, the former may be regarded as a descendant or nephew of the latter. In what follows I shall for the most part ignore Zd, which may be assumed to agree with Zu. But I shall cite Zd when the reading of Zu has been corrected: it will be seen that Zd normally agrees with Zuᶜ.

ζ do not form a unified class. Two or more of them sometimes agree in unique readings; but there is no consistent pattern in these agreements. In the following list I offer a single example of each combination which is found of two or more members of ζ when they share a reading which is unique to them, and I add in brackets how many more instances of such unique combinations are found:

hyp. 1.5 ἐκφέρεςθαι] ἐκφέρειν ZbZu (+2), [ZZm]; 92 δῆτά μοί τι] τί μοι ZZcZm (+0); 345 ἕτερον (ZZmZu+) uel ἄλλον ἕτερον (Zc+)] ἄλλων ἕτερον ZcⁱˢZmⁱᶜ (+0); 433 τοῦ ante Παλαμήδου(ς) add. ZZb (+3); 606 δυςτυχέςτερον] δυςχερέςτερον ZʸᵖZmⁱˢZu (~Zuʸᵖ) (+0); 770 ὥςπερ] ὡς ZbZmᶜ (+0); 774 (τί) λέγειν χρή] τί χ- λ- ZZu (+4); 829 ἐξανάψηι] -ης ZZc (+2); 848 ὑμᾶς] post ζῆν ZmZu (+4); 892 λόγους] -οις ZZm (+3); 899 còν ante cύγγονον add. ZʸᵖZbZu (+1); 1006 μεταβάλλει] -βάλοι ZZbZm (+3); 1207 τάλας] φίλος ZZbZcʸᵖ (+0); 1268 ὅδε] ὧδε ZZcZmⁱˢZuᵘᵛ (~ZˢZcⁱˢ ZdZuᶜ) (+0); 1281 ἀκοὰν] -àς ZZcZu (+2); 1339 εἰςιδεῖν] ἰδεῖν Zc

Zu (+3); 1368 ἔχει] -οι ZbZmZu^s (+o); 1459 δίνασεν] δίνησεν ‹Zu²›Zv (~ZdZu^c) (+o).

The 51 readings on Turyn's list give a fair picture of the relationships which exist between the members of ζ and the other manuscripts. No single member of ζ shows an especial connection with any other single manuscript or group of manuscripts. Unique agreements with other manuscripts or groups do occur: in particular with L or P or both, with Aa, Cr, Rf, Rw, and with members of Θ. But no pattern is discernible in these agreements. I offer a selection:

(i) L/P: 87 πεπραγότας] -χότας ZZcZmP‹T^z› (~Zc^1sT^c); 161 ὦ τάλας om. ZbP (~Zb³) (ὦ om. T^t3); 215 δ' om. ZuL; 233 πόδας] πόδα ZcZmZuP; 405 δέμας] σῶμα ZcP; 434 οὔκουν] οὗ γ' οὐ ζLP T^z (~Zb³) (οὗ γ' οὐ MOPr, οὔκ οὐ fere B^2/3ACF, οὔ*οὐ B, ὅ γ' οὐ M²); 467 ἀπέδωκ'] ἀποδέδωκ' ZmZuL; 475 ἀσπάσασθαι] ἀποσπάσασθαι ZbP; 758 μακρῶν] μικρῶν ZZc^1sZmZuP; 803 εἴ] ἤν ZbP (ἐάν Pr^1s); 856 ἤκεις] ἦκες ZmZuLTa^gl; 880 τε] δὲ ZuL; 914 πέτροις] -αις PZu (-ης Z); 941 ὁ om. ZbZmZuL; 1023 τάδ' om. ZP; 1069 πρῶτα] πρῶτον ZL; 1388–9 'Ερινὺν] post ξεστῶν ZP; 1495 διαπρό] δὴ πρὸ ZZcZmZuL; 1504 εἰσορῶ] post πρὸ δωμάτων (ἐκ προδ- L) ZmZuL; 1528 ἐν om. ZuLP.

(ii) Aa: 552 μέν] γὰρ ZbAa; 747 τόδε] τάδε ZZbZcZmAa; 752 μᾶλλον] post πατρός ZAa (om. CrFSa); 1194 δέρηι . . . αὐτῆι] -ην . . . -ἠν ZuAa^rs; 1209 ἄν post γένοιτ' add. ZbZmAa; 1392 εὐνέτα] -άτα ZAa^γρ.

(iii) Cr: 54 δὲ] δὴ ZZc^1sCr; 529 τάλας] γόοις ZCr; 753 κοὐκ] οὐκ ZbCr (~Zb^1c); 1412–13 τὸ κεῖθεν . . . τὸ κεῖθεν (uel τὸ 'κ- . . . τὸ 'κ-)] τὸκεῖθεν utroque loco ZCr; 1529 cε om. ZbCr (et Th, ~Th^s).

(iv) Rf: 186 ἥσυχον] ἡσύχως Zu^γρRf; 1527 με om. ZvRf (et gB).[34]

(v) Rw: hyp. 1.15–16 ἅμα] post γυναικός ZuRw; 1.16 ἐπεβ-άλ(λ)ετο] ὑπεβάλλετο ZuRw (ὑπεβάλετο AAn); 28 μὲν om. ZcRw (et AnTh); 73 cύ τε om. ZbRw (~Rw^s); (τε om. Zb^1cAbFPRSSa); 92 πίθοι' ἄν uel sim.] πείθοιο ZZcZmRw; 103 τ'] τῶ(ι)δ' ZZcZm ZuRw^uv‹T^z²› (~T^t1; τῶδε τ' Rw^cuv); 273 ὁρᾶθ'] ὁρᾶc θ' ZuRw; 1391 Γαν(ν)υμήδεος] -διος ZuRw.

(vi) Θ and associates: hyp. 1. 9 ἀποκτείνειν] -κτεῖναι ZbZcZuCr MnS, [ZZm]; 126 ἐν om. ZbF (et Thom. Mag. Ecl. p. 384. 8 Ritschl cod. La); 313 cτρωτοῦ] -ῶ(ι) ZuF (~F²); 390 ὄνομ'] οὔνομ'

[34] Zv and Rf share almost identical colometry: see p. 149.

Z²ZbS; 406 γ' post Πυλάδης add. ZcZmSa;³⁵ 425 δή om. ZuFSa; 468 δ' post ποῖον add. ZZbAbMnRS; 502 τ' om. ZbAb (et Ad); 525 καί (alterum) om. ZuSa; 526 ὦ τάλας] post ψυχήν ZbZmZuMn (post τίν' Z); 545 λυπήσειν] λυπῆσαι ZuVMnPrʸᵖR²Sᴵˢ (~Mnʸᵖ); 549 ὅ μ'] ὅμμ' ZuS; 594 ἔκτανον] κατέκτανον ZZbAbR; 768 καὶ cέ] post τἀμά ZmZuCrFSa (om. Aa); 925 κάθεον] ἄθεον ZbMnS (et Th); 940 κατακτανεῖτε] κτανεῖτε ZZcFSa (et ThXcXd); 953 φάσγαν'] φάσγανον ZVAbMnRS (et ᵍˡOᴵAaʳ); 1022 κίγ' uel cίγ'] cύ γ' ZZcZmZuAa³ˢFMnᶜPr (~ZˢZmᴵˢF²ˢPrʸᵖ); 1093 καλόν] post ποτὲ ZbCrMnS; 1132 γάρ om. ZuFSa (~F²Sa²); 1149 οὖν] αὖ ZuAbF MnPrʸᵖRSSa²ʸᵖ (~Mnʸᵖ); 1154 γένοc] λέχη Zuʸᵖ, λέχοc VAbMn PrʸᵖSSa²ʸᵖ (~Abᴵʸᵖ); 1207 ἁμαρτήcηι] -cειc ZcᴵᶜZuAaPrSa, -cηc Aa³F (~PrᴵˢSa²ˢ); 1340 χεροῖν] -οῖc ZbPrSa (~Zbᴵᶜ); 1465 ὤμοι] ἰώ μοι ZbAaFPrSa; 1477 πέτρουc] -αc ZmAaFMnᴵˢRw, -αν AbR (~ZmᴵˢAbᴵˢF²Rwᴵˢ); 1494 κόραν] κούραν ZmAaPrSa; 1513 τριπτύ χουc] διπτύχουc Z‹Zuⁱ›Ab (~ZuᶜZd).

There is very little trace of any connection between members of ζ and HMBOV or A: 280 θεῖc' uel θεῖc] τιθεῖc' ZmA; 323 φόνον] -ου BZdZuᴵˢ (-ων ZᴵˢZmᴵˢ, -ουc Ab²ˢ);³⁶ 1098 εἰc] ἐc ZO; 1148 cπάcω μέλαν] cπαcόμεθα ZuʸᵖV (-ώμεθα ʸᵖCPr); 1476 ἄλλοθεν] ἄλλοcε ZO; 1479 ἦλθον] -εν ZOXa; 1650 cοι] cε ZcO. There is equally little trace of a connection with G and K: 1220 εἰc uel ἐν] ἐc ZGK; 1326 τί δ'] τάδ' Z²ZaGK; 1604 γάρ om. ZcK. And there are only sporadic agreements in readings peculiar to members of ξ: hyp. 1.19 καθαρθέντι] -των ZcZuXa, [ZZbZm]; 1.20 post ἄρχειν add. ἠξιώθηcαν ZcZuXa, ἠξιώθη G, [ZZbZm]; 2.2 καί om. ZcXa; 153 ὦ om. ZcXaTh (~Xaᴵᶜ); 1228 ὑπό] ὑπὲρ ZuX (~Zuᵍˡ); 1438 κόραν om. ZuX (~ZdZuˢ); 1465 ἀνίαχεν ἴαχεν] ἀνίαχεν fere MRw, ἀν- ἀν- ZbZmZuMt+, ἴα- ἴα- ZcZvMtᶜξ.

The agreements which have been illustrated in this chapter are manifold, but the conclusions which may be drawn are straightforward. The members of ζ, whether singly or in company with each other, regularly share readings which are attested, sometimes widely, in manuscripts contemporary with or later than the date of Thomas. It is not uncommon for all members of ζ to agree among themselves. But it is rare for them to do so in a reading unique to

---

³⁵ γ' (conjectured by Kirchhoff) may well be right.
³⁶ See CQ n.s. 40 (1990) 109 n. 39.

themselves.[37] No member of ζ (with the exception of the pair ZdZu) shares a relationship significantly more close to any one member than to another.[38] These manuscripts are not the offspring of one or two exemplars fashioned by Thomas. They reflect the wide variety of readings which had become available in that much wider variety of manuscripts which was available in the time of Thomas than is available now.[39]

[37] But if T^z is considered as a member of this class, there are three readings unique to the class ζT^z (286, 509, 741, all on Turyn's list). See further below, p. 95–6.

[38] Mastronarde (*GRBS* 26 [1985] 99–102) detects a close relationship between Zv and Zm in *Ph*. No such relationship exists in *Or*.

[39] My conclusions are similar to those of Matthiessen 95–100, Mastronarde 121–36, Smith, *Studies* 8 n. 12, 132–3 n. 18, 225 n. 109. Zuntz, *Inquiry* 169 (in the course of an admirable discussion of 'Thoman' readings) goes astray when he perpetuates Turyn's belief in 'Thomas's two master copies'. For Aeschylus (where, again, Turyn posited two 'Thoman recensions') see Dawe, *Coll. & Inv.* 18–22; for Sophocles (again, two 'recensions' posited), Dawe, *Studies* i. 60–80, E. C. Kopff, *TAPA* 106 (1976) 241–66; for Aristophanes, Smith, *GRBS* 17 (1976) 75–80. But belief in Thomas as an editor dies hard: see Schartau, II. 88 n. 39, Eberline 87.

CHAPTER XI

T, Ry, Tp

(i) *T*

Turyn[1] detected three separate stages in Triclinius' work on T. He distinguished these stages by the following criteria: (i) at the earliest stage, the use of black ink and rounded breathings; (ii) at the second stage, the use of black ink with angular breathings; (iii) at the third stage, the use of brown or yellow ink with angular breathings. Triclinius' other autograph manuscripts show that the change from rounded to angular breathings occurred $c.1319$. Turyn dates the original hand T^z to 1300–10, the first stage of Triclinius' revision to $c.1315$, the second to $c.1319$–25, the third to $c.1325$.[2]

During the earliest stage Triclinius made corrections to the text of T^z and added Thoman scholia and glosses, the Thoman prefatory material, and some scholia of his own. He also substituted for pages written by T^z some pages written by himself containing iambic trimeters, trochaic tetrameters, or anapaests (for *Orestes* these are fol. 71r–71v [lines 772–98] and fol. 104r [lines 1682–93]).[3] During the second stage he added Moschopoulean scholia and glosses and perhaps made further corrections to the text. During the third stage he substituted (whether for pages written by T^z or for pages already substituted by himself at the second stage) replacements written by himself for nearly all the pages containing lyrics, together with some iambic and trochaic pages, mainly adjacent to the lyric pages. He also added his own metrical scholia at this stage.

Such, in essence, is Turyn's analysis. Now I offer some obser-

---

[1] Especially 25–33.

[2] T^z is identified as the scribe of the Aristophanes manuscript Par. suppl. gr. 463, which was also revised by Triclinius (Turyn 32 n. 49, Smith, *Studies* 43). The view of W. J. W. Koster (*Autour d'un manuscrit d'Aristophane écrit par Demetrius Triclinius* [1957]) that the scribe was Triclinius himself appears to be untenable: for bibliography on this issue see Matthiessen 52 n. 4, Smith, *Studies* 99 n. 80, Eberline 49–77. On the date of Triclinius' change from round to angular breathings see also Turyn, *Dated Greek Manuscripts of the thirteenth and fourteenth Centuries in the Libraries of Italy* 1 (1972) 124–5, Smith, *Studies* 43–4.

[3] Except that 1682 is written by T^{t3}, as I explain below (p. 95).

vations of my own on the three stages of Triclinius' work. I distinguish these stages by the symbols T^{t1}, T^{t2}, T^{t3}.

The original scribe T^z writes in an ink which appears as either very dark brown or, more commonly, black. The text has been extensively corrected by a scribe using black ink, which is usually indistinguishable from that of T^z. Many of these corrections are made *in rasura* and are exceptionally difficult to detect. Some of them may have been made by T^z; but occasionally the shape of the letters enables us to identify the hand of Triclinius. Breathings are rounded. Turyn ascribes nearly all these corrections to Triclinius. He may be right to do so. But where there is no positive indication of Triclinian authorship I attribute them to T^c.

More easily identifiable as Triclinian are very small supralinear additions and variants written in a similar black ink. If they have angular breathings I label them T^{t2}. If breathings are not in evidence I label them $T^{t1/2}$.

Unmistakable is a smaller number of corrections in brown, some of which declare themselves by their nature (often violent) to be Triclinian conjectures. These I label T^{t3}, since they are written in the same colour of ink which Triclinius uses on the pages of lyrics substituted by him (these pages I also label T^{t3}).

Brown ink, however, is not associated only with the third stage. Triclinius uses brown, with rounded breathings, in writing occasional scholia. He also does so in the following circumstance. At the foot of fol. 76v he adds, in brown and with rounded breathings, lines 950–1. Fol. 77r (beginning with line 952) is the first of a set of substituted pages written by T^{t3} in brown and with angular breathings (lyrics begin at 960). Whatever may have induced Triclinius to start fol. 77r with line 952 and not with line 950, we are bound to conclude that he wrote lines 950–1 before he wrote the substitute page 77r. Perhaps this is an indication that Triclinius inserted earlier replacements for the lyric sections before making his final fair copy.[4] By contrast, at the end of these lyrics, on fol. 8or, which is written by T^z (lines 1024 ff.), Triclinius adds at the top of the page line 1023, in brown and with angular breathings. Presumably the preceding page, as written by T^z, ended with line 1023, whereas the page substituted by T^{t3} ends with 1022.

The final page of the play, 104r (the anapaests 1682–93), is a re-

---

[4] As Turyn (25) had surmised.

placement by T^{tt} (black ink with rounded breathings), except for
the first line (1682), which is written by T^{t3} (brown ink with angular breathings). The preceding page (103v), written by T^z, contains
only 17 lines (1665–81) instead of the customary 18. But it is clear
from the gap which now exists between 1681 and the scholia that
1682 originally stood at the foot of this page and must have been
later erased by T^{t3} so that all the anapaests might stand on the same
page.

'The original scribe T^z followed a manuscript of the Thoman recension,' claimed Turyn (49), later specifying the second Thoman
recension as the model (168). In the preceding chapter I have rejected Turyn's belief in 'recensions' by Thomas. But his claim that
T^z is affiliated to the 'Thoman' manuscripts is right to this extent,
that T^z generally agrees with at least one member of ζ and occasionally agrees with all or all but one of ζ in readings which are attested either weakly or not at all in other manuscripts.

A selection of readings will illustrate the affinity of T^z and ζ:

3 ἀνθρώπου] -ων M(Mn)S^{uv}SαζT^z (~S^{c}Zm^{1s}); 13 τ’ post πόλεμον
add. V$^{1/2c}$SαζT^z (~T^{t3}); 53 Τροίας] -ης AaLZcZmZuT^z (~Aa^{3s}T^c);
87 πεπραγότας] -χότας PZZcZm<T^z> (~Zc^{1s}T^c); 92 τῶν ante θεῶν
add. ZZcZm<T^z> (~T^c); 231 ἀνακύκλει] κάνα- PZb^{3}Zc<T^z> (~T$^{tt/2}$)
(καὶ Z^{2s}); 286 εἰς ante ἔργον add. ζ<T^z> (~T^c); 292 ἤμελλε] ἔμ-
ZT^c+, ἔτ’ ἤμ- CZ^{c}ZaZbZcZmZu<T^z> (~Zm^c); 434 οὔκουν] οὖ γ’ οὐ
LPζT^z (οὖ γ’ οὐ MOPr, οὔκ οὐ fere B$^{2/3}$ACF, οὖ*οὐ B, ὄ γ’ οὐ M^2);
482 ὅδ’ ante ἐστιν add. ZZc<Zm$^?$>Zu<T^z> (~(Zm^{1c})T^c); 489 κτήσο-
μαι] κεκτήσομαι CFPZZc<Zm>(Zu)<T^z> (~(P^c)Zm^{c}T^c); 491 οὐ ante
cοφίας add. Xa^{2s}<Z>ZaZbZc^{2}Zm^{1γρ}T^z (~Z^c), ante cοφίας duo litt.
spat. uac. P; 502 ἂν τῆς] ἀντὶ LMnPPrSaZbZcZmZuT^z (~L^{2}T^{ttγρ}
T$^{tt/2s}$), ἀντὶ τῆς Z;^{5} 509 ἀνταποκτενεῖ] ἀποκτενεῖ ζ<T^z> (~T^c); 695
γὰρ ante καὶ add. MCLZc<Zm>Zu<T^z> (~Zm^{c}T^c); 699 ὑπείκοι] -ει
C$^?$LPZZbZcZuT^z (~C$^{1c?}$P^{1c}T$^{tt/2s}$); 741 ἢ ante καὶ add. ζ<T^z>
(~Zb^{3}T^c); 922 ἀκέραιος] -ον FLPζT^z (~Zb^{3}T^c); 945 ἠγόρευε] -σε

---

^{5} ἀντὶ must be right. West (endorsed by Willink in the Addendis Addenda to his second
edition) defends the 'ablatival genitive' τῆς cυμφορᾶc by reference to *Med.* 534. Such a genitive (found also in *Rh.* 467) signifies 'in return for', and forces us to refer cυμφορά to the
murder of Agamemnon ('he would have got credit for sanity out of the calamity'), which is
scarcely effective or appropriate sense. The argument demands 'Orestes would have gained
τὸ cῶφρον instead of cυμφορά' (i.e. he would have acted sanely, and would now be sane, instead of being in his present plight). For ἔλαβ’ ἄν ('a type of elision found mainly in emendations', West) see *Studies* 100, 120.

VLPZcZmZu‹Tᶻ› (~Tᶜ); 1127 ἐκκλείcομεν] ἐγκλ- CrLPZZcZm
Tᶻ; 1200 παρῇ(ι)] -ῇν BᶦᶜLPrRfᶦᶜSaζ‹Tᶻ› (~ZᶜTᶜ).

Is Tᶻ related more closely to one member of ζ than to another?
I have tabulated 363 readings in which the members of ζ are divided among themselves. I have ignored corrections and variants,
isolated errors of individual manuscripts, and some (but not all)
minutiae. In a few cases the reading either of Tᶻ or of a member of
ζ is not certain. For these reasons my calculations are rough and
ready. But, since the total number of readings at issue is so large, a
certain amount of imprecision will not distort the overall picture.

Out of these 363 readings, Tᶻ agrees with Zc in 261 (Zc is absent
for 10 of the 363), with Z in 225, with Zm in 223, with Zu in 193,
with Zb in 167 (Zb is absent for 18). When one of ζ, disagreeing
with the remaining members, agrees with Tᶻ and other manuscripts, its total of agreements with Tᶻ is: Zc 15, Z 7, Zm 4, Zu 4,
Zb 3. The totals of unique agreements between members of ζ and
Tᶻ are: Zc 5, Z 1, Zb 0, Zm 0, Zu 0. These unique agreements,
however, are not good evidence of affiliation: 140 δ᾽ante ἴχνοc add.
Zc‹Tᶻ²› (~Tᶜ pot. qu. Tᶻ); 438 ἑῶc᾽] ἑῶcιν ZcTᶻ (~Tᶜ); 574
Ἑλλάδοc] ἑλα- ZcTᶻ (~ZcᶜTᶜ); 1114 Ἑλλὰc] ἑλὰc ZTᶻ (~ZaTᶜ);
1158 Αἴγιcθον] -ιcτον ZcTᶻ; 1640 cυνήγαγον] ξυν- ZcTᶻ.

A clear enough picture emerges. If ZZbZcZmZu are to be
treated as members of a single class, then Tᶻ must be assigned to
that class. The closest relative of Tᶻ is Zc, the next close Z, the least
close Zb.

I now examine the activities of Triclinius. I begin with corrections
which may be ascribed to Tᵗ¹ or Tᵗ² (if there is doubt I label the
correction Tᵗ¹/² or Tᶜ). Usually the corrected reading is well or
moderately well attested in other manuscripts, and so affords no
clue to Triclinius' source. Occasional unique agreements between
Triclinius and individual members of ζ are compatible with a belief
in Triclinian influence on ζ, as well as with the reverse belief.[6] The
one certainty is that Triclinius had access to some, at least, of the
readings which are characteristic of ξ: 228 μέλη] δέμαc
GᶦᵞᵖRwξTᵗ¹/²ᵞᵖ; 378 ἐξέλιπον] -λειπον ξTᶜ (pot. qu. Tᶻ); 424 ἔφυc
κακόc] εἰπὼν κακῶc ξ, εἰπών Tᵗ²ᵞᵖ; 535 τοῦτον] αὐτὸν ξTᵗ²ᵞᵖ; 698
fere αὐτῶ(ι) uel αὐτὸν] αὐτὸc ξTᶜ (αὐτὸc Aa³, αὐτῶ γ᾽P, αὐτ** Tᶻ);

---

[6] See pp. 87–8.

779 μολόντι] -τα ξT^{tι/2s} (u. scr. T^{tι}); 1115 δοῦλον (alterum)] δούλων XXa^{ιc}Xb^rT^{tι/2s}; 1596 μή γ'] μήτ'ξT^{tι/2s}. A few metrical corrections are common not only to Triclinius and ξ but also to one or both of GK: 523 ἀμύνω] ἀμυνῶ Aa³GK^{ιc}ξT^c; 594 πειθόμενος] πιθ- Aa^{ιs}G^c KXXa^cXbT^{tι/2}; 1622 οὐχί] οὔκουν GKξT^c. And Triclinius has the following unique agreement with GK: 933 Δαναΐδαι] δαναοὶ δὲ fere AaCrFPPrRfSaZbZm, δαναΐδαι δὲ GKT^{tι/2}. A few other metrical corrections either are unique to Triclinius or, if attested elsewhere, may still have been made by him independently: 258 coîc ἐν] coîc G, ἐν coîc RyT^{tι/2uv},[7] 575 ἔcωcεν] ἔcωc' T^{t2/3} (the c was probably written by T^{t2}, the apostrophe by T^{t3}); 791 κατάcχωcι(ν)] -ωc'Kξ T^{t2} (u. scr. T^{tι}); 897 πόλεως] πόλεος H^cMBAGKT^{tι/2} (~B^{2/3}); 901 λέγοι uel λέγει] del. T^{tι/2}, sed λέγ (omisso compendio) suprascr. T^{tgl}; 1196 Μενέλεως] -λαος T^t (ao scr. T^{tι/2}, c T^{t3}); 1239 cε] c'ξT^c; 1598 τάδε] τάδ'ξT^{t2}; 1605 cε] c'ξT^{t2}; 1606 μητέρα] μητέρ'ξT^{t2/3}.

I turn to the corrections of T^{t3} on pages not written by T^{t3}. There are fewer of these at issue, and I ignore trifles. Among these corrections is a greater proportion of Triclinius' own conjectures than was found in the corrections of T^{tι} and T^{t2} and a smaller proportion of readings characteristic of ξ. Of the latter I find only two: 747 τίδε (uel τάδε) γάρ] τοῦτο γὰρ V, τοῦτό γ'ξT^{t3}, [T^z]; 786 τὸ om. LRfξT^{t3} (u. scr. T^{tι}). Here are four readings elsewhere weakly attested: 86 εἶ] ἡ VL²PT^{t(3?)} (~V^{ιs}P²), ἡ F (~F²); 497 ὑπέρ] ὑπαὶ ZbT^{t3} (~Zb³);[8] 1123 κείνη(ι)] ᾽κείνη PZm, ἐκείνη(ι) AaAtXcMsZ T^{t3}; 1189 cυλλάβεθ'] ξυλλάβεθ'CrL(Zb)ZmT^{t3} (~<T^{t2}>), cυλλάβεcθ' CGKMn^cPr^{uv}ZZu<T^z> (~K^{ιc}Pr^{cuv}), cυλλαβόμεθ'Zc.

These are the possible or certain Triclinian conjectures: 143 κοί-τας] λέχουc MnRyZcT^{t3}, [T^z];[9] 410 εὐπαίδευτα uel ἀπ- (ἀπ-ζ<T^z>+)] ἀπαίδευτον S^{uv}T^{t3};[10] 515 ἀνταποκτείνειν uel -κτεῖναι]

---

[7] The interpretation of what can be seen in T is problematical (see Turyn 191). Visible is ἀτρέμ^{ac}ἐ⟨.⟩δεμνίοιc. The ac and ἐν are probably written by T^{tι/2} in an erasure. The [⟨.⟩] indicates a strip of paper pasted onto the page and obscuring the script. Above this strip two traces are visible. The former looks like the top of the compendium for οιc, and the latter looks like a circumflex. By holding the page up to the sunlight I was able to see enough of the writing obscured by the pasted slip to confirm that my impression was probably right. Further confirmation is provided by Ta (a copy of T, or a copy of a copy of T [see p. 13]), which has ἀτρέμαc ἐν coîc. Perhaps the original reading of T^z was ἀτρέμαc ἐν δεμνίοιc (with coîc accidentally omitted), or ^{coîc}ἐν, and perhaps Triclinius erased ac and ἐν and wrote ἐν in the place left by ac, which he now wrote above the line. The slip was presumably pasted in later, to repair the damage to the page which (as the reverse of the page shows) had been caused by the erasure.

[8] See p. 87. [9] See pp. 99–100. [10] See p. 155.

ἀποκτείνειν T^{t3}; 527 ἐξέβαλ(λ)ε] ἐξέβαλε τὸν T^{t3} (τὸν Ab^{2gl}); 586
γὰρ τὸ κείνης] τὸ κείνης γὰρ T^{t3};[11] 782 τὸ πρᾶγμʼ] τὸ πρᾶγμα γʼξ,
τὸ πρᾶγμα δʼGK, μὴν τὸ π- T^{t3} (u. scr. T^{t1}); 782 τὸ] τῷ(ι) Aa^{rs}GK^{1c}
LξZu^{γρ}, καὶ τὸ T^{t3} (u. scr. T^{t1}); 798 μητρὸс] μητέρος GKξ, τῆς
μητρὸς T^{t3} (u. scr. T^{t1}); 861 τε καὶ ante τίνες add. T^{t3}; 1092 λέχος]
λ- γʼ K, τὸ λ- T^{t3};[12] 1094 ἀκρόπολιν] -πτολιν OGKXaXb, τὴν
ἀκρόπολιν T^{t3}, [T^z]; 1236 δʼ] δέ γʼT^{t3}. Triclinius' conjectures are
so inferior to the readings of GKξ at 782 (twice), 798, 1094 (the last
not necessarily conjectural in GKXaXb) that I am loth to believe
that he was acquainted with the superior readings. And it should
be remembered that not all of the manuscripts which are commonly associated with ξ attest these readings.[13] One may equally
wonder whether Triclinius was aware of Ζηνός for Διός at 1684, a
reading which, by contrast, is almost universally attested by the associates of ξ.[14]

Finally I turn to the pages written by T^{t3}. These pages cover not
only the lyrics but also some stretches of iambics and trochaics
contiguous with lyrics.

In the iambics the following may be assumed to be Triclinian
conjectures: 303 χροῖ] χροὸс RyT^{t3} (~Ry^{2uv}); 313 γʼ post ἄγαν add.
RyT^{t3}; 1330 and 1571 ἄραρε(ν)] ἄρηρε(ν) T^{t3} (in 1330 also Zb^cZd
Zu or Zu^c);[15] 1345 ἐμοί] ἔμʼT^{t3}, ἐμ* Zb (~Zb³T^{t3s}). I shall discuss
the first two of these passages later.[16]

Triclinius introduces the following readings characteristic of
ξ into lyrics:[17] 186 ὦ om., 1254 ἔνεπε, 1294 σκοποῦς' ἄπαντα, 1299
ἀέναον, 1323 με (~T^{t3s}), 1357 πρὶν ἄν, 1372 τριγλύφας, 1449
στέγης. In 982 Triclinius modifies a conjecture found in ξ: καὶ post
μέσον add. ξ, ante μέσον T^{t3}.

That Triclinius had access to an older tradition[18] is proved by

[11] Triclinius' conjecture should probably be accepted. It has been almost universally rejected (West alone, of modern editors, accepts it) in favour of Canter's διὰ τὸ γὰρ κείνης,
where the position of γὰρ is anomalous. Denniston, Greek Particles 95–8, quotes only one
instance of the order preposition, article, γάρ (Pl. Symp. 209b ἐν τῶι γὰρ αἰσχρῶι). The
same order would be equally anomalous with δέ instead of γάρ (Denniston 186). For the
order preposition, article, genitive, γάρ, see Tr. 1020 ἐν τοῖς Ἀλεξάνδρου γάρ, and similar
passages (with adjective instead of genitive) cited by Denniston 96.

[12] See p. 156.

[13] See p. 79. Triclinius' failure to make the correction ἀκρόπολιν at 1094 is particularly
remarkable, since -πτολις for -πολις was within his conjectural repertory (Smith, Studies
121, 185–6, 192).   [14] See pp. 62, 79.   [15] See p. 87.   [16] See pp. 100–1.

[17] For the full attestation of these readings see pp. 54–6.

[18] See also Turyn 193, 302–3, Browning (cited above, p. 62 n. 53) 14, Zuntz, Inquiry
154–5, Matthiessen 103–5, Mastronarde 143–6, Smith, Studies 3, 185 n. 49.

823 μεγάλη] ποικίλα ᵞᵖM¹(C), ποικίλη T¹³. Here are other weakly attested readings to which he had access: 1288 ἐν ὅπλοις] ἔνοπλος Aa³ˢMnRRw¹ˢST¹³ˢ (~R¹ᵞᵖ); 1507 προσπίπτων] -πιτνῶν OGKZv T¹³, -πεσών ξ.

(ii) Ry

'We can with good reason postulate the existence in the past of several Triclinian stages of the Euripidean triad, although some components of the former stages probably disappeared in the wastebasket of Triclinius and were not copied at all by other copyists; if they ever were, no copies of it have survived, so far as we know' (Turyn 32–3).

The fragmentary manuscript Ry, unknown to Turyn, has been discussed in detail by Zuntz.[19] And Zuntz has argued that Ry is just such a copy of an earlier stage of Triclinius' work.

Ry has several readings which may be held to be Triclinian conjectures. And yet it does not have all the Triclinian conjectures found in T. From this Zuntz concluded that it reflects a version of Triclinius' work earlier than that reflected by T. As parallels he adduced the Aeschylean manuscripts FGE, which reflect a version of Triclinius' work earlier than that reflected by the Triclinian autograph Tr, and the Euripidean P, which in the alphabetical plays reflects the first but not the second and third stages of Triclinius' work on L.[20] Zuntz's conclusions have not been universally accepted.[21] They may now be tested in the light of the additional evidence which is available.

These are the places where Zuntz claims that Ry has a Triclinian conjecture:

143 κοίτας] λέχους RyT¹³MnZc (τῆς κοίτης Ryᵍˡ); [Tᶻ]. The first page of lyrics written by T¹³ is fol. 52r (145 ff.). But the lyrics begin at 140 on fol. 51v. Triclinius left this page (written by Tᶻ) in place, but erased and rewrote 142–3, dividing thus: ἄπο πρόβατ' ἐκεῖ |c' ἀπόπρο μοι λέχους. Tᶻ had also written 142–3 as two lines. Ry is the

---

[19] Bulletin of the John Rylands Library 49 (1967) 497–517.

[20] For Aeschylus see Zuntz, Inquiry 204–11, Dawe, Coll.&Inv. 189–94, J.J. Helm, TAPA 103 (1972) 575–98, Smith, Studies, passim; for Euripides see my remarks in Sileno 10 (1984) 101–6.

[21] They are accepted by Schartau I, and by Smith, Studies 93, but not by Matthiessen, 100 n. 38 (see below, p. 103 n. 39).

only manuscript to follow T^z and T^{t3} in writing 142–3 as two lines. The remainder write them as a single line. But Ry divides at ἐκεῖc' |. We do not know whether T^z divided differently from T^{t3} (Zuntz suggests that the division may have been at ἐκεῖc' |, as in Ry; it is equally possible that T^z wrote ἐκεῖcε, as do many manuscripts), nor do we know whether T^z had λέχουc or κοίτας. That λέχουc is also the reading of MnZc was unknown to Zuntz and is not recorded by Turyn. Zc is the member of ζ most closely related to T^z;[22] and there are some points of contact between Zc and Triclinius.[23] The appearance in Mn of a reading otherwise attested only in manuscripts associated with the scriptorium of Thomas and Triclinius, while surprising, is not without parallel.[24] It is hard to resist the conclusion that λέχουc is a metrical conjecture, creating responsion with the antistrophe (Triclinius analyses 142–3~154–5 as each consisting of paeon + iambus [i.e. ⏖ ⏑–|⏑–, *bis*]). If it is (and the only alternative is to suppose that it is a careless trivialization), its author is presumably Triclinius.

258 ἀτρέμας coῖc ἐν] ἀτρέμα coῖc ἐν BLXc^{c}Zu (~B^{2}Zu^c), ἀτρέμας coῖc GVa^c, ἀτρέμας ἐν coῖc T$^{t1/2uv}$TaRy, [T^z].[25] Again, the conclusion that this is a Triclinian metrical conjecture is hard to resist. Whether the truth in LZu is conjectural or inherited (it is presumably inherited in B),[26] we cannot tell. The reading of G is certainly conjectural.[27]

303 χροϊ] χροὸc T^{t3}Ry (~Ry^{2uv}). A metrical conjecture, in a page of iambics written by T^{t3}, and conceivably right; better, at any rate, than τῷ χροϊ (if that is conjectural) in SXe (τῷ Aa^{3gl}).

328 ὦ uel ὁ] om. T^{t3}RyAd (ὦ T^{t3gl}, ὁ Ry^{2}Ad^{1s}). The (wrong) omission of ὦ (ὁ) is presumably conjectural, creating correspondence between οἵων τάλας and 344 λάβροιc ὀλεθρ- (Triclinius marks -εθρ- as a long syllable). T^{t3} has the same remedy (this time correctly) at 160–1 (omission of ὦ before μέλεος and τάλας). In all three places (328, 160, 161) Triclinius writes ὦ above the line, but

---

[22] See p. 96.   [23] See pp. 87–8.   [24] See p. 31.

[25] For an explanation of what may be seen in T see p. 97 n. 7.

[26] The original reading of B is reported rightly by Turyn (190) as ἀτρέμα coῖc, wrongly by Prinz (*ap.* Wecklein) and Spranger (*CQ* 33 [1939] 187) as ἀτρέμας οῖc. Although there is more space than usual between c and οιc, similar uneven spacing is found elsewhere in B. It is above all the position of the accent (there was almost certainly no breathing) which suggests that the scribe intended coῖc.

[27] See p. 155. For attestation of ἀτρέμα(c) in the indirect tradition see p. 123.

as a gloss not as a correction.[28] A similar remedy was adopted by
T^{t3} at 162 (anticipated by M^{c}O)[29] and 186 (anticipated by ξ).

332 ἰώ] ὦ T^{t3}Ry (~Ry³) et Aa³ˢJʳ. A (correct) conjecture, creating
correspondence between ὦ Ζεῦ and 316 αἰαῖ. The conjecture has
Triclinian parallels.[30]

335 ὦ(ι)] ὅ T^{t3}Ry². A bad conjecture, creating correspondence
between μέλεον ὅ and 319 θίασον ἐλ-. Triclinius all but claims it as
his own: ὅ γράφε ἀντὶ τοῦ ὅςτιc ΣTᵗ.

337 δόμους] δόμον T^{t3}Ry. A correct conjecture, again for metrical responsion. Triclinius' scholion (quoted on 335 above) contin-
ues . . . καὶ δόμον μὴ δόμους. The truth appears also to be preserved
in Σ^{bvc} (133. 3, 25 Schwartz).

349 πολλῆι δ'(uel sim.)] πολλῆ(ι) T^{t3}Ry. A bad conjecture, which
mends the metre with an appalling correption.[31]

To these eight passages adduced by Zuntz I can add a ninth:

313 γ' post ἄγαν add. T^{t3}Ry. This is from a page of iambics written by T^{t3}. The letter which I identify in Ry as γ' is damaged, but
there was certainly an extra letter after ἄγαν, and it is unlikely to
have been anything other than γ' (with which the surviving traces
are fully compatible). Addition of γ' after ἄγαν is a Triclinian
trademark.[32]

Zuntz observed that Ry is ignorant of the following three
Triclinian conjectures: 154 τίνα . . . τίνα] ποίαν . . . ποίαν T^{t3} (οὕτως
ἐγράφη παρ' ἡμῶν ΣTᵗ); 261 ἱέρειαι] ἱερίαι LT^{t3} (ἱερίαι γράφε ΣTᵗ)
(~L²), ἱέριαι OXcZb³ᵘᵛ; 331 γᾶc om. T^{t3} (ἐξεβλήθη παρ' ἐμοῦ ΣTᵗ).
And there are several other Triclinian readings which are absent
from Ry: 86 εἴ] ἡ VL²PTᵗ$^{(3?)}$ (~V¹ˢP²); 118 τε] γε ZbZcTᶜ; 119
Ἀργείων] ἀργεῖον Tᶜ+; 140 λεπτὸν] λευκὸν Tᵗ¹ᐟ²+; 147 ὑπώροφον]
ὑπόρ- T^{t3}+; 148 οὕτως] οὕτω T^{t3}Tp; 150 λόγον T^{t3}+: λόγον δ'Ryᵘᵛ+;
214 εὐκταία] -τέα T^{t3}; 217 εὔφρανας] ηὔ- T^{t3}+; 294 ἀνακάλυπτ' ὦ]
ἀνακαλύπτου B²Tᵗ¹ᐟ² (ἢ ἀνακαλύπτου ὦ ΣT).[33]

The conclusion to be drawn from the nine passages quoted above
is unequivocal. Ry has nine metrical conjectures which may be im-
puted either with certainty or with probability to Triclinius. Since

---

[28] Other words omitted by Triclinius and added by him as glosses: 186 ὦ, 191 ὅ, 901 λέγ
(see p. 97).   [29] See p. 69.   [30] See Zuntz, *Inquiry* 23, 195.
[31] Turyn (191) rightly diagnoses Triclinius' intention (he marks -ῆι as short). Modern
scholars would treat this as synecphonesis. But a change of label does not improve the product.   [32] See Fraenkel on A. *Ag.* 1241, Zuntz, *Inquiry* 208–9.   [33] See p. 155.

Ry is ignorant of other metrical conjectures of Triclinius and of
other readings introduced by him into T, it is unlikely that Ry took
these conjectures directly from T. Between Ry and the manuscript
T no connection appears to exist. In addition to the disagreements
between Ry and T^t which I have listed, there are several disagreements (in readings untouched by Triclinius) between Ry and T^z:
61 συμφοράν] -άc Ry+; 128 ἀπέθριξε] -ιcε Ry+; 234 γλυκύ] ἡδύ RyP
(et JThgBgE); 287 ηὔφρανε] εὔ- Ry+; 374 παιδὸc] θυγατρὸc Ry+.

Nor does there appear to exist any especial connection between
Ry and the members of ζ. Zuntz observes that Ry has only one
reading which Turyn held to be characteristic of ζ, and he suggests
that it is significant that Triclinius allowed that reading to stand in
T^z. In fact, I believe that the reading in question (at 35) is not original to T^z but was imported by Triclinius himself.[34] Equally absent
from Ry, as Zuntz observes, are most of the readings which Turyn
held to be characteristic of ξ: 69 ὀχούμεcθ', 116 cτᾶcά γ', 228 δέμαc,
286 ἔργον ἐc, 326 ἐᾶτ', 327 κακῶν μόχθων, 345 ἄλλον, 373 ἁλιτύπων.
Zuntz might have added (from Turyn's list) 281 coι. From my
supplement to Turyn's list I add 101 ἐc, 350 ὁρᾶται, 355 εὔχου. All
of these readings are similarly absent from T^z and T^t (except that
T$^{t1/2}$ added δέμαc as a variant at 228).[35] Ry shares only one unique
error with another manuscript, and the agreement is of no
significance: 112 δόμων] δωμάτων RyTa, δομάτων Zm. The confusion is common: 1474 (H), 1495 (MnRS), 1499 (PrSa), 1506 (R, δομάτων Ms^{γρ}), 1524 (At).

Two features of Ry have been established: (i) it has some but not
all of Triclinius' conjectures—and these conjectures occur in both
the iambics and the lyrics; (ii) it has no especial connection with ξ
or ζ or T^z.

There appear to be only two hypotheses which will explain why
some, but not all, of Triclinius' conjectures are present in Ry: the
scribe of Ry (or of the model of Ry) either (a) chose some and rejected others, or (b) was aware of only some and ignorant of others.
The first hypothesis implies that the final work of Triclinius (as
represented by T) was available to the scribe of Ry (or its model),

---

[34] See p. 84.

[35] Ry does have two readings which Turyn regarded as characteristic of ξ (61 συμφοράc
and 212 τε). The former is shared by RyΠ³GKSξ, the latter by Ry²Π⁵Rξ. I regard both as
inherited truth (see p. 52) and therefore not especially characteristic of ξ.

who picked and chose as he saw fit.[36] But the nature of Ry's text
suggests that its scribe is most unlikely to have been acquainted
with T.[37] The absence from Ry of readings which are characteristic
of ξ and ζ and T^z suggests that its text is basically pre-
Moschopoulean, in other words that Ry was copied from a manuscript typical of those which must have been available in the time
of Moschopoulos. Ry has acquired the Thomano-Triclinian hypothesis,[38] Moschopoulean scholia, and Moschopoulean and
Thoman glosses. The assembly of such a collection of explanatory
material, as Zuntz has observed, is characteristic of Triclinius. Ry
has not acquired the Triclinian scholia which appear in T. But
these scholia presumably reflect the final thoughts of Triclinius,
and so their absence is no cause for surprise.[39]

I therefore consider that Zuntz's hypothesis, that Ry is copied
from a manuscript which incorporated some of Triclinius' earlier
work, is likely to be right.

(iii) *Tp*

The metrical scholia on the triad in Tp were discussed by O. L.
Smith in 1975[40] and were published by him, together with the accompanying text of the lyrics, in 1977.[41] Turyn (32 n. 49) had already noted the similarity between these scholia and the metrical
scholia on Aristophanes in Par. gr. 2821; and Smith has now shown
that the scribe of both manuscripts is one and the same.[42] Turyn
(32 n. 49 and 202–4) argued that the scholia in Par. gr. 2821 represent the earliest metrical work of Triclinius on Aristophanes. His
argument is endorsed by Smith, who argues that the scholia in Tp
likewise represent the earliest metrical work of Triclinius on the

---

[36] J (see pp. 74–5) does not provide an adequate analogy, since (*a*) it is probably later in
date than Ry, and possibly much later, and (*b*) it has a text of a very different kind from Ry,
a text fundamentally akin to ξ, with the admission of only a small number of Triclinian conjectures, which it has presumably acquired from a copy of T.   [37] See p. 102.

[38] For the description of this as Thomano-Triclinian rather than simply Thoman see
Schartau, II. 88 n. 36.

[39] And so I cannot accept Matthiessen's reasoning (100 n. 38) that their absence tells
against Zuntz's hypothesis.   [40] *Studies* 81–94.

[41] *Scholia metrica anonyma in Euripidis Hecubam, Orestem, Phoenissas.*

[42] *Mnemosyne* ser. iv 27 (1974) 414–15, *Studies* 82, 95–113, *Scholia* xi–xii, *Cl&Med* 33
(1981–2) 253–6. See also Eberline 24–5, 113–23, Schartau, *ICS* 6.2 (1981) 223 (in the
course of a discussion of the exegetical, as opposed to the metrical, scholia of Tp).

Euripidean triad.[43] Mastronarde (137–8) has added some evidence from *Phoenissae* in support of Smith's view. My discussion of the evidence from *Orestes* will take two parts. First, I shall try to discover the nature of the text on which the metrician Tp based his work. Second, I shall consider the evidence which might associate Triclinius with this work.

Smith describes the text of Tp as 'predominantly Moschopulean with some Thoman interpolations and some stray but absolutely certain *old* readings'.[44] This description does less than justice to the composite nature of the text of Tp. I illustrate the nature of its text under five headings.

(*a*) The evidence of Tp is available for 31 of the 110 readings which I listed as characteristic of ξ.[45] Tp has only 8 of these 31 (832 γῆν, 982 μέcον καὶ, 1294 cκοποῦc' ἅπαντα, 1372 τριγλύφαc, 1449 ἄλλον ἄλλοcε, 1449 cτέγηc, 1465 ἤ, 1491 τλήμων), unless we add as a ninth a reading which might be a modification of the reading of ξ (1465 ἴαχεν ἴαχεν ξ, ἴαχεν γ' ἴαχεν γ' Tp). Three of these readings are of no significance (832, 1465, 1491), since Tp regularly substitutes Attic η for Doric α. Of the remaining five (or six) four are shared by Triclinius, and one (982) was modified by Triclinius.

(*b*) The evidence of Tp is available for 11 of the 51 readings which Turyn listed as 'Thoman interpolations'.[46] Tp has only 3 of these 11, and shares two of the three with Triclinius and other manuscripts (147, 1011), the third with Z (168 ἔβαλεc ἐξ] ἐξέβαλεc TpZ et ^{gl}MBVξZc+). Other unique or nearly unique agreements with members of ζ: 145 πνοά] πνοή TpZ; 153 μ' post μετάδοc add. TpZ (μοι add. ZcTh; ἐμοί ^sZ^rZm^{gl}Rf^{gl}); 319 ἐλάχετ' ἐν] ἐλάχετε TpZP (-ητε Ab); 816 ἐξαμείβων] ἀμείβων TpZmL; 1275 δέ] δαί Tp ZZbZcZm; 1480 ὁ om. TpZc.

(*c*) Tp has the following 'old' readings which are absent from ξ and ζ (or the majority of ζ) and Triclinius: 1003 ἔcπερον] ἐcπέραν TpMV+; 1004 προcαρμόcαc] -caca TpV²G (~V²/³); 1005 δρό-μημα] δραμήματα TpMMnS (~S^{γρ}), δρομήματα G^{1c}Pr^{γρ}ξ, δράμημα

---

[43] Smith's discussion (*Studies* 87–8) of *Ph.* 260 will puzzle those who do not detect that in transcribing the metrical note on this line (*Scholia* 28. 23) he has accidentally written ἰωνικόν for ἰαμβικόν (as we can see from the photograph in *Studies*, Plate 6).

[44] *Studies* 86, following Turyn 149 ('The text is inconsistent, but it is predominantly Moschopulean'). Similarly Schartau, *ICS* 6.2 (1981) 224. Turyn adds a few agreements between Tp and ξ in the non-lyric parts.

[45] See pp. 52–6.   [46] See pp. 82–5.

BAC; 1300 ἐπίκουρον] -ος TpMBOVaZuᶜ+; 1373 γᾶ semel TpOC
Zu (~Zuˢ); 1446 cυνεργὸc] ξυν- TpBVa+.

(*d*) Tp shares with Triclinius the following 'old' readings which
are absent from ξ and ζ (or the majority of ζ): 1391 Γαννυμήδεος]
γαιυ- TpΠ¹⁸HMBOZvTᵗ³+; 1403 ἀνήρ om. TpHOZvTᵗ³ᶜ+.

(*e*) Tp has the following readings which are absent from the
older manuscripts (HMBOV) and from ξ and ζ and Triclinius: 196
με om. TpAbFLPRfZbᶜ? (~F²Zb³); 1287 ἐκκεκώφηται uel -ηνται]
-ωται TpF²MnS; 1358 δόμοιc] δόμοιcι TpAbMnRRwS (δόμοιcι
τοῖcδε Tᵗ³); 1414 ἱκεcίουc] -ίας TpAbMnS (~Ab¹ˢ); 1431
ἠλακάται] ἠλεκ- TpMnRwS (~S¹ˢ); 1447 ἀλλ'] ἀλλ' TpMnRS;
1452 ἀποπρο (diuersis acc.)] ἀπόπροθι TpPrSa¹ˢ; 1461 cταθέντεc]
cτάντεc TpRf; 1467 μέλεον] μελέαν TpAa; 1469 ἔφερεν bis] ἔφερον
bis TpRf.

No pattern is discernible in the agreements between Tp and ξ
or ζ or Triclinius or the remaining manuscripts. The text of Tp
must not be described as 'predominantly Moschopulean', because
it lacks most of the readings which are characteristic of ξ. Nor does
Tp show any especial affinity to ζ or to the final Triclinian text as
represented by Tᵗ³. Rather, the text of Tp may be described as basically a pre-Thoman text. It has acquired a small number of readings characteristic of ξ (of which all, or nearly all, were adopted by
Triclinius), it shares a few trivial slips with individual members of
ζ, it has preserved a few old readings which are absent from ξ and
ζ and Triclinius, and it has acquired a few readings which are not
certainly old and are equally absent from these manuscripts.

Investigation of the colometry of Tp might be expected to reveal
something of its affiliations.⁴⁷ But the result of such an investigation is disappointing.⁴⁸ There is only one unique agreement with
Triclinius: 1389 ἐριννὺν ὀττοτοῖ | (analysed by both Tp and
Triclinius as a brachycatalectic iambic dimeter). Only one other
agreement with Triclinius (where Tp and Triclinius analyse very
differently) deserves to be recorded: 983 αἰωρήμαcι (-cιν Tᵗ³) πέ-
τραν | (etiam Zm) ... φερομέναν | (etiam RwZm). Further agree-
ments with Rw will be reported below. There is one unique
agreement with Zm: 808 μέγα ... Ἑλλάδα | .

---

⁴⁷ See Smith, *Studies* 91, Mastronarde 164–6.
⁴⁸ In this and the following sections I give the spelling and accentuation of Tp and
record variations in other manuscripts only where they need to be known.

The largest number of unique or nearly unique agreements is with Z: 175 τῶν πολυπόνων βροτῶν | (etiam Sa); 188–9 θανεῖν . . . πόθον |, 319 αἴ . . . ἐλάχετε | δάκρυσι (ἐλάχετ᾽ ἐν | Sa, ἐλάχετ᾽ | ἐν C); 325–7 τὸν . . . ἐάсατ᾽ | (etiam C) ἐκλαθέϲθαι . . . φοιταλέου |, 329–31 ἄν . . . δά|πεδον . . . λέγονται |, 343–4 πόνων . . . λάβροιϲ |, 349 Μενέλαοϲ . . . πολλῇ δ᾽ | (πολλῇ | δ᾽ Z), 353–4 εἰϲ . . . αὐτὸϲ | (etiam Cr).

There are three unique or nearly unique agreements with ξ: 161 ὦ . . . ἆ ἆ |, 1434 ϲκύλων . . . ἀγάλματα | (etiam Aa), 1491–2 ἐπὶ . . . τλάμων | (etiam O). There is a further agreeement with Aa (in addition to 1434 cited above), in which Aa is in part joined by Mn or MnS: 1459–64 ὡϲ . . . ἀντίοι (ἀντίϲ Tp)[49] | (etiam MnS) ϲτάντεϲ (TpRf: ϲταθέντεϲ cett.) . . . κατθανῇ | (etiam Mn) κακὸϲ . . . καϲιγνήτου | (etiam Mn) . . . γόνον |. There is a further agreement with MnS at 1246–7: Μυκηνίδεϲ . . . πρῶτα | κατὰ . . . Ἀργείων |. And Cr (which was associated with TpZ at 353–4 cited above) joins TpMnS and then continues in unique agreement with Tp at 1381–2: Ἴλιον . . . ἄϲτυ | (etiam MnS) . . . ϲτένω |. For further agreements between Tp and MnS see 1430–2 and 1437–40 cited below.

There is one unique agreement with RfRw, and there are a few agreements with RfZv: 1285–6 ϲφάγια . . . εἰϲακούουϲιν | ὦ . . . κακῶν | (RfRw), 1405–7 θραϲὺϲ . . . πολέμου | . . . ἡϲύχου | (RfZv), 1430–2 βάρβαροι . . . λῖνον | (RfZvAbMn) ἠλεκάτα . . . ἕλιϲϲε | (Rf ZvAb), 1437–40 προϲεῖπε . . . κόραν | (RfZvAbCrMnS) . . . ἀποϲ-τᾶϲα | (RfZv).

From this investigation it emerges that colometry alone tells us little about the affiliations of Tp. But when we compare such results as have emerged with the lists of unique or nearly unique agreements in readings in the text given above (under *b*, *c*, and *e*), we find that several manuscripts which share with Tp a unique or nearly unique reading also share with Tp unique or nearly unique colometry: notably Z (readings at 145, 153, 168, 319, 1275, colometry at 175, 188–9, 319, 325–7, 329–31, 343–4, 349, 353–4),[50] MnS (readings at 1005, 1287, 1358, 1414, 1431, 1447, colometry at

---

[49] ἀντίϲ is presumably not a conjecture but a corruption of ἀντίοι, which is implied by the analysis (hypercatalectic trochaic trimeter).

[50] It should be remembered that Z itself has come under suspicion of direct influence by Triclinius: see pp. 87–8.

1246–7, 1381, 1430, 1437, 1459–63), Rf (readings at 196, 1461, 1469, colometry at 1285–6, 1405–7, 1430–2, 1437–40).

We may now look for evidence of a connection between Tp and Triclinius. Unique agreements are few and trivial: 148 οὕτως] οὕτω TpTᵗ³; 837 δρομάcι] -cιν TpTᵗ³ (but Tp uniquely has εὐμενίcιν for -cι at 836); 1011 ἤλυθε] -εν TpTᵗ³. There are a few readings which Tp and Triclinius share with only a small number of other manuscripts: 822 εἰc] ἐc TpTᵗ³C²⁷GKLZm; 1414 χεῖρας] χέρας TpTᵗ³AaAt; 1430 βαρβάροιcι] -οιc TpTᵗ³Rw; 1447 αἰεί] ἀεί TpTᵗ³ BOVaCr.

We have seen that Tp has only 8 (or 9) readings characteristic of ξ, and that of these only 5 (or 6) are significant, and that these five were adopted or modified by Triclinius. It is noteworthy that of the other readings characteristic of ξ (from the total of 31 for which Tp is available) Triclinius adopts only three more (186, 1299, 1357). There is, then, a very large measure of agreement between Tp and Triclinius in their choice of readings characteristic of ξ. And it is at least arguable that Tp has gained all such readings by courtesy of Triclinius.

There are two places where Tp and Triclinius light upon a metrical anomaly but offer different solutions:[51]

143 κοίτας] κλίνας Tp, λέχους Tᵗ³MnRyZc, [Tᵛ]. I have argued that λέχους is an early Triclinian conjecture.[52] If κλίνας is also Triclinian, it was a yet earlier conjecture, as its faulty prosody suggests. Tp analyses 142–3 as an iambic trimeter.

960 κατάρχομαι cτεναγμῶν ὦ Πελαςγία. Tp recognizes the anomaly and calls the syllable -μῶν 'common'.[53] Tᵗ³ writes cτεναγ- μόν (as do ⟨K²⟩VaᶜPrᴵˢ, ∼Kᴵᶜ), with an accompanying note that metre requires a short syllable.

It is possible, then, that in these two places we find Triclinius improving on his earlier thoughts.

At this point I wish to emphasize a feature of Tp which is not mentioned by those who have discussed the text and scholia of Tp:

---

[51] For examples of this in *Ph.* see Mastronarde 138.   [52] See pp. 99–100.

[53] The only other places where Tp has recourse to this plea are 1498 ἤτοι φαρμάκοιcιν ἢ μάγων τέχναιc ἢ θεῶν κλοπαῖc (catalectic trochaic tetrameter) and *Hec.* 1066 εἴθε μοι ὀμ- μάτων αἱματόεν βλέφαρον (hypercatalectic dactylic tetrameter). For the term 'common syl- lable' and Triclinius' more sophisticated treatment of the phenomenon see Fraenkel, *Ag.* i. 18–20, Turyn 247 n. 232, Smith, *Studies* 59 and (for the text of Triclinius' treatise Περὶ cη- μείων τῆc κοινῆc cυλλαβῆc) 256–7.

that Tp is profoundly ignorant of prosody. We have seen that Tp scans κλῖνας. The following lines, as emended by Tp, are iambic trimeters: 146 λεπτοῦ δόνᾱκος ὦ φίλα φώνει ⟨γέ⟩ μοι, 823 τὸ δ' αὖ κακουργεῖν ἀcέβειά (ᾱc-?) ⟨γε⟩ μεγάλη (ποικίλη T^{t3}, ποικίλα ^{γρ}M(C)), 1283 τί μέλλεθ' οἱ κατ' οἶκον ἐν ⟨γ⟩ ἡcῡχία (ὡc ἡcῡχία T^{t3}). The following is a dactylic hexameter: 1381 Ἴλιον Ἴλιον ὦ μοι μοι ⟨φεῦ⟩ Φρῡγιον ἄcτυ. Such prosodical ignorance causes no surprise in itself,[54] and even Triclinius offends on occasion.[55] But ignorance on this scale is not characteristic of T^{t3}.

Can anything be learned from an examination of the kinds of change which are characteristic of Tp? His most characteristic remedy is interpolation of γε, of which I have already quoted several examples. Here are some, but not all, of the others (iambic trimeters, unless otherwise noted): 207 ἁ μέλεοc εἰc τὸν αἰὲν ἕλκω ⟨γε⟩ χρόνον, 964 νερτέρων ⟨γε⟩ Περcέφαccα καλλίπαιc θεά (hyper-catalectic trochaic trimeter), 1448 ἐκλήιcεν δέ ⟨γ⟩ (ἐκλήιcε δ' fere cett.) ἄλλον ἄλλοcε cτέγηc, 1461 cτάντεc (TpRf: cταθέντεc cett.) ἐννέπουcι κατθανῇ ⟨γε⟩ κατθανῇ (metre as 964), 1465 ἢ δ' ἴαχεν ⟨γ⟩ ἴαχεν ⟨γ⟩ (ἀνίαχεν ἴαχεν fere cett.) ὤμοιμοι (dactylic tetrameter), 1468 φυγᾷ δὲ ποδὶ τὸ χρυcεοcάνδαλον ⟨γ⟩ ἴχνος, 1493 cκύμνον ⟨γ⟩ ὀρείαν ἐν χεροῖν (cκύμνον ἐν χ- ὀ- fere cett., ὡc cκύμνον [etiam JZZcMn^c] ἐν χεροῖν ὀρίαν [-ίαν T^{t3c} pot. qu. T^{t3}] T^{t3}) ξυνάρπαcαν (-άρπαcαν etiam ThXd, -ήρπαcαν cett.), 1501 Μενέλαοc ἀναcχό-μενοc ⟨γ⟩ ἀνόνητον ἀπὸ Τροίαc (anapaestic trimeter). Interpolation or substitution of γε is found in T^{t3}: 171 cόν ⟨γ⟩, 313 ἄγαν ⟨γ⟩,[56] 828 càν uel cὴν] γε, 965 δέ ⟨γε⟩, 1236 δ⟨έ γ⟩. Such employment of γε is characteristic of Triclinius;[57] although the example of *Ph.* 615 (δέ ⟨γε⟩ ξT^s) shows that he was not the first so to employ it.

Another characteristic of Tp is omission: 814 καί, 991 πόντου, 1409–10 Πάριc γυναικόc, 1441 ἐπί, 1446 Φωκεύc. Equally charac-teristic is interpolation of colourless words: 1275 ἔτι ⟨δή⟩, 1419 ⟨ἄλλοc⟩ δόλοc, 1464 ⟨φεῦ⟩ θανεῖν, 1466 ⟨ἐν⟩ cτέρνοιc⟨ι⟩. Such omis-sion and interpolation are practised by T^{t3}: 181 οὐχί] οὔ μεν ουν, 331 γᾶc om., 527 ἐξέβαλε ⟨τόν⟩, 812 ⟨τῆc⟩ χρυcέαc, 814 ⟨τε⟩ θοινή-

---

[54] For illustration see Turyn 168 n. 182, J. Jackson, *Marginalia Scaenica* 3, 241, M. L. West, *BICS* 28 (1981) 73–6, Wilson 255.

[55] See Zuntz, *Inquiry* 99.

[56] See p. 101.

[57] See Zuntz, *Inquiry* 115, 194, 197, 208–9, Smith, *Studies* 89, Mastronarde 141, Eberline 75.

μ̄ατα, 1248 ‹cὺ› πότνια, 1276 μοι om., 1304 ἐκ om., 1305 ‹τὰν› λειπόγαμον, 1464 ‹τὸν› κασιγνήτου.[58]

We may also note that the creation of iambics out of dochmiacs (illustrated in Tp by 142–3, 146, 207, cited above) is found in T^{t3}: 1358 καθαιμακτὸν ἐν δόμοις (δόμοισι TpAbMnRRwS) κείμενον] αἱμακτὸν ἐν δόμοισι τοῖςδε κείμενον T^{t3}. Triclinius' ignorance of the dochmiac metre is well known.[59] But he was not the first reader who attempted to turn dochmiacs into iambics, as is proved by *Ph.* 301–3.[60]

The evidence which I have presented does little either to strengthen or to weaken the case, as argued by Smith and Mastronarde, for Triclinian authorship of the text and scholia in Tp. And, if we confine ourselves to this evidence (and that offered by Smith and Mastronarde), it is possible to argue a seemingly plausible case for Triclinian authorship. The argument might be formulated under two heads. (*a*) That the text and metrical analysis of Tp are very different from the text and metrical analysis of T^{t3} says nothing against Triclinian authorship. We are dealing here (we should naturally assume) with a very immature Triclinius, ignorant of both prosody and strophic responsion. That Triclinius was at one time ignorant of the principle of strophic responsion is a proposition which is self-evidently correct, since it was he who discovered that principle. And that the young Triclinius was more ignorant of prosody than the later Triclinius is at least a logical assumption. (*b*) We know of no Byzantine scholar before Triclinius who attempted to understand and expound his understanding of the metre of Euripidean lyrics and who engaged in the systematic emendation of the lyrics in the light of that knowledge.

But the evidence is incomplete, and the argument based on it is vulnerable. To complete the evidence, we need to examine the nature of the metrical scholia in Tp in the light of Triclinius' metrical annotations in both T and other manuscripts. This examination has been performed by Dr H. C. Günther, who has kindly shown me his results. He concludes that the nature of the

---

[58] For omission and interpolation as characteristic Triclinian remedies see Zuntz, *Inquiry* 194–5, Smith, *Studies* 122, 128, 236, Mastronarde 140–1, Eberline 75.

[59] See Zuntz, *Inquiry* 30–1, 214, Smith, *Studies* 72.

[60] Discussed by Jackson, *Marginalia Scaenica* 241, Mastronarde 51, 159. See also Willink, *CQ* n.s. 39 (1989) 49.

metrical scholia in Tp is hard to square with the pattern of development in Triclinius' metrical knowledge which we may form from our other sources. He prefers to detect in these scholia the hand of an associate of the early Triclinius, belonging perhaps to the school of Planudes and Moschopoulos, who may have had access to some of Triclinius' earliest work. I suspect that, when Dr Günther's arguments are published, they will be found convincing.[61]

[61] A somewhat similar conclusion was reached by Eberline 123.

CHAPTER XII

LP

The bonds which unite LP in the other plays do not exist in the triad.[1] There are scarcely any unique agreements in *Or.*: 478 μὴ εἰ-δέναι] μὴ 'δέναι LP; 1242 δίκης] δίκας LP (~P[1s]). Here are a few agreements which are almost unique: *Inscriptio* Εὐριπίδου Ἠλέκτρα LPZXc; 20 Μενέλεως] -λαος LPJK; 266 ἐγώ] 'γὼ LPZm[c]; 298 ἴσχα(ι)νε] ἴσχναινε LPM[γρ]C[γρ]; 608 μ' (prius) om. LPGZm (~L²Zm[1c]); 838 Ἀγαμεμνόν(ε)ιος] -μέμνονος LP[c], -μεμνόν⁎(⁎)ος P; 1528 ἐν om. LPZu.

L and P are typical of the time and place of their copying. The sources which have contributed to their texts are so varied that it is impossible to bring them into any stemmatic relationship either with each other or with the remaining manuscripts.[2] I have illustrated the connections which exist between them and members of ζ.[3] I now illustrate such connections as are discoverable between them and the remaining manuscripts.

L has several readings which are characteristic of Θ and associates (it shows a connection, slight but unmistakable, with Cr): 184 διὰ ante στόματος add. LAb; 347 τὸν] τῶν LAaAbMnPr⁵RRwSSa (~Aa[rs]); 532 καὶ om. LMn (~L²); 539 εἰκὸς ἦν αὐτήν] ἦν εἰ- αὐ-LSa (εἰ- αὐ- ἦν Z; εἰ- ἦν CrPRw, ~Rw[1c]; ἦν εἰ- AtF); 598 οὖν om. LCr (~L²Cr[1s]); 734 coι om. LCr (~L²); 775 ἔδρασας] ἔπραξας LV Ab[gl]MnPr[γρ]S (~Mn[γρ]); 815 τεκέων uel τοκέων] τέκνων LMnRRfS Sa²[gl]X[gl] (~L²Rf²[s]); 855 λόγωι] λόγων LAbMnPr[1s]SSa (~L[1c?]Sa[1s]); 869 ἔφερβε] ἔφορβε LMnS; 906 ἔτ'] ὥστ' L et (super περι-) [gl]VAa; 1129 τ(ε)ίνειν] κτείνειν LAbCrMnS, κτίνειν R; 1144 τὸν om. LCr (~L²); 1275 μοι om. LCrG; 1314 βοήν] βοάν LAaAtCr; 1333 cὺ μὴ] μὴ cὺ LAdCr; 1578 coυ] cὴν LCrZcZmZu.

P similarly agrees with Θ and associates: 63 οἴκους] οἶκον PFSa Zb; 73 τε om. PAbFRSSaZb[1c] (cύ τε om. RwZb, ~Rw[s]); 418 εἰcὶ(ν)] εἰcὶν οἱ PAaRfRwZb; 519 πρώτην] πρῶτον PAb[1s]R[1s]; 539

---

[1] See Turyn 298–306, 309–10, Zuntz, *Inquiry* 151–74, Matthiessen 35 n. 4, 55, 63–4, Mastronarde 49.

[2] In saying this I am expressing reservations about the complicated analysis offered by Turyn, as well as about the stemmatic relationship devised by Zuntz (170–4).

[3] See p. 90.

112   LP

αὐτὴν om. PCrRw (~Rw¹ᶜ);⁴ 1051 πάρα uel ἄρα] μέτα P et ᵞᵖM²Mn PrS; 1149 ἦν] εἰ PMnᵞᵖ; 1268 ἄρ'om. PRw; 1405 δ'post θρασὺς add. PMnRSgE (τ'O); 1567 χερί] χεροῖν PF²PrSaZdᵞᵖ; 1569 ϲυνθραύϲω] ϲυνθλάϲω PAaRfZv (ϲυνθράϲω M). Possible Triclinian readings in P are:⁵ 831 καὶ] ἢ PTᵗ³J; 975 φονία] φοινία PTᵗ³(Π¹⁴). There is one unique agreement between L and Triclinius: 261 ἱέρειαι] ἱερίαι LTᵗ³ΣTᵗ³ (~L²), ἱέριαι OXc Zbᵘᵛ. L has one unique agreement with O: 1399 Ἀίδα] ἀίδαο LO. Note also 232ⁿ χο. uel om.] ἠλ. LOCr; 1102 τι om. LOCAd. And P has one unique agreement with V: 1621 Δαναῶν] δαναιδῶν PV. Note also 86 εἶ] ἡ PVL²Tᵗ⁽³·⁾ (~V¹ˢP²), ἢ F (~F²); 758 δ'om. PVF; 861 ἐν Ἀργείοιϲ uel (ἐν) Ἀργείων] ἀργείοιϲ PVRf¹ˢ; 1518 ϲίδηροϲ] ϲίδαροϲ PVH.

---

⁴ For L see the preceding paragraph.
⁵ See Turyn 300–1.

gBgE

gB is present for 121, gE for 406 lines or parts of lines. Their value for the editor of *Orestes* is negligible.[1] Neither offers a true reading unknown to the other manuscripts, with one exception: 1114 ὥcθ’] ὡc gE, coni. Wecklein (see Willink). I regard this as a happy slip, since gnomologies have no reliability in the transmission of connecting words at the beginning of the line.[2] Neither gB nor gE shows any clear relationship with a single manuscript or group of manuscripts. Here are the more notable agreements:

   (i) agreements in old but weakly attested readings: 69 ὀχούμεθ’] ὠχ- MFgE; 238 ἐῶcί c’] ἐῶcιν c’ AAa, ἐῶcιν MCRgE; 298 ἴcχανε] ἴcχναινε M¹ʸᵖC¹ᵖLP, ἴcχαινε BPr¹ˢRfgE; 702 ἔνεcτι δ’] ἔνεcτιν BCrFSagB (~gE); 804 κτᾶcθ’ ἑταίρουc] κτᾶcθαι φίλουc BgB (~Bᶜ); 918 εὐωπόc] εὔοπτοc M¹ʸᵖOGK, εὔωπτοc B¹ʸᵖgE.

   (ii) agreements with Θ: 1 οὐδὲν om. PrgE et testes nonnulli;[3] 577 πόcει] πόcιν SagE (~Sa¹ˢ), πόc** G (~G¹ᶜ); 694 μὲν γὰρ] μὲν AAt Xb¹ᶜ, γὰρ CrKSSagE, om. gB; 1072 μέ] post ζῆν FSagB (~gE); 1135 ἔκτειν’ (-νεν PrSaZd)] ἔκτανεν FgE; 1405 δ’ post θραcὺc add. MnPRSgE; 1677 καὶ (prius) om. MnSgBgE (~Mnˢ).

   (iii) agreements with Rf/Rw: 698 ἐντείνοντι] ἐκτ- RwgE, coni. Wecklein;[4] 1527 με om. RfZvgB; 1691 cεμνὴ νίκη] cεμνὰ νίκα RfgB.

   (iv) agreements with ζ: 671 ἐμῶν] ἐγώ ZcgE (et ᵍˡAaʳAb+);[5] 1206 ζῆν] post μᾶλλον ZmgB; 1514 γλώccηι] -ηc ZvgB; 1667 ἄρ’] ante ἦcθ’ ZmZugE (om. AtRRfRw).

   (v) agreements with L/P: 234 γλυκύ] ἡδύ JPRyThgBgE et testes nonnulli;[6] 280 κρᾶτα uel κράτα] κάρα PgE; 740 χρόνιοc] post ἦλθε gE, om. P;[7] 1669 κλύειν] κλύων LgE.

   (vi) agreements with At/J/Ms: 268 Λοξίου] λοξία AtgE; 938 δὲ

---

[1] Cf. Matthiessen, *Hermes* 94 (1966) 409–10, Mastronarde 173–4.
[2] Cf. 236 δὲ om. gBgE (et A), 279 γὰρ om. gB, 773 ἀλλ’ ὅταν] ὅταν δὲ gB. For the same fault in gV see p. 22. [3] See p. 125.
[4] Wrongly (contrast 1114 above), and again at 381 (μηνύcω uel cημανῶ] μηνύω gE, coni. Wecklein).
[5] Rightly (see Willink). It is possible (though quite uncertain) that V also had ἐγώ. All that is visible is ἐμῶν written in an erasure by V².
[6] See p. 126.   [7] See p. 21 n. 15.

om. MsgE; 1072 δέ] δη Π[15], δὲ δὴ J[?], δὲ δεῖ J[2]gB; 1214 νιν] ante πέλας At, om. gE;[8] 1545 τέλος (alterum) om. AtgB.

(vii) other agreements: 236 δέ om. AgBgE; 602 εὖ om. XagE (~Xa[1c]) et Stob. 4. 22. 81; 1581 κἀφ'] καθ' CgE.

---

[8] See p. 21 n. 15.

CHAPTER XIV

The Papyri[1]

Π[1]   P. Oxy. 2455 [Pack² 453] fr. 3 col. iii–fr. 4 col. iv + fr.   ii p.C.
        113 + fr. 141: part of hyp. 1. See W. S. Barrett, *CQ* n.s.
        15 (1965) 67–8, W. Luppe, *ZPE* 49 (1982) 20–1, 60
        (1985) 16–20, 65 (1986) 29–30, J. Diggle, *ZPE* 77
        (1989) 1–11.
Π²   P. Strasb. WG 307 uerso [Pack² 1592]: uu. 9, 10, 6   *c*.250 a.C.
        (in that order). See D. J. Mastronarde, *ZPE* 38 (1980) 38.
Π³   P. Oxy. 1616 [Pack² 409, Donovan 21]: uu. 53–61, 89–97.   v p.C.
Π⁴   P. Köln 131 = 252: uu. 134–42. See M. Gronewald, *ZPE*   ii–i a.C.
        39 (1980) 35–6, J. O'Callaghan, *Studia Papyrologica*
        20 (1981) 15–19, O. Musso, *ZPE* 46 (1982) 43–6.
Π⁵   PL III/908: uu. 196–216. See R. Pintaudi, *SCO* 35   150–100 a.C.
        (1985) 13–23, V. Di Benedetto, ibid. 25–7, M. C.
        Martinelli, ibid. 29–35, R. Kassel, *ZPE* 64 (1986)
        39–40, Di Benedetto, ibid. 70 (1987) 11–18,
        J. Diggle, *Papyrologica Florentina* 19 (1990) 145–8.
Π⁶   P. Columb. inv. 517A [Pack² 410]: uu. 205–47. See C. W.   i a.C.
        Keyes, *Cl.Ph.* 33 (1938) 411–13.
Π⁷   (*a*) P. Berol. 17051: uu. 290–300, 321–30. See W.   vi–vii p.C.
        Müller, *Festschr. z. 150jähr. Bestehen d. Berl. Äg. Mus.*
        (1974) 398, J. Lenaerts, *Pap. litt. grecs* (Pap. Bruxell.
        13 [1977]) 19–23, J. O'Callaghan, *Stud. Pap.* 20 (1981)
        19–24.
        (*b*) P. Berol. 17014: uu. 304–9, 333–9. See W. Müller,
        Staatl. Mus. z. Berlin, Forsch. u. Ber. 6 (1964) 9–10,
        Lenaerts, loc. cit.
Π⁸   P. Vindob. G 2315 [Pack² 411]: uu. 338–44. See H.   *c*.200 a.C.
        Hunger and E. Pöhlmann, *WS* 75 (1962) 76–8, G. A.
        Longman, *CQ* n.s. 12 (1962) 61–6, J. Solomon, *GRBS*
        18 (1977) 71–83, E. G. Turner, *Greek Manuscripts of
        the Ancient World*² (=*BICS* Suppl. 46 [1987]) 70, 150.

---

[1] In the following list Pack² refers to R. A. Pack, *The Greek and Latin literary Texts from
Greco–Roman Egypt* (2nd edn., 1965), Donovan refers to B. E. Donovan, *Euripides Papyri.
I: Texts from Oxyrhynchus* (1969). The only papyri which I have inspected personally are
Π¹, Π⁵, and Π¹¹. Dr R. A. Coles kindly sent me photographs (from the collection in the
Ashmolean Museum) of Π⁹.

Π⁹   P. Oxy. 1370 [Pack² 402]: uu. 445–9, 469–74, 482–6,   v p.c.
        508–12, 685–90, 723–9, 811–17, 850–4, 896–8,
        907–10, 934–6, 945–8, 1246–65, 1297–1306, 1334–45,
        1370–1.

Π¹⁰   P. Cairo inv. 56224 [Pack² 412, Donovan 8]: uu. 754–64.   i–ii p.c.

Π¹¹   PSI 1475 (ined.): uu. 867–81. Some readings are reported   ii p.c.
        by Di Benedetto.

Π¹²   P. Berol. 21180: uu. 884–95, 917–27. See H. Maehler,   v–vi p.c.
        ZPE 4 (1969) 108–9.²

Π¹³   P. Oxy. 3716: uu. 941–51, 973–82.   ii–i a.c.

Π¹⁴   P. Geneva inv. 91 [Pack² 413]: uu. 1062–90.   ii–iii p.c.

Π¹⁵   P. Ross.-Georg. 9 [Pack² 1576]: uu. 1155–6.   ii a.c.

Π¹⁶   P. Oxy. 1178 [Pack² 414, Donovan 1]: uu. 1313–26,   c.100 a.c.
        1335–50, 1356–60.

Π¹⁷   P. Oxy. 3717: uu. 1377–95.   ii p.c.

Π¹⁸   P. Oxy. 3718: uu. 1406–12, 1431–43, 1620–35, 1649–60.   v p.c.

Π¹⁹   P. Mich. 3735c: uu. 835–46. See L. Koenen and P. J.   i a.c.
        Sijpesteijn, ZPE 77 (1989) 261–6.

The papyri offer welcome confirmation of several readings over
which HMBOV are divided, and none of these readings should any
longer be controversial:

91 ἀπείρηκ᾽ ἐν] -κεν (Π³)ΜΒΚ (~Bᶜ) (-κε C, -κα ἐν Rf, -κα
VRw); 204 γόοις] γόοισι Π⁵Hᵘᵛ (coni. Porson);³ 291 μήπω] μή ποτε
⟨Π⁷⟩BFGK+; 946 πετρουμένους] πετρούμενος (Π⁹)HMV²⁵+ (coni.
Elmsley); 1082 ὄνομ᾽] ὄμμ᾽ Π¹⁴VAR+;⁴ 1350 βάλλοντες uel βαλλόν-
τες] βαλόντες (Π¹⁶)VaA+; 1382 καὶ Π¹⁷MO¹ˢ+: om. HBOV+.

The papyri confirm the antiquity of some false readings found
in one or more of HMBOV:

224 κόραις] νόσω(ι) Π⁶Μ¹ʸᵖC⁽ʸᵖ⁾; 298 ἴσχναινε Μ¹ʸᵖC⁽ʸᵖ⁾LP: ἴσχαινε
BPr¹ᴳRfgE: ἴσχανε ⟨Π⁷ˀ⟩MOV+; 298 θ᾽] τ᾽Π⁷O; 1064 τολμήμασι(ν)]
βουλεύμασι(ν) Π¹⁴V+ (~ V²ᐟ³ˢ); 1072 ἑταιρίας] -είας Π¹⁴BA+ (~B¹ˢ
Aʳ); 1079 ἑταιρίαν] -είαν Π¹⁴BA+ (~B¹ˢ); 1359 τοῦ uel του] που

² In view of the surmise (Lenaerts 20, W. Luppe, Archiv f. Pap. 27 [1980] 241, M.W.
Haslam, Oxyrhynchus Papyri liii [1986] 131, Koenen and Sijpesteijn, ZPE 77 [1989] 261 n.
1) that Π⁷ and Π¹² might be parts of the same papyrus, I consulted Prof. Maehler, who
kindly informed me (on the authority of Dr G. Poethke in Berlin) that they are not.
³ See Papyrologica Florentina 19 (1990) 145–6. Beck and Wecklein wrongly attribute the
conjecture to Heath.
⁴ Turyn (323) claimed to find ὄνομ᾽ as a variant in R. I could not find it.

Π¹⁶Ο; 1371 τέραμνα] τέρεμνα Π⁹HOVa+; 1383 c' om. Π¹⁷OVa+; 1633 ὑπό] ἀπὸ Π¹⁸ᵘᵛB³V+;⁵ 1650 βραβῆc OᵘᵛAd: -εῖc Π¹⁸ʔMBV Ad¹ᶜ+.

In one place, where MBOV are divided, the papyrus does not help, for I believe that neither ancient reading is right: 238 ἐῶcι c' Π⁶BOV+: ἐῶcιν MCRgE: ἐῶcιν c' AAa (et ἔωc' pro ἔωc Aa): ἐῶc' R¹ʸᵖ.⁶ I believe that the truth is ἔωc c' ἐῶcιν (Brunck), because (a) the enclitic c' is then better placed, nearer the beginning of its clause,⁷ and would be more easily omitted after ἔωc than after ἐῶcι, and (b) the omission of c' in MCRgE is a possible indication that the word may originally have stood elsewhere than after ἐῶcι.⁸ Conceivably ἔωc' in Aa preserves a vestige of the truth. A close parallel for the corruption is 1020: c' ἰδοῦc' ἐν Porson: ἰδοῦcά c' ἐν MBO+: ἰδοῦcά c' M¹ʸᵖB¹ʸᵖV+: ἰδοῦc' ἐν A+: ἰδοῦc' Mn. Similarly 1626 c'] post Φοῖβοc B¹/²ᶜA+: post παῖc O+: om. MV+.

In a further place the papyrus confirms the antiquity of both readings attested by MBOV: 1658 ὧ(ι) Π¹⁸ˢMB+: ὥc Π¹⁸ᵘᵛO+: ὅ V: ὅc MnS (~Mnʸᵖ). I believe that the papyrus' supralinear variant, which has the stronger support from the medieval tradition, is the choicer reading.

In several places the papyrus agrees in truth or possible truth with later manuscripts against HMBOV:

hyp. 1.19 λαβεῖν] λαβεῖν γυναῖκα (Π¹)Ad, γ- λ- Xa;⁹ 59 πετρῶν] πέτρων (Π³)B²/³AaʳˢRyξZuTᵗ¹ (πέτ[Π³), πέτρον Aa (~Aa²); 61 cυμφοράν] -άc (Π³)GKRySξ;¹⁰ 138 ἐμοί] ὅμωc Π⁴ᵘᵛAb¹ʸᵖCr (ομω[pot. qu. ομο[Π⁴, ὅμ[Ab¹ʸᵖ); 212 γε] τε Π⁵RRy²ξ;¹¹ 232ⁿ Xo. MBV²+: ἠλ. OCrL: om. Π⁶C²RRyZuᶜ²: [VA]; 343 κατέκλυcε] -cεν Π⁸AdJXbTᵗ³; 761 ἄcτεοc] ἄcτεωc Π¹⁰Aa³GKL; 975 φονία (φονεία VF)] φοινία (Π¹³)PTᵗ³; 1073 cὴν] τὴν AdKPrʸᵖSSa¹ʸᵖ (~Sʸᵖ), cὺ <Π¹⁴ʔ>CrMnʸᵖ Pr; 1380 ἔcτ'HMO+: ἔcθ'BVa+: ἔcτιν (Π¹⁷ᵘᵛ)GKMtˢξᵍˡTᵗ³; 1659 μενεῖ] μένει Π¹⁸ᵘᵛCrJLTh (~Π¹⁸ᶜᵘᵛ), μενεί Ad: [C].

Several of these agreements between the papyrus and the later manuscripts may be fortuitous, since the truth was recoverable by conjecture, and metre pointed to the need for conjecture (343 κατ-

---

⁵ I count ἀπὸ as an error (see Willink); but one cannot be sure.
⁶ Presumably the variant in R reflects ἐῶcίν (intended as ἐῶcι(ν) c') in R's model.
⁷ See p. 59.   ⁸ See p. 21 n. 15.
⁹ See pp. 49, 62, 71. In the same line we should have another such agreement, if the papyrus were rightly identified as having cυνοικίcαι (so RfSa: -ῆcαι cett.). But the identification is very uncertain: see ZPE 77 (1989) 1–2.   ¹⁰ See p. 52.   ¹¹ See p. 52.

ἔκλυcεν, 761 ἄcτεωc, 975 φοινία, 1380 ἔcτιν). But such a plea can‑
not be made in the case of hyp. 1.19, 61, 212, all of which I have
previously discussed. Nor can it be made in the case of two other
readings on the list: 138 ὅμωc and 1073 cύ. The latter has been
rightly commended by Di Benedetto, Willink, and West. The for‑
mer calls for full discussion. Gronewald, who first published Π⁴ as P.
Köln III 131, labelling it 'Adespotum: Prosafragment (?)', deciphered oμo[. The papyrus
was correctly identified by Gronewald (ZPE 39 [1980] 35–6) and
O'Callaghan. Merkelbach (ap. Gronewald 35 n. 6) suggested
oμω[c, and this suggestion was endorsed by Musso. In republishing
the papyrus as P. Köln VI 252 Gronewald remarked 'Vor der
Lücke sehr wahrscheinlich o[, nicht ω['. But the photograph makes
clear that oμω[is just as likely as oμo[. 'If ἀλλ' ὅμωc were indeed
attested as a variant,' writes Willink, 'one might consider accepting
it and bracketing 139.' I have now found ὅμωc in Cr and as a
marginal variant in Ab. The evidence of AbCr (where ὅμωc cannot
possibly be conjectural and must be inherited) puts beyond all
reasonable doubt that the papyrus too had oμω[c. I should accept
ὅμωc, and Willink's deletion of 139. With ἐμοί (and line 139) the
sentence runs very awkwardly. There is certainly 'anacoluthon', as
Willink calls it; and Denniston, Greek Particles 5–6, to whom he
refers, offers nothing fully comparable. The problem is that μέν,
placed where it is, suggests that both πρευμενήc and cυμφορά are
predicates of φιλία: not (what we want) 'Your φιλία, on the one
hand, is πρευμενήc, but to awaken Orestes will be a cυμφορά', but
'Your φιλία is on the one hand πρευμενήc, but it (φιλία) will be a
cυμφορά to awaken Orestes'. This is, at worst, absurd; at best, very
lax writing. The idiomatic ἀλλ' ὅμωc frequently invites interpola‑
tion.¹²

The papyri offer testimony of great importance in these last five
passages (hyp. 1.19, 61, 138, 212, 1073). They prove that the later
manuscripts had access to old, and sometimes true, readings which
had evaded their elders. We might also cite, as evidence for the
preservation of old readings in the younger manuscripts, at least

¹² See Willink on 1024, which must be deleted (in 1023 Cʸᵖ offers οἰκτρὰ μὲν ἀλλ' ὅμωc
φέρε). Having established the credit of Cr, I mention in passing its curious ἔννυκτοc for
νυκτὸc at 404. If one believes (as I do, and the possibility is entertained by Willink) that
νυκτὸc should be changed to ἐκτὸc (Wecklein olim), one may at least contemplate the notion
that the reading of Cr is derived from ἐκτὸc.

some of the following readings, either probably or certainly false, which the younger manuscripts share with papyri: 137 κτύπος] ψόφος Π⁴Aaʳˢ; 511 ποῖ] post κακῶν Π⁹AbAt (~<Π⁹ᶜ>); 1081 δέ] τε Π¹⁴A AaCrLPRfZZbZmZu; 1627 θ'] δ'Π¹⁸AtCCrFKMnPrRRwSSaZc Zu. The last two are probably genuine old variants. The first (137 ψόφος) implies that the papyrus had the widely attested variant κτυπεῖτε for ψοφεῖτε earlier in the line, where its evidence is lacking. The reading at 511 is a trivial slip, which might have occurred independently of the papyrus in the later manuscripts.

The papyri offer a few readings which are new and either possibly or certainly true: 472 εἰc] ἐc Π⁹; 836 φόνω(ι)] φόνου MnᵛˢPrRfSaᵛˢS (~PrᵛˢSᵛˢ; ἕνεκα φόνου ᵍˡVZu), φοβωι Π¹⁹ (coni. Paley), unde φόβον proprio Marte Koenen, Diggle (φόνον Wilamowitz); 976 ἰὼ ἰὼ] ἰὼ Cr (coni. Wecklein), ιω ω Π¹³ (coni. Hartung); 1340 ἀλλ'] ἀγ'Π⁹ (~Π¹⁶) (coni. Weil); 1394 om. Π¹⁷ (cf. Σᵐᶜ οὗτος ὁ cτίχος ἐν πολλοῖc (τῶν) ἀντιγράφων οὐ γράφεται [φέρεται Wecklein]); ΣPrSa τινὲc λέγουcιν ὅτι οὗτος ὁ cτίχος οὐ φέρεται ἐν τοῖc πολλοῖc τῶν ἀντιγράφων); 1441 ἕδραν] εδρανα Π¹⁸. Whether or not ἐc should be printed for εἰc in 472 and in places where metre admits either form, we have no means of knowing.[13] In 836 an accusative is decidedly preferable to a dative; and φόβον is at least as good as φόνου.[14] In 976 ἰὼ ὢ, if rightly deciphered, solves the metrical problem and deserves to be right (so Willink, against West). In 1340 ἀγ' would have deserved acceptance, even without the support of the papyrus (see Willink). The omission of 1394 pleasingly confirms the scholia. In 1441 there is no fault in ἕδραν, but ἕδρανα, if rightly deciphered, deserves acceptance, as the editor of the papyrus (Haslam) recommends.

But the papyri have their share of falsehood from which the manuscripts are immune: 141 μηδ' ἔcτω κτύπος om. Π⁴ ut uid. (et Dion. Hal. comp. 11.63); 142 ἀποπρο (diuersis acc.) uel ἀπόπροθι] αποπ]ρομα Π⁴; 206 ἄτε] οτε Π⁵; 208 πέλας] παρος Π⁵;[15] 216 φρενῶν]

[13] See Mastronarde 175–7.

[14] Orestes may perfectly well be described as having blood-red eyes (see Willink). But it is more appropriate here to allude to the terror in his eyes, since he is both a hunted man (835 Εὐμενίcι θήραμα) and a madman (835 βεβάκχευται μανίαιc). See 38, 532, and, for terror in the eyes of a madman, A. ScT 497–8 ἔνθεος δ' Άρει | βακχᾶι πρὸς ἀλκήν, θυιὰς ὥς, φόβον βλέπων. See further Koenen and Sijpesteijn, loc. cit. 264–6, and my note on Herc. 871 in PCPS n.s. 20 (1974) 12 and Studies 54.

[15] For this reading (correcting that of the ed. pr.) see Papyrologica Florentina 19 (1990) 145.

ακων Π⁶; 240 δ' εἰc] δ' ἐc AnCr, δε Π⁶; 339 ante 338 Π⁸; 877 Ὀρέcτην] ορεcτη]c Π¹¹; 1072 δὲ] δη Π¹⁵, δὲ δὴ J², δὲ δεῖ J²gB; 1315 βρόχουc] βρο]χοιc Π¹⁶; 1320 τἀξειργαcμένα] τὰν δόμοιc] κακα Π¹⁶ (suppl. Hunt); 1335 δόμοc] δομ]οιc Π¹⁶, δόμ∗∗ M (~M³), δόμουc B² (~B²), δόμ∗c Rw (~Rwᶜ); 1386 κυκνόπτερον] κυανοπτε̣[ρο]ν̣ Π¹⁷; 1627 ὅc] ὡc MnS (~S¹⁵), ὁ Π¹⁸.
Some of these are simple errors (208, 240, 1072,¹⁶ 1386, 1627). Others invite brief comment. At 1315 the dative might lead one to suspect that earlier in the line the papyrus had ἐμπεcοῦca not εἰcπεcοῦca. But ἐμπεcοῦca . . . βρόχοιc does nothing to help with the problem (on which see Willink). At 1335 M may originally have had the same reading as the papyrus, δόμοιc; but equally it may have had δόμουc. The remaining readings on this list have all been espoused as true or near to the truth. At 141 the omission is accepted by West, and by Barrett on Hi. 738; but Willink explains why it is unacceptable. At 142 it is idle to base conjectures on]ρομα (ἄ]δρομα Merkelbach ap. Gronewald, ZPE 39 [1980] 35 n. 6), since ἀποπρό is clearly right. At 206 ὅτε, although it has been hailed as the solution to this intractable problem, is not acceptable, for reasons which I have given elsewhere.¹⁷ In 216, if ακων represents ἀκῶν, it is inept; if ‹κ›ακῶν, inferior. The location of 339 before 338 is impossible, without further unacceptable changes (such as are proposed by Longman).

¹⁶ δή is not impossible, but δὲ is more idiomatic (see Denniston, Greek Particles 175).
¹⁷ See Papyrologica Florentina 19 (1990) 147, and below, p. 134 n. 8.

CHAPTER XV

Testimonia[1]

There are few places where the indirect tradition is right or probably right and the Euripidean tradition is wrong or probably wrong:

45 ἀπό] ὑπό Herwerden ex Athen. 108B (=Eubul. fr. 75. 6 Kassel–Austin). The merits of ὑπό were explained by Barrett *ap.* R. Carden, *The Papyrus Fragments of Sophocles* (1974) 217 n. 103. See also R. L. Hunter, *Eubulus: The Fragments* (1983) 169. We cannot be certain that Eubulus is borrowing from Euripides, in view of S. fr. 444. 6 Radt] εἰ πῶλος ὡς ὑπὸ ζυγοῦ. But imitation of Euripides by Eubulus is more likely than imitation of Sophocles (see Hunter's index, p. 255, s.u. Euripides, and Kassel–Austin on Eub. fr. 6. 2).

349 πολλῇ(ι) δ’] πολλὴ δ’ M¹ᶜC, πολλῇ γ’ Aa²ᵞᴾ et Dio Chrys. 2. 42 codd. PW, πολῇ δ’ V (~V¹ᶜ), πολλῇ(ι) RyT¹³, πολὺ δ’ HMBOK¹ᶜ (~B²O¹ᶜ) et ¹Σᵛ et Σᵛ et Dio cod. V et (a Dione deriuatum) Σᵗ H. Od. 4. 97 (ii. 756 Dindorf), πολ δ’ S, (πολ)ὺς ˢV²ᐟ³Rw¹, πολὺς δ’ ¹ΣRw, πολὺ Dio codd. UB. Willink conjectured πολὺς, unaware of the attestation for πολὺς δ’ in the Euripidean tradition. I believe that the conjecture is right, and that Dio's πολὺ (without δ’ in UB) may be a genuine preservation of what is nearest to the truth. The Homeric scholia are derived from Dio, as a glance at the surrounding context of this citation shows, and so have no

---

[1] A very full and mostly accurate list of testimonia is given by Biehl 108–33. Citations which should be added are: 1–2 (–πάθος) Men. Asp. 424–5; 14 Symeon Magistros ep. 91. 20 (ed. J. Darrouzès, *Épistoliers Byzantins du xᵉ Siècle* [1960] 152); 136b and 140–1 Psellus, Eur. et Georg. Pisid. comp. (ed. A. R. Dyck, *Michael Psellus, The Essays on Eur. and George of Pisidia and on Heliod. and Ach. Tat.* [1986] 44–6); 211–12 Theophylactus Achridensis (11th cent.; cf. D. Obolensky, *Six Byzantine Portraits* [1988] 34–82) ep. 32 (ed. P. Gautier, *Théophylacte d'Achrida, Lettres* [1986] 237; =126. 392 Migne); 232 Men. Asp. 432; 258 Theoph. Achr. ep. 103 (Gautier 517; 126. 465 Migne); 428 id. ep. 93 (Gautier 477; 126. 440 Migne), ep. 109 (Gautier 529; 126. 472 Migne); 450–1 id. ep. 93 (Gautier 477; 126. 440 Migne); 1115 id. (ed. Gautier, *Théoph. d'Achrida, Discours, Traités, Poésies* [1980] 313); 1384 Phot. *A* 2835 Theodoridis; 1469 ΣTzetz. in Ar. Ran. 1354; and several citations in Nicephorus Basilaca (12th cent.), which may be found by reference to Garzya's edition (1984). Biehl also ignores many allusions in *Chr.Pat.*: these may be found by reference to Tuilier's edition (1969). I mention without enthusiasm the disagreeable controversy relating to the testimonia between E. Degani, *BPENC* n.s. 15 (1967) 19–21, *QIFC* 3 (1968) 18–27, and V. Di Benedetto, *Maia* 20 (1969) 152–4.

independent value. It does not matter, for this purpose, whether this chapter of Dio is genuine or (as suggested by Wilamowitz *ap.* von Arnim) interpolated. At all events, the reverse relationship (interpolation of Dio from the Homeric scholia) is excluded.

351 τῶν Ταντaλιδῶν] τοῦ Ταντaλιδᾶν Dio, τοῦ Ταντaλιδῶν Σᵗ H. Od. τοῦ may well be right, as Willink (followed by West) argues, since the corruption of τοῦ to τῶν was much more likely than the reverse. But I should not accept Ταντaλιδᾶν (accepted by West, but not by Willink). As parallels for the Doric ending of the patronymic in non-lyric anapaests one might quote A. *Ag.* 44 Ἀτρειδᾶν (-δῶν Aldina), 1569 Πλεισθενιδᾶν (-δῶν Trˢ), where Fraenkel, citing H. W. Smyth, *HSCP* 7 (1896) 139–65, pleads that such Doricisms are permissible in the case of proper names. I regard this plea as unconvincing. Doric forms are from time to time imported by scribes into non-lyric anapaests: for example, in the lines which immediately follow Ἀτρειδᾶν at *Ag.* 44 we find: 45 χιλιοναύτην MᶜTrˢ: -ταν MVFGTr; ἴλιον αὐτὰν ᵞᵖMF; 47 ἀρωγήν MᶜTrˢ: -γάν MVFTr. Even more telling (from iambic trimeters) is S. *El.* 10 Πελοπιδᾶν Lᵃᶜ. For other examples of Doric forms imported into trimeters see Mastronarde 177.

593 omitted by Clem. Alex. *protr.* 7. 76. 3,² who cites 591b–2 and 594–6a; deleted by Nauck, and stigmatized by Willink as 'a clumsily superfluous line'. The deletion (accepted also by West) is probably right. But no argument should be based on Clement, who quotes the passage very loosely, adding a linking word between 592 and 594 (ποτὲ μὲν τὸν Ἀπόλλωνα, ὃς μεσομφάλους ἕδρας ναίει βροτοῖσιν εἰς cτόμα νέμων cαφέστατα [for ναίων βροτοῖcι cτόμα νέμει cαφέcτατον], διελέγχων, κείνωι [for τούτωι] πειθόμενος κτλ.), and subjoining 417 to 596a.

1295 cκοποῦcα πάντα (-τη) uel cκοποῦc' ἄπαντα] cκοπεὺc ἀπατᾷ anon. Ambrosianus de re metrica ap. Studemund, *Anecdota* (1886) 226. Since the metrician cites the words as an instance of bacchiac rhythm, Nauck (*Lexicon Vindobonense* [1867] 258) conjectured cκοπεύουc' ἀπαντᾶι. This (but with ἀπάντα or ἀπάνται or -cα πάντα(ι))³ is almost certainly right.

1384 ἁρμάτειον ἁρμάτειον μέλος om. Demetrius Laco ap. P.

---

² But not by ps.-Iustin. de mon. 107E (ii. 142 Otto²), who cites 591–8a.
³ See Schwyzer, *Gr. Gramm.* 1. 550, Barrett on *Hi.* 563, Diggle, *CQ* n.s. 33 (1983) 352 n. 58.

Herc. 1012 (re-edited by E. Puglia, *Cron. Erc.* 10 [1980] 32). Since we have independent evidence that in antiquity these words (or words hereabouts) were regarded as a παρεπιγραφή (Σ 220. 22–3 Schwartz, Phot. *A* 2835 Theodoridis; see O. Taplin, *PCPS* n.s. 23 [1977] 125, A. R. Dyck, *HSCP* 85 [1981] 101, 103), and since they are difficult to interpret and to fit into the structure of the sentence, I should accept Murray's deletion, as does Willink.

In a few places the truth, preserved by the indirect tradition, is preserved by only a minority of Euripidean manuscripts:

212 γϵ] τϵ Π⁵RRy²ξ et Stob. 4. 36. 1 et pars codd. Plut. mor. 165E (~Theoph. Achr.).⁴

232ⁿ χο. MBV²+: ἠλ. OCrL: om. Π⁶AtC²JRRyZuᶜ⁽ et Stob. 4. 36. 3: [VA].

258 ἀτρέμας] etiam Olympiod. in Pl. Alc. 170. 11–12 (p. 108 Westerink), Plut. mor. 465C ap. Stob. 3. 29. 79, Liban. decl. 23. 69 codd. plerique: ἀτρέμα BLXcᶜZu (~B²Zuᶜ) et Erotian. uoc. Hipp. coll. Σ 29 (p. 79 Nachmanson), Liban. cod. V, fort. Galen. x. 13 Kühn: utrumque codd. Plut. mor. 465C, 501C, 788F, 901A, 1126A: om. Theoph. Achr.⁵

545 cὲ uel cϵ] γϵ AtMnᵘᵛPrʸᵖSʸᵖZZc (~Mnᶜ) et lex. Vind. *O* 31 codd. Vind. 169 et Vat. 12 (~cod. Vat. 22), γϵ cὲ Sa. The *Lexicon Vindobonense*, compiled *c*.1300,⁶ was edited by Nauck from a single Viennese manuscript. But it exists in at least two other manuscripts: see F. Benedetti, *BPENC* 14 (1966) 85–92, A. Colonna, ibid. 19 (1971) 13–16. The transmitted text cannot stand. Either we must accept γϵ and Musgrave's τι for τϵ (cf. *Ph.* 383 μή τι cὴν δάκω φρένα) or we must delete the line (Paley).⁷

667 χρή] δεῖ B¹ˢV et Ar. eth. Nic. 1169b. 8, [Ar.] magna mor. 1212b. 28, Plut. mor. 68E. The two words are often confused: 564 χρή] δεῖ OV+; 666 χρή] δεῖ O¹ˢ; 864 δεῖ] χρή V+; 911 χρή] δεῖ H; 1074 δεῖ] χρή Z; 1652 χρή] δεῖ Cr.

922 ἀκέραιοc] -ον FLPζT²gE (~Zb³Tᶜ) et Hesych. *A* 2331, Chr. Pat. 395. I believe, like Willink, that the accusative is right and that the imitation by Men. *Epitr.* 910 ἀκέραιοc ἀνεπίπληκτοc αὐτὸc τῶι βίωι lends further support to ἀκέραιον ἀνεπίπληκτον (as against ἀκέραιοc ἀνεπίπληκτον).

---

⁴ See p. 52, and (for Theoph. Achr.) p. 121 n. 1 above.
⁵ See p. 100.   ⁶ Cf. Mastronarde 72.   ⁷ See *CQ* n.s. 40 (1990) 101–5.

1382 καὶ Π¹⁷ΜΟ¹ˢAbMnRSZZc et ⟨Demetr. Laco⟩: om. cett. Further welcome support for the antiquity of this reading.[8]

1633 κἀπὸ] κ᾽ ὑπὸ BOACMt²⟨Tᶻ?⟩ (~B³AᵞᵖMtᶜTᶜ), καὶ ὑπὸ MR, χ᾽ ὑπὸ ΣLyc. 510 pars codd. I believe that χὑπὸ is right. Whether ΣLyc. have ὑπὸ by preservation, by corruption, or by contamination with the Euripidean tradition,[9] we cannot tell.

In the following places the reading of an external source has sometimes been espoused as true:

141 μηδ᾽ ἔστω κτύπος non hab. Π⁴ ut uid., om. Dion. Hal. comp. 11. 63.[10]

696 ὅταν γὰρ ἥβαι δῆμος εἰς ὀργὴν πεσών] ὅταν γὰρ ὀργῆι δῆ- μος εἰς θυμὸν πέσηι Stob. 4. 5. 14; cf. [Men.] sent. 112 βλάπτει γὰρ ἄνδρα θυμὸς εἰς ὀργὴν πεσών. Nauck's θυμὸς for δῆμος, sup- ported by M. D. Reeve, *GRBS* 14 (1973) 157, seems to me uncalled for (see Willink). Faith in Stobaeus is not enhanced by his ἔποιτο for ὑπείκοι in 699.

700 ἐκπνεύσειεν· ὅταν] ἐκπνεύσει·· ὅταν Stob. 4. 5. 14 cod. M (~codd. SA), coni. Duport. This (though accepted by West) is less plausible than Nauck's ἐκπνεύσειεν· ἦν.

I add three further readings, which may appeal to some:

141 τιθεῖτε (ψοφεῖτε VK, ~V¹ˢK¹ᵞᵖ; τίθετε Porson) μὴ κτυ- πεῖτε (ψοφεῖτε Aaᵞᵖ) μὴ δ᾽ ἔστω κτύπος] ciγᾶτε μὴ κτυπῆτε μὴ ἔcω κτύπος Psell.[11] I doubt if Psellus' μὴ ἔcω makes Elmsley's μὴ 'cτω any more attractive.[12]

251 νῦν] τοι Plut. mor. 88C, Orio anth. 1. 16. We do not want τοι with an imperative: see N. V. Dunbar, *CR* n.s. 20 (1970) 272, my app. crit. at *El.* 659.

1381 ὤμοι μοι] ωμοι κ]ακων Demetr. Laco. There is no good reason to prefer this.

I turn now to errors which are shared by the indirect tradition and a part of the Euripidean tradition. Not all of these agreements are evidence for the antiquity of the variant. Some of the errors may have arisen independently. Equally, I believe that in some cases the independent tradition has been contaminated with the Euripidean tradition.[13]

---

[8] See p. 116.   [9] For this possibility see below, n. 13.
[10] See pp. 119–20, 132.   [11] See p. 121 n. 1.   [12] See p. 132.
[13] For an instance of this in *Hi.* see Barrett, pp. 429–30.

1 οὐδέν] etiam Men. Asp. 424, Luc. Iupp. trag. 1, Dio Chrys. 4. 82, Orio anth. 8. 6, Stob. 4. 34. 48 cod. A^c, Olympiod. in Pl. Alc. 132. 16 (p. 88 Westerink), Sud. Α 3819 (i. 344 Adler), ps.-Luc. Timar. 1, ΣΑ. Pe. 714 (pars codd.), ΣPlan. in Hermog., v. 424 Walz (pars codd.): om. PrgE et Σ^m (95. 27–8) et ¹Σ^v et Stob. 4. 34. 48 (SMA), ΣΑ. Pe. (pars codd.), ΣPlan. (pars codd.), Theod. Prodr. p. 142 La Porte du Theil (*Notices et extraits des mss. de la Bibl. imp.* viii.2 [1810]). The coincidence of Pr and gE, which have no especial affinity,[14] suggests that the omission of οὐδέν may once have enjoyed a greater measure of diffusion in the Euripidean tradition than is now apparent.

2 ξυμφορά (uel cυμ-) θεήλατος] etiam (Luc.), Orio, Stob. cod. S., Sud., Theod. Prodr., ps.-Luc. (nom. interpr. Cic. Tusc. 4. 63): -άν . . . -ον M‹B›O^{1γρ}VC (~M²B^cV^{1s} et ^{γρ}Σ^{mvc}) et Stob. codd. MA et (Dio). The accusative is evidently an ancient variant.

3 ἀνθρώπου] etiam Zonar. i. 307 Tittmann, Dio, Orio, Stob. codd. MA, Sud., Σ^t H. Il. 24. 49, Theod. Prodr., ps.-Luc.: -ων MS^{uv}SaζT^z (~S^cZm^{1s}) et Luc. ocyp. 167: om. Stob. cod. S. The plural is evidently an ancient variant.

127 κεκτημένοις] κεχρημένοις ^{γρ}Aa^rAb²R¹ (κεχρωμένοις Ab²^{γρ}) et G^{gl} et Liban. or. 64. 46 cod. V (saec. xii) et interpr. Eust. Il. 172. 43 (χρωμένοις), coni. F. W. Schmidt. Schmidt's conjecture, which is now found to have support both in the Euripidean tradition and in the indirect tradition (though it is not clear that this variant is an old one), must be rejected, since the perfect of this verb does not, in tragedy, have the requisite sense. And so it would serve no good purpose to adduce in its support (as parallels for καλῶс χρῆςθαι) 705, *Hi.* 1035, *Andr.* 242. For καλῶс κεκτημένοις see *Tr.* 737 εὖ . . . τὰc τύχαc κεκτημένη (ταῖc τύχαιc κεχρημένη Hartung), fr. 187. 1 (*Antiope* fr. VIII Kambitsis) εὖ βίον κεκτημένος, fr. 417. 1 κέκτηсο δ᾽ ὀρθῶς. The reverse corruption is found at *Ph.* 534 (κτωμένων O, ~O^{1c}) and A. *Pe.* 829 (κεκτημένοι P^{γρ}). It is noteworthy that Aa, which offers κεχρημένοις as a variant here (Aa^{rγρ}), offers χρῆμ᾽ for κτῆμ᾽ as a variant at 230 (Aa²^{γρ}), and that Eustathius, who implies κεχρημένοις, also implies χρῆμ᾽ at 230 (Il. 1261. 40 τὸ δέμνιον . . . χρῆμα ἡ τραγωιδία φησίν).[15] Euripides is echoing Theogn. 472 πᾶν γὰρ ἀναγκαῖον χρῆμ᾽ ἀνιηρὸν ἔφυ.

¹⁴ See p. 113.
¹⁵ Other examples of κτῆμα and χρῆμα confused: 703 (χρῆμα gB), *Ph.* 555, *Ba.* 1152, S. *OT* 549, *Ant.* 684, *Phil.* 81.

128 *ἀπέθριcε(ν)*] etiam Hesych. *A* 5881 (Cyrilli codd.): *-ξε* Ab CrGKLMnPrR^{1s}RfRwSSaζT^{z} et (*-εν*) Hesych. (cod. Marc.) et ΣTr A. Ag. 536 (i. 143 Smith). Presumably an old corruption.

140^{n} *χο.* (uel *ἡμιχ.*)] etiam Σ^{mbvc} Ph. 202 et anecd. Par. i. 19 Cramer: *ἡλ.* arg. 2.19, Cleanth. (SVF i. 610) ap. Diog. Laert. 7. 172, Dion. Hal. comp. 11. 63 (Usener–Radermacher), Psell.[16] Confusion over the distribution of parts was evidently ancient.[17]

140 *λεπτὸν*] etiam ΣNic. alex. 423: *λευκὸν* <HB>OV (~H^{c}B^{2}O^{1γρ} V^{3γρ}) et ^{γρ}K^{1}R^{1}ξT$^{t1/2}$ et ΣPh., Dion., anecd.: utrumque arg. 2.19 et codd. Diog. Evidently an ancient variant.

142 *ἀπόπρο μοι*] *ἀπόπρο* Rf, *ἀπόπροθι μοι* ZZbZm, *ἀπόπροθι* O^{gl}CrLMnRf^{gl}SSaZu (~Mn^{γρ}) et Dion. cod. V (saec. xvi). It seems likely that Dion. cod. V gained its reading from the Euripidean tradition.

229 *δέμνιον*] *δέμνια* Ab^{1s} et Stob. 4. 36. 2. I do not think that this reading lends support to Hermann's conjecture (*δέμνια . . . ὄντα*). The plural probably reflects an awareness (conscious on the part of Ab^{1s}, unconscious on the part of Stobaeus or his source) that the plural *δέμνια* is regular in tragedy, the singular *δέμνιον* almost non-existent. I believe that Willink's *δεμνίων* is right.

230 *ὂν* om. AAtZc<T^{z}> (~T$^{t1/2}$) et Stob. codd. SM (*μὲν* cod. A). The omission (haplography after *ἀνιαρὸν*) probably occurred independently.

234 *γλυκύ*] etiam Ar. rhet. 1371a, eth. Nic. 1154b, eth. Eud. 1235a, com. fr. adesp. 115. 1 Kock, Ammon. diff. 316, Apostol. 11. 31b, Eust. Od. 1799. 31: *ἡδύ* JPRyThgBgE et Eust. Il. 1093. 52, Od. 1404. 55, 1910. 30, ΣPlan. in Hermog., v. 438 Walz et (in paraphrasi) Dion. Hal. comp. 12. 69, Phoebammon, viii. 492 Walz. Cf. 1112 below.

279 *αὖ* om. MAaFPrXagB (~Xa^{2}) et Sud. *H* 36 (ii. 548 Adler), Apostol. 6. 88d, Ar. ran. 304 pars codd., Σ^{rv} et Tzetz. in Ar. The omission of *αὖ* after *αὖθιc* was an easy error, and presumably occurred independently in the Euripidean and Aristophanic traditions. Whether it occurred independently of these traditions in the Suda and Apostolius, we cannot say.

417 *γ'* om. VCrMnRSXaXb et Clem. Alex. protr. 7. 76. 4 (~ps.-Iustin. de mon. 107d [ii. 142 Otto^{2}]). The omission could be an independent error by Clement; or it may have been an old one.

[16] See p. 121 n. 1. [17] For the evidence of Π^{4} see p. 132.

485 ἐν βαρβάροις] etiam Tzetz. ep. 13 (p. 21. 13 Leone), lex. Vind. X 8: ἀφ' Ἑλλάδος ᵧᵖM¹V³C et [Ap. Ty.] ep. 34 (i. 352 Kayser, p. 48 Penella) (ἐβαρβαρώθην οὐ χρόνιος ὤν ἀφ' Ἑλλάδος ἀλλὰ χρόνιος ὤν ἐν Ἑλλάδι). The citation[18] appears to prove the antiquity of the variant.

515 ἀνταποκτείνειν] -κτεῖναι VAbMn²PPrRSZZbZm et Phot. A 2055 Theodoridis (who less plausibly refers the entry to 509 ἀνταποκτενεῖ). Probably an ancient variant.

606 δυστυχέστερον] δυστυχέστατον XXa et Stob. 4. 22. 196, δυσχερέστατον Xb. It is possible, but far from certain, that Stobaeus has gained his reading from the Euripidean tradition.[19]

637 τότε] τάδε OSa (~O¹ˢ) et Orio anth. 1. 2. Since O and Sa have no especial connection, Orio may be reflecting a variant which was once more widely disseminated. But colourless disyllables of this kind are easily substituted for one another; and so Orio (and O and Sa) may have committed an independent slip.

643 πατρὸς ἐμοῦ λαβών] πατρὸς λαβὼν ἐμοῦ Z, ἐμοῦ λαβών Aa, ἐμοῦ πατρὸς λαβών et. Gud. i. 202 de Stefani. An interesting coincidence between the direct and indirect traditions in the often related phenomena of transposition and omission.[20]

721 ἄρ'] om. VRfRw (~V²), ante ἄφιλος MnS, ante ἧϲθ' Caecil. Calact. fr. 75 Ofenloch, Niceph. Basil. ep. 2 (p. 113. 19 Garzya). See on 643 above.

729 προβαίνων] om. Sa (~Saʳˢ) et Ioseph. Rhacend., iii. 500 Walz, προβαίνειν Aaʳˢ et ΣPlan. in Hermog., v. 525 Walz (pars codd.) (~ΣHephaest. p. 314. 34 Consbruch, [Castor] de metr., iii. 717 Walz). The agreements are perhaps fortuitous.[21]

750 ἀρίϲταϲ] ἀρίϲτουϲ ZZc<Tᶻ˙> (~T^{ti/2}) et [Trypho] de trop., viii. 758 Walz (pars codd.). Perhaps fortuitous.

876 ἀνεπτέρωκε] -κεν BO et Chr. Pat. 384 codd. BCN, -ϲε Ab CrF²ˢ˙MnPPrRRfSSa¹ˢZb˙ (~P¹ᶜZb¹ᶜ), -ϲκε Chr. Pat. cod. A. The latter seems to reflect contamination with the variant -ϲε.[22]

877 πόλεος HᶜMBAGKT^{ti/2} et disertim Theodos. canon., gr. Gr. iv, i. 10 Hilgard (-εωϲ pars codd.), unde Choerob. ΣSophron.,

---

[18] On which see R. J. Penella, *CQ* n.s. 38 (1988) 571. For allusions to this line in Byzantine writers see Wilson 205, Obolensky (above, p. 121 n. 1) 58, 61.

[19] See pp. 52, 86.   [20] See p. 21 n. 15.

[21] Nauck (*Lex. Vind.* 254. 13) attributes προβαίνειν also to anon. Ambros. de re metr. He is silently corrected by Studemund, *Anecd.* 223.

[22] The dates of the manuscripts of *Christus Patiens*, according to Tuilier, are: B 1300–50, C 1250–1300, N 1310–20, A early 14th cent.

128   TESTIMONIA

iv, i. 20 Hilgard, Sophron. excerpta, iv, ii. 389 Hilgard, Greg. Cor.
p. 402 Schaefer: πόλεωc HB²/³OV+.

933 Δαναΐδαι] etiam Eust. Il. 357. 31, Eust. ad Dion. Perieg. 347
(p. 278. 35–6 Müller) pars codd.: δαναοίδε PrRf: δαναοὶ δὲ AaAt
CrFPSaZbZm et Eust. ad Dion. pars codd.: δαναΐδαι δὲ GKT^{t1/2}
et Eust. ad Dion. pars codd. The manuscripts of Eustathius on
Dion. Perieg. have clearly been contaminated with the Euripidean
tradition, in which δαναοὶ δὲ and δαναΐδαι δὲ appear to be conjec-
tural.²³

982 καὶ ante χθονός add. ξTp et ΣPi. Ol. 1. 91a cod. E. Turyn
has argued that Pindar's manuscript has been contaminated with
the Euripidean tradition.²⁴

984 ἀναβοάcω] -cωμαι J², -cομαι ΣTzetz. in Ar. Plut. 639
(~ΣPi.). I do not know what to make of this agreement.²⁵

1005 τε om. An (~An²) et ΣArat. 257, Eust. Od. 1713. 7
(~Philopon. in Ar. met. p. 102. 3 Hayduck). Probably fortuitous.

1005 Πλειάδος] πελειάδος KRw^{1cuv} et Eust. (~Philopon.,
ΣArat.). The reading of K is certainly conjectural.²⁶ The agreement
of Eustathius is perhaps fortuitous; I should certainly not regard it
as evidence for the antiquity of the reading.

1101 ἀνάμεινον] etiam lex. Vind. A 126: ἄμεινον MR (~ˢM¹
M^{gl}R¹), ἄμμεινον M³. I report the reading of lex. Vind. here only
because it has been misreported by both Biehl (καὶ ἄμεινον) and
Degani (⟨ἀν⟩άμεινον).²⁷

1112 ἐνόπτρων] κατόπτρων ^{gl}B³/⁴Aa³F³ et Aelian. nat. an. 7. 25.
The coincidence between the prose writer and the glossator's pro-
saic substitute is no cause for surprise and no evidence for a connection. Cf. 234 above.

1204 ἄρcεναc] ἄρcενος F²X et Stob. 4. 22. 8 codd. MA (~cod.
S et Apostol. 18. 71a); -ac an -oc L incertum. Perhaps fortuitous.

1287 ἐκκcκώφηται] etiam Ter. Maur. 963, anon. in Greg. Cor.
p. 909 Schaefer: -ηνται AaAtF²ᵞᵖPrRwSa et Clem. Alex. strom. 2.
107. 1, Eust. Il. 964. 56, Od. 1539. 60: et -ηται et -ηνται agnoscit
Σ^{mbc}: -ωται F²MnSTp: -ωνται B²ˢAaᵗᵞᵖ et Ar. Byz. ap. Σ^{mc}. The
plural is evidently an ancient variant.

1369 βαρβάροιc ἐν] etiam et. ma. p. 393. 18: -οιcιν ἐν MZ: -οιc

---

²³ See p. 156.   ²⁴ See p. 55.
²⁵ Turyn (207, 212) cites ἀναβοάcωμαι also from U (Harl. 5725), which is closely related
to J.   ²⁶ See p. 156.   ²⁷ For Degani see p. 121 n. 1.

AAaGMtZb: -οιciv Cr et et. gen. B p. 133 Miller. The latter agreement is presumably fortuitous.

1523 ὁρῶν] etiam Stob. 4. 52. 6 codd. AS^{ιc}: ὁρᾶν VAtCrGJKPξ ZZcT^{t3}gVgBgE (~Cr^{ιc} et ^sJ^rZ^rZcT^{t3}) et Stob. cod. S. Probably ancient variants.

Finally I mention one place where the truth is uncertain, our manuscripts are divided, and the testimonia disappoint us by offering a new corruption of their own:

694 cμικροῖcι μὲν γάρ] cμικροῖcι μὲν AAtXb^{ιc}Th (etiam γὰρ Xb^{1s}), cμικροῖcι γὰρ K^{ιc}SSagE (coni. Barnes), cμικροῖc γὰρ CrK, cμικροῖcι gB, (c)μικροῖc δὲ Cyrill. c. Iulian. 9. 308 (76. 973b Migne), Didym. de trin. 1. 105 (39. 440a Migne). The citation by Cyril and Didymus of 694–5 is mistakenly printed as TrGF adesp. 123b by Kannicht and Snell.

CHAPTER XVI

Colometry

The Alexandrian colometry can usually be recovered.[1] When our manuscripts agree in rational colometry, this colometry is presumably the ancient one.[2] When (less commonly) they agree in demonstrably false colometry, we cannot be sure whether the fault lies with them or with the Alexandrian metrician. But more often than not it will lie with them; and sometimes they are convicted of error by the evidence of papyri.

The preservation of true colometry by a handful of manuscripts, when the majority are in error, may be a valuable index of the integrity of their source. Equally, agreement in false colometry may be an index of affiliation among manuscripts, and may usefully supplement the evidence for affiliation provided by agreements in error in the poetical text. I shall examine all the places where the greater (or the older) part of our manuscripts has corrupted what may be assumed to be the Alexandrian divisions. And I shall report the transmitted colometry in places where it may have a bearing on the constitution of the text. I shall pay particular attention to the colometry of the papyri: not only because their evidence is often a more reliable guide to the ancient divisions than that of the medieval manuscripts, but also because, in some places, where a papyrus is lacunose, we shall be able to establish its colometry with a greater degree of probability than its original editor was able to do, by the application of our knowledge of the colometry of the medieval tradition. And finally I shall consider whether the evidence of colometry can throw any light on the question whether our medieval manuscripts are derived from a single ancient source or more than one.

---

[1] See Zuntz, *Inquiry* 27–35, and *Drei Kapitel zur griechischen Metrik* (Sitzb. Öst. Akad. Wiss., phil.-hist. Kl., 443 [1984]) 50–8, Barrett, *Hippolytos* 84–90, Mastronarde 151–66. For *Hecuba* see Daitz's edition (1973), xiv, xvii–xxii, 85–102.

[2] It is not necessarily the right one. But, if we reject it, we must have good reason for doing so. I shall draw attention to several places where the ancient colometry is preferable to that of modern editors.

(i) *140–207 (Parodos)*

141~154. At 141, where dochmiacs are needed, the manuscripts offer an iambic trimeter τιθεῖτε μὴ κτυπεῖτε μηδ' ἔστω κτύπος. But M uniquely divides τιθεῖτε μὴ κτυπεῖτε | . This apparently irrational division perhaps reflects an original dochmiac division τίθετε (Porson) μὴ κτυπεῖ|τε. The omission of μηδ' ἔστω κτύπος (μὴ 'στω Elmsley) by Π⁴ and Dion. Hal.³ will have been all the easier if (as M's colometry suggests) the Alexandrian colometry presented these words (or whatever is the true version of them) on a line of their own.

I transcribe the text of Π⁴ in 139–42, in order to show how the lines must have been aligned:

139 τονδεξεγειραιcυμφοραγε]νηcεται
 cιγαcιγαλεπτονι]χνοcαρβ[υλης
τιθετεμηκτυπειτ(ε)]
142 αποπροβατεκειcαποπ]ρομαμοικοιτ[ας.

140 was evidently indented, and so presumably was 141.⁴ Indentation often indicates a change of metre,⁵ as here at 140. At 142, where there is no change of metre, it presumably indicates change of speaker. And so (since 142 belongs to Electra) the papyrus is likely to have attributed 140–1 to the chorus.⁶ Even if (what seems most improbable) 141 began level with 139 and 142, there is no room for μηδ' ἔστω κτύπος or for the original uncorrupted dochmiac. Nor is it likely that the original dochmiac stood at the beginning of 142, for (if we assume that 142 began level with 139) αποπροβατεκειcαποπ] exactly fits the space.

147–8~160–1. The correct dochmiac division is preserved in the antistrophe (160 ἐργμάτων |) by nearly all manuscripts, in spite of the interpolation of ὦ at the beginning of the line. But the corresponding division in the strophe (147 φέρω |) has been corrupted in all manuscripts, presumably as a consequence of the widespread corruption of ὑπόροφον to ὑπώροφον. The only trace of

---

³ See pp. 119–20, 124.
⁴ Rightly O'Callaghan, *Studia Papyrologica* 20 (1981) 16–17; wrongly Gronewald, *ZPE* 39 (1980) 356, but rightly in his republication of the papyrus (P. Köln 6 [1986] 252).
⁵ So also in Π⁵ (εἴcθεcιc of 203–7). Cf. E. G. Turner, *Greek Manuscripts of the ancient World* ² (=*BICS* Suppl. 46 [1987]) 8, 12.
⁶ For the rival attributions of 140–1 to the chorus and Electra in the manuscripts and testimonia see p. 126.

dochmiac division which survives at 147 is in V, which divides after the first dochmiac (ὡc |). The majority (including V) divide at βοάν |. But HMB divide at ὑπώροφον | as well as at βοάν |, while AAaAbZcT divide only at ὑπώροφον | (AaAbZcT are among the handful which transmit ὑπόροφον). These divisions appear to reflect a (later) iambic interpretation of a text with the (evidently old) corruption ὑπώροφον.

149–52~162–5. Whether or not the ancient colometry offered dochmiacs in 149~162, the division inherited by the manuscripts offers iambics (or trochaics) at the beginning (ἀτρέμας | ἀτρέμας ~ ἔλακεν | ἔλακεν), and dochmiacs do not appear until ὅτι | . . . ποτε | . . . εὐνάζεται | ~ τρίποδι | . . . ἐδίκαςε | . . . ματέρος | (the division at ὅτι | in 150 is corrupted in OAaCrRwSaZb, which divide at ἀπόδος |).

167–8~188–9. Many manuscripts divide correctly in the anti-strophe (at 188 ἄλλο |, or, if they have the interpolated γ' or γ' εἶπας or the like, either before or after the interpolation). But in the strophe only MnRRfSaξT divide correctly at 167 τάλαινα |. MBACLZcZmZu divide at ἔβαλες |, while HOV and most of the remainder do not divide at all. Here, then, is an instance of true colometry preserved in a minority of late manuscripts (MnRRf SaξT).

174–86~195–207. The evidence of Π⁵, which is present for the antistrophic passage, enables us to establish the Alexandrian colometry. In 174 the manuscripts preserve the correct division at νύξ |, but in 195 they have lost the corresponding division at ὦ |. They divide either at | ὦ (HMB+) or at τεκομένα | (VAbGK) or at με | (MnRSaξ) or at μᾶτερ | (OCr+) or not until ὤλεςας | (L, where the majority correctly divide). I assume that Π⁵ divided cor-rectly.[7] The correct division at ὦ | was also restored by Triclinius, who then uniquely divides after the next dochmiac (μᾶ|τερ). In 181–2~203–4 the Alexandrian division was διοιχόμεθ' οἰχόμεθα | κτύπον ἠγάγετ' οὐχὶ | cῖγα ~ βίου τὸ πλέον μέρος ἐν | ςτοναχαῖcί τε καὶ γό|οιcι. This division is preserved by most manuscripts in the strophe but has been variously corrupted in the antistrophe. Π⁵ MBVAKMnPRZbZcT divide rightly at ἐν |, but CRfξZu divide at μέρος | and HO+ do not divide. Π⁵ and K divide at γό|οιc(ι),

---

[7] Even if Pintaudi is right to identify τεκο]με[να (which, to judge from the photograph, is a precarious identification) it remains far from certain that there is room for ὦ before it.

the rest (apart from a few which divide erratically) divide at γόοιϲ
|. Division at 184 ϲτόματοϲ | ~ 205 ἄγαμοϲ | is almost universal
(OCr divide in 205 at ἄτεκνοϲ |), and Π⁵ confirms the antiquity of
this division. Π⁵ uniquely preserves the right division at 206 ά |
(~ 185 ἤ|ϲυχον), where the manuscripts divide wrongly (206 | ά
the majority, no division OCrL; 185 | ἤϲυχον the majority, ἤϲυχον
| OAaCr, no division L). The agreement of K and Π⁵ in preserv-
ing the division γό|οιϲ(ι) at 204 is remarkable. It cannot be right.
But it must be the Alexandrian division, in view of the universal
division at 181 οὐχὶ |. The text of 206 was already corrupt in
Alexandrian times (Π⁵ has the unbearable ἐπι δ; its οτε for ατε
does not solve the problems)⁸ and the unexpected (Alexandrian)
division at 184 ϲτόματοϲ | ~ 205 ἄγαμοϲ | was evidently designed
to yield an iambic dimeter in 185~206.⁹

(ii) *316–47 (First Stasimon)*

Π⁷ is present for 321–30 and so covers that part of the ode which
presents textual and metrical difficulties. The colometry of the
manuscripts enables us to establish the colometry of the papyrus
with certainty in 321–8 and with probability in 329–30.¹⁰

321 μελαγχρῶτεϲ Ε]ὐμενίδε[ϲ αἵτε
τὸν ταναὸν αἰθ]έρ' ἀμπ[άλλεϲθ' αἵματοϲ
τινύμεναι δί]καν τινύ[μεναι φόνον
καθικετε]ύομαι καθι[κετεύομαι
325 τὸν Ἀγαμέμ]νονοϲ γό[νον ἐάϲατ' ἐκ-
λαθέϲθαι λ]ύϲϲαϲ μα[νιάδοϲ φοιτα-
λέου φεῦ] μόχθων[
οἵων ὦ τά]λαϲ ὀρ[εχθεὶϲ ἔρρειϲ
τρίποδοϲ] ἄπο φά[τιν ἂν ὁ Φοῖβοϲ
330 ἔλακεν ἔλα]κε [δεξάμενοϲ ἀνὰ δάπεδον.

The division at 321 αἵτε | is shared by Π⁷ with only AbMnRSa

---

⁸ I have commented in *Papyrologica Florentina* 19 (1990) 147 on Di Benedetto's defence
of ἐπὶ δ'... ὅτε. I add that, in view of the appearance of ἐπὶ δ' in Π⁵, we cannot accept
Wilamowitz's notion (as reported by Murray) that it intruded as a corruption of the scholia's ἐπειδή, which rather is an interpretation of ἄτε.

⁹ For Π⁶ (205–6) see *Papyrologica Florentina* 19 (1990) 146 n. 2. There is insufficient evidence to justify Barrett's statement (*Hippolytos* 84 n. 4) that it divides 'quite otherwise than
the medieval mss.'.

¹⁰ My colometry should be compared with that of Lenaerts and O'Callaghan, which is
wrong at 321–2 and 325–8 and has misled W. Luppe, *Archiv f. Pap.* 27 (1980) 241.

ξTp. The correct division at τὸν | is preserved by HMBOV and most other manuscripts (and all divide rightly in the antistrophe at 337 ἀλαςτόρων |). At 325 Π[7] shares the correct division ἐκ|λαθέcθαι with HMOVACrFGKPPrRRySaξZcT, slightly corrupted by Ab (ἐκλε|λαθέcθαι) and BS (ἐκλα|θέcθαι), while AaLRfZmZu wrongly divide at ἐκλαθέcθαι |, CZTp at ἐάcατ' |, Rw at λύccac |.[11] At 326 Π[7] shares the correct division φοιτα|λέου with HMBOVACG KξZc, while AbAnFMnPRSSaZZmZuTp divide wrongly at φοιταλέου | and CrRyTp at μανιάδοc |. In the antistrophe the divisions which correspond to ἐκ|λαθέcθαι and φοιτα|λέου are 342 θοᾶc | and 343 δεινῶν |. The manuscripts correctly transmit the division at θοᾶc |, but in 343 BVAbFMnRS SaξZcT wrongly divide at κατέκλυcεν | and AaRf at πόνων |. The divisions of Π[7] at 327 μόχθων | and 328 ἔρρειc | are shared by most manuscripts.

The only uncertainties are at 329–30, since we do not know whether Π[7] had ὁ Φοῖβοc (omitted by HMACCrGKRf) and ἔλακεν ἔλακε(ν) or only ἔλακε(ν) (as OAAaCrGKLRwRyζTTp). If Π[7] did have ὁ Φοῖβοc, then it is likely to have had the text and colometry printed above, and it would share them with BVAbFMnRSaξ. The theoretical alternatives are τρίποδοc] ἄπο φά[τιν | ἂν ὁ Φοῖβοc ἔλα]κε̣[(ν ἔλακε), which is found in OLPSZZmZuTp but is too long for the space, and τρίποδοc] ἄπο φά[τιν ἂν | ὁ Φοῖβοc ἔλα]κε̣[(ν ἔλακε), which would introduce a division (ἂν |) not found in any manuscript. If Π[7] omitted ὁ Φοῖβοc, then the possibilities are τρίποδοc] ἄπο φά[τιν ἂν | ἔλακεν ἔλα]κε̣[, with unparalleled division at ἂν |, and τρίποδοc] ἄπο φά[τιν | ἂν ἔλακεν ἔλα]κε̣[(as HMCRf), which is too long for the space.[12] And so, by elimination of the impossible and the improbable, the likelihood emerges that Π[7] did have the text and colometry printed above.

The division at Φοῖβοc | matches the commonest division in the antistrophe at 345 (οἶκον ἄλλον | (ἕτερον) BVAAaAbFGKMnPRS SaξZcZmT, of which Aξ omit ἕτερον). There the remainder, which have οἶκον ἕτερον only, divide at οἶκον | (HMCLZZuTp) or at ἕτερον | (CrRfRw) or not at all (O). What is the right text and colometry in 329–30~345–6 remains uncertain.[13]

[11] Mn has ἐκ . . . |λαθέcθαι. I cannot read the three letters at the end of the line.

[12] |ἂν ἔλακ' ἔλα]κε̣ would fit (and Willink tentatively proposes this as a conjecture). H has ἔλακε ἔλακεν, no manuscript has the elided form.

[13] For suggestions see Willink and my *Studies* 20. West's colometry cannot be right: not

Π⁷ also preserves 333–9. It divides | τίс ἔλεος... ἔρχεται | ...
δάκρυα | ... cυμβάλλει | ... ἀλαстόρων | ... ἀναβακχεύει | ...
κατολοφύρομαι |, like most of the manuscripts. The only variations
of note are at the beginning, where the division | τίс... ἔρχεται |
is shared with Π⁷ by only OFLPRfZZcTp, while MB divide | τίс
... ἀγών | ... ἔρχεται |, AaCrGRw | ἰώ... ἔρχεται |, K(S) | ἰώ...
ἔλεος | ... ἔρχεται |, and the remainder | ἰώ... ἀγών | ... ἔρχ-
εται |.

Lines 338–44 are partly preserved by Π⁸, the 'musical papyrus',
with 339 placed before 338. Division is correctly marked between
dochmiacs at (the second) κατολοφύρομαι |, ἀναβακχεύει |, βρο-
τοῖς |, and θοᾶς |. For a reconstruction of the remaining lines see
J. Solomon, *GRBS* 18 (1977) 71–83.

(iii) *807–43 (Second Stasimon)*

807–18~819–30. Π⁹ is present for 811–17. It divides 811–13,
with the majority, at δόμων |, ἀρνόс |, and Ταντταλίδαιс |. But in
814–15, where MBOV+ rightly divide at καὶ | (at οἰκτρότατα |
AtMnS, cφάγια | SaZ, γενναίων | Ad, no division AbFRw), Π⁹
apparently divided at θοινάματα |, with only CCrTp (but Tp
omits καὶ). At the corresponding place in the antistrophe all
manuscripts (except RRw, which have no division) divide 826
wrongly at τάλαινα | instead of at τάλαι|να. In 815–16 Π⁹ again
apparently had wrong division at ὅθεν |, but this is shared by
MBO+, while the correct division at τεκέων | is preserved by VA
AbAtCrFMnRwSSa (ACr omit ὅθεν), and R has no division. At
the corresponding place in the antistrophe the correct division at
827 ὅcια | is almost universal (κτείνων | MnS, ματέρα | AaFPr
RfSa). In 816–17 Π⁹ may have divided at ἐξαμείβων |, like the
majority (αἵματος | FSa, no division AaZcZu). The original editor
prints [φον]ω̣ʹφον̣[ος εξαμει|βων δι] ạ[ιματος and remarks that the

only because of the irregularity of 328~344 (dochmiac with resolved anceps, on which see
CR n.s. 34 [1984] 68) but also because the anadiplosis in 329 (ὁ Φοῖβος ἔλακεν ἔλακε δε|ξ-)
is not in accord with Euripidean usage. In verbal anadiplosis in iambics or trochaics the two
verbs either occupy the whole metron (1416 ἔθὄρὄν ἔθὄρὄν |, 1461 κᾱτθᾰνῇ | κᾱτθᾰνῇ |,
Alc. 266, 872, *Su.* 818, 1123, *Tr.* 1077, 1090, *Hel.* 331, *Or.* 188 [if Lachmann's ‹θανεῖν› is
accepted], *Ph.* 681, 1018, 1030, 1054, 1568, *Hyps.* fr. 64. 92 [p. 48 Bond]), or they overrun
it by one short syllable (986 ὃс ἐτέκεν ἐτέ|κέ, 1481 ὃν εἴδὄν εἴ|δὄν, *Herc.* 1072, *Tr.* 1235,
Ion 705, *Hel.* 195, 214, 1118, *Ph.* 679?, 1350?, 1716). This should be taken into account in
establishing the colometry of 1468.

trace printed as ạ 'would suit ο or σ better than α, so that ἐξαμ-
ειβων δι| αιματ]ο[ϲ is possible'. This division would have no par-
allel in any manuscript. My photograph does not help in the
identification of the doubtful letter; but the available space would
be suited by δι' αἵματ]ο[ϲ. Division at ἐξαμείβων | is matched by
almost universal division in the antistrophe at 829 πατρώιαν |
(τιμῶν | MnS, not until ἐξανάψηι | AaFPrRfSa). In 817–18~
829–30 (Π⁹ being no longer available) the manuscripts for the most
part divide at προλείπει | ~ ἐξανάψηι |.
831–43. No manuscript divides 831–2 correctly at καὶ |.
MBOV+ divide at ἔλεοϲ |, the remainder at δάκρυα | (AaAbMn
PrRRfS) or τίνα | (FSa) or (the second) τίϲ | (Tp). Lines 833–41
are correctly divided by the majority. But no manuscript divides
the iambics correctly at 842 πατρώι |αν. MBOV+ divide at μα-
τέρα |, a few have no division in 842–3, and two divide erratically
(μαϲτὸν . . . ϲφάγιον | . . . ἀμοιβάν Aa, μαϲτὸν . . . ἔθετο | . . .
ἀμοιβάν Cr), and Mn divides at πατρώιων |, and this same division
suits the space available in Π¹⁹ (division at παθέ |ων, suggested by
the editors of Π¹⁹, is not found in any manuscript and assumes indentation of 843).

(iv) 960–1017 (Third Stasimon)

960–70~971–81. Π¹³ is present for parts of 973–81. There is
nothing exceptional (aberrations of individual manuscripts apart)
in the behaviour of the papyrus or the manuscripts before 976–7.
Here Π¹³ alone has the right division at ἐφαμέρων |. The
manuscripts divide at ἔθνη |, except for MnS, which divide at
πολύπονα |.
982–1004. Π¹³ is present for only four lines more. It offers al-
most certain proof that the Alexandrian division was οὐρανοῦ | . . .
τεταμέναν | αἰωρήμαϲι(ν) | πέτραν . . . .¹⁴ This division is found in
MBVACLZu. A few other manuscripts (AaMnPRξZ) also divide
at αἰωρήμαϲι |, but do not divide at τεταμέναν |. All those which
divide at αἰωρήμαϲι | divide next at φερομέναν |, with the excep-
tion of Aa, which divides at χρυϲέαιϲι |. Those which do not di-
vide at αἰωρήμαϲι | divide both at τεταμέναν | and either (a) at
χρυϲέαιϲ(ι) | (CrGKPrRf(S)Sa)¹⁵ or (b) at φερομέναν | (FZbZc) or

¹⁴ -ιν only VXTᵗ³; Π¹³ has α[ι]ωρημ[.
¹⁵ χρυϲέαιϲ only CrZbTᵗ³ and ΣPi. Ol. 1. 91a.

138   COLOMETRY

(c) at πέτραν | and φερομέναν | ((Rw)ZmTTp), except that O has no division between οὐρανοῦ | and χρυϲέαιϲι |. If (as I assume) division at αἰωρήμαϲι(ν) | is the Alexandrian division, it is likely that the next division came at φερομέναν | (so all manuscripts, except those which divide at χρυϲέαιϲ(ι) |), which gives an iambic trimeter.[16]

At 989–90 the almost universal division is at ϲτόλωι | (except for Πέλοψ | MnS, τεθριππο|βάμονι Aa, no division CrG). Then MBO+ divide Πέλοψ ὅτε πελάγεϲι (-εϲϲι MBOP¹ᶜ) διε|δίφρευϲε Μυρτίλου φόνον |, the remainder at διεδίφρευϲε | (AaMnRwSSa ZbZuTp) or at πελάγεϲι | (VG; -εϲϲιν | T) or at ὅτε | (Cr) or not at all (OFPrRξ). Division at διε|δίφρευϲε is presumably the Alexandrian division.[17] This, with πελάγεϲϲι (MBOP¹ᶜ), gives an iambic dimeter. Editors have generally preferred an iambic trimeter (τεθριπποβάμονι . . . ὅτε), which is found uniquely in Cr. But such a trimeter would have one feature which is unwelcome, lack of caesura,[18] and another which is unbearable, *breuis in longo*.[19] We should perhaps accept πελάγεϲϲι.[20] This entails divided resolution (Πέλοψ ὅτ͡ε͡π͡έ |), but there are parallels enough for this (such as 1414 πέρι δὲ͜ γ͡ό͡ν͡υ͜ι͡χ͡έ|ρᾶϲ ἱκέϲι͡ουϲ).[21] Other possibilities exist, such as ὁπότε (V³ˢAa^rsL²MnS), adopted by West, and ὅτ'

---

[16] What is the right colometry after αἰωρήμαϲι(ν) remains doubtful. Willink suggests πέτραν ἀλύϲεϲι χρυϲέαιϲ | φερομέναν δίναιϲι, iambic dimeter and syncopated trochees (‿ ‑ ‑ · | ‑ · ‑ ‿). As an alternative I suggest | ‑(ϲι) φερομέναν δίναιϲ ‹ἀε›ί. The long anceps in the second iambic metron is no obstacle: see *Cycl.* 63, *Alc.* 227, 254, *Andr.* 297~†305†, *El.* 480, *Su.* 1156~1162, *Ion* 693~711, *Hel.* 171, 1108~1138, *Or.* 842, 1462, 1545, *Rh.* 702.

[17] The tendency of manuscripts is to eliminate division within a word, not to introduce it: see p. 147. For the overlap of more than one syllable see *Herc.* 1072–3, *Or.* 1498–9 (below, p. 147).

[18] In over 150 lyric iambic trimeters (including catalectic trimeters, but excluding those which, even though amid lyrics, are shown by their admission of Attic forms to be non-lyric) there are few certain or possible examples: *Hi.* 878, *Andr.* 291, *Su.* 615 (better divided θεοὶ | πάντων |), *El.* 1221, *Tr.* 1305~1320 (see the next note), *Hel.* 342, 368, *Or.* 966, *Ph.* 673 (text doubtful; avoidable by Porson's transposition of πάλιν, which is omitted by AtPRw), 1717 (whole passage spurious), *Ba.* 991 = 1011.

[19] A lyric iambic trimeter, unless it ends with sense-pause, may be expected to stand in synapheia with following iambics. Synapheia is demonstrable at *Su.* 923 (elision), *El.* 1183 (elision), *Herc.* 910 (resolved final syllable), *Tr.* 316 (πατρὶδα͡ τέ, with resolved final syllable, not πατρὶδα τέ, with *breuis in longo*). At *Tr.* 1305 ~1320 (which also lacks a caesura: see the previous note) the truth is still to seek (see T. C. W. Stinton, *JHS* 96 [1976] 127, ibid. 97 [1977] 149, M. L. West, *BICS* 31 [1984] 189–90). By contrast, the synapheia which editors present between 1489 and 1490 (iambic trimeter, ending in strong sense-pause, elided before dochmiacs) I judge to be impossible: see *CQ* n.s. 40 (1990) 122–3.

[20] For the epic form see *PCPS* n.s. 20 (1974) 22 n. 2, *Studies* 2, 97.

[21] See L. P. E. Parker, *CQ* n.s. 18 (1968) 245–9.

ἐ‹πὶ› (Burges), adopted by Willink, whose claim that a preposition is needed is answered by S. *Tr.* 114–15 (κύματα) εὑρεῖ πόντωι | βάντ' ἐπιόντα τ'.²² But the testimony of MBO for πελάγεccι should not be lightly discarded. At 1001–4 the majority conspire in this wrong division: ὅθεν ... ἀελίου | ... ἑcπέραν | ... προcαρμόcαc |. Only AaFSSa divide rightly at πτερωτόν |. This may be a lucky accident rather than preservation of a superior tradition, since none of these four divides where division ought next to occur, at ἄρμα |: AaFSa share the common division at ἑcπέραν |, and S divides at πρὸc |. One manuscript, however, surprises us with impeccable divisions: Cr gives two trochaic tetrameters by dividing only at ἄρμα | and προcαρμόcαc |. Rw also earns some credit: having divided wrongly at τε |, it next divides at ἄρμα | and (uniquely) at κέλευθον |.

(v) *1246–1310*

1249–50. The editor of Π⁹ assumes the division πότνια] | π[α]ρ[αμένει γὰρ, claiming that π is more likely than γ (the photograph in Plate VII allows no decision), and thereby rejecting the division πότνια παραμένει] | γ[ὰ]ρ. But only T divides at πότνια |. The remainder divide rightly at παραμένει | (MBO+) or wrongly at γὰρ | (V+). So I suspect that Π⁹ had the right division παραμένει] | γ[ὰ]ρ.

1269–70. The correct division at ἀμ|φὶ is preserved by MBOAJ KLΞZbZmZu. The remainder divide at προcέρχεται | (AdCrZc T) or τίc | (ZRfRw) or ὅδ' | (AtMn) or ἄρ' | (VaAaFGPrRSa) or ἀμφὶ | (CP).²³ The correct dochmiac division at ἀμ|φὶ (in MBO+) has survived even the intrusion of προcέρχεται. And this is a good indication that we must not simply delete προcέρχεται but must restore a dochmiac.

1302–10. Π⁹ is visible for only one line-end, and (if rightly deciphered) confirms the division at 1306 πλείcτουc |. The inherited divisions appear to be ὄλλυτε | (MBVa+) ... φάcγανα (πέμπετε) | (MBOVa+) ... ἱέμενοι | (MBVa+) ... πλείcτουc | (Π⁹?MBO+) ... Ἑλλάνων | (MBOVa+) ... ὀλομένουc |. These have been corrupted in a minority: AaAtFPrSaZbT divide at δίπτυχα | instead of at ὄλλυτε |; OGRw at τὰν | (the word is omitted by half

²² See also (for the locative dative in general) KG 1. 441–2, A.C. Moorhouse, *The Syntax of Sophocles* (1982) 86–7.
²³ I ignore S, which writes these lyrics as prose.

the manuscripts) instead of at ἱέμενοι |; VaAbMnRSXXaZcT at λιπόγαμον | instead of at πλείστουc |; AaAtFPrSa at ἔκανεν | instead of at Ἑλλάνων |; and AbMnR at δορὶ | instead of at Ἑλλάνων |.

In 1308–10 it is convenient to work backwards, since the majority agree in ending the ode with two dochmiacs (βέλεcιν ἀμφὶ τὰc Σκαμάνδρου δίναc | MBVa+). In 1308–9 there are three alternative readings: ἔπεcε and cυνέπεcε(ν) and cυνέπεcεν ἔπεcε. The manuscripts which end with two dochmiacs have the following divisions: ὅθι δάκρυα δάκρυcιν | ἔπεcε cιδαρέοιcι (MBVaK), ὅθι δά- κρυα δάκρυcι cυνέπεcε(ν) | cιδαρέοιcι | (Lξ), ὅθι δάκρυα δάκρυcι(ν) cυνέπεcε(ν) cιδαρέοιcι | (AdAtFGPrSa), ὅθι δάκρυα δάκρυcι cυνέπεcεν | ἔπεcε cιδαρέοιcι | (CRfZZu), ὅθι δάκρυα δάκρυcι cυν- έπεcεν ἔπεcε cιδαρέοιcι | (Zm). The remainder divide as follows: ὅθι . . . δάκρυcιν | ἔπεcε . . . δίναc | (AbS), ὅθι . . . δάκρυcιν | ἔπεcε . . . βέλεcιν | (Mn), ὅθι . . . cυνέπεcε | . . . δίναc | (RwZbTp), ὅθι . . .cυνέπεcε . . . βέλεcιν | (R), ὅθι . . . cυνέπεcε cιδαρέ|οιcι . . . δί- ναc | (Aa), ὅθι | . . . cυνέπεcεν | . . . βέλεcιν | (T), ὅθι . . . cυνέπεcεν | ἔπεcε . . . δίναc | (Cr), ὅθι . . . cυνέπεcεν ἔπεcε | . . . δίναc | (Zc), ὅθι . . . cυνέπεcον (sic) ἔπεcε . . . βέλεcιν | (O), ὅθι . . . cυνέπεcεν | ἔπεcε . . . βέλεcιν | (AMtP). Although text and colometry remain a matter for dispute in 1308–9, there should be no cause to doubt the two final dochmiacs (so, rightly, Willink, against West and others).

(vi) *1361–5*

Perhaps as a consequence of the corruption in all manuscripts of ἐc to εἰc no manuscript recognizes the dochmiac νέμεcιc ἐc Ἑλέναν. But Va and others at least offer διὰ . . . Ἑλέναν as a single colon. The remainder go astray by dividing at εἰc | Ἑλέναν (HMB ΛCKLMtZZcZm) or νέμεcιc | εἰc (OAdAtCrFPSTp) or ἔβα | θεῶν (T).

(vii) *1369–1502* (*Phrygian's Monody*)

1369–72. Π⁹ is present for 1370–1 and shares with the majority the divisions at εὐμαρίcιν | and τέραμνα |. VaFMnPrSSa divide at κεδρωτὰ | and VaFPr not again before τριγλύφουc, MnSa not again before τε |, and S divides at Δω|ρικάc.

1376–92. Π¹⁷ is present from ἢ (1376b) onwards. It offers several abnormal divisions, but none which are unique. I transcribe the passage, with a speculative reconstruction of the Alexandrian colometry, and then I append some comments in justification:[24]

1376a πᾶι φύγω ξέναι | [HMBO+]
1376b πολιὸν [PrSaZc] αἰθέρ' [FMnS] ἀμπτάμενος [Π¹⁷Va+]
ἢ |[HMBRw]
1377 πόντον [Tp] Ὠκεανὸς [MnPrSSaZbZc] ὂν | [HMBO+]
1378 ταυρόκρανος [Π¹⁷AaAbAtFZu] ἀγκάλαις |
[VaGRRfRwZcZmTp]
1379 ἑλίσσων [MnPrSSa] κυκλοῖ χθόνα | [Π¹⁷HMBOVa+]
1380 τί δ' ἔστιν Ἑλένης πρόσπολ' Ἰδαῖον κάρα |
[Π¹⁷HMBOVa+]
1381 Ἴλιον Ἴλιον ὤμοι μοι | [HMBOVa+]
1382a Φρύγιον [PrSa] ἄστυ [Π¹⁷CrMnSTp] καὶ |
1382b καλλίβωλον [HMBOVa+] Ἰ-|
1383a -δας [Ab] ὄρος ἱερὸν [Π¹⁷MnSTp] ὥς |
1383b σ' [PrSa] ὀλόμενον στένω | [Π¹⁷HMBOVa+]
1384 ἁρμάτειον [FMnSZu] ἁρμάτειον [PrSaT] μέλος |
[HMBVa+]
1385a βαρβάρωι [Aa] βοᾶι | [Π¹⁷HMBOVa+]
1385b διὰ τὸ τᾶς [PrSa] ὀρνιθόγονον [Cr] ὄμμα |
[Π¹⁷HMBO+]
1386a κυκνόπτερον | [MBOVa+]
1386b καλλοσύνας [Π¹⁷Cr] Λήδας | [HMRwZm]
1387a σκύμνον [AaGKξZcTp] Δυσελένας | [Π¹⁷²MBOVa+]
1387b Δυσελένας (om. Π¹⁷²+) [Π¹⁷²ZbZu] ξεστῶν | [HMBO+]
1388 περγάμων [Π¹⁷AaCrRf] ἀπολ-| [MBA(C)GKMt(S)ξ]
1389a -ωνίων [ZbZuTTp] Ἐρινύν |[Π¹⁷HVaAdFLPPrSaZZm]
1389b ὀττ(οτοτ)οτοῖ | [HMBO+]
1390 ἰαλέμων ἰαλέμων | [Π¹⁷MVaT]
1391 Δαρδανία [SaTp] τλᾶμον | [Π¹⁷HMBOVa+]
1392 Γανυμήδεος [T] ἱπποσύνα Διὸς εὐνέτα ||.

1376a. For the hypodochmiac see 1382b, 1385a, 1388.

1376b. We cannot be sure whether the Alexandrian divison was at ἀμπτάμενος | or at ἢ |, since both divisions give intelligible metre (the former ⏔ ⏑ – |⏑ – ⏑ ⏔, the latter ⏔ ⏑ – |⏑ – ⏔ ⏑ – or

---

[24] I print each dochmiac or hypodochmiac on a single line. Whether they were originally written singly or in pairs is of no consequence.

‿ ‿‿ ‿‿ ‿ | ‿‿ ‿ ‿). Division after the prepositive ἤ was perhaps more likely to be corrupted (see below on 1382a καὶ |).

1377. Division at ὅν | appears irresistible. It leaves straightforward cola to follow in 1378–9, and in 1377 it gives (‾) ‾ ‿ ‿ | ‿‿ ‿ ‾. The division of Π¹⁷ at ταυρόκρανος | yields a scarcely intelligible colon in 1377a.

1382–3. The divisions at καὶ | and Ἰ |δας have been universally corrupted but seem certain. Corruption was easy. The division of Π¹⁷ at ἄστυ | attests a reluctance to divide after prepositive καὶ (which, in fact, is omitted by all except Π¹⁷MO¹ˢAbMnRSZZc), and the well-nigh universal division at καλλίβωλον | attests a reluctance to divide in mid-word, one syllable later, at Ἰ |δας (Ab divides after Ἰδας). It is noteworthy that PrSa, whose divisions in this passage are often erratic, isolate 1383b as a single dochmiac.

1385b–6a. There is corruption at the beginning of 1385b, and this may be the cause of the surprising division (shared by Π¹⁷ with HMBO+) at ὄμμα |. We certainly expect ὄμμα κυκνόπτερον | to be a dochmiac; and so it may have been presented in the Alexandrian colometry. But at least the majority do divide correctly at κυκνόπτερον | and convict Π¹⁷ of error (its κυκνόπτερον καλλοσύνας | is not an acceptable colon in this context).

1386b–9a. Π¹⁷ begins a new line at ξεστῶν, but we do not know whether it had Δυσελένας once (like AbFGKMnPrRRwSSaξZv Tp) or twice. Neither Λήδας σκύμνον Δυσελένας | nor Λήδας σκύ-μνον Δυσελένας Δυσελένας | has any appeal (the former division is found in Cr, the latter nowhere). Π¹⁷ continues by offering an impeccable dochmiac ξεστῶν περγάμων | (of the other manuscripts which divide at περγάμων |, Aa offers Δυσελένας Δυσελένας ξεστῶν περγάμων |, CrRf offer Δυσελένας ξεστῶν περγάμων |), but we must reject it, for the division in mid-word at Ἀπολ |λωνίων (MBAGKMtξ, slightly corrupted by C to Ἀπολλω |νίων, by S to Ἀπο |λλωνίων) is presumably the ancient division. I have discussed elsewhere in greater detail the text and colometry of this passage.²⁵

1391. Division after the dochmiac is well-nigh universal and should be accepted.

1395–1402. The true colometry in 1395–9 is disputed. The inherited colometry appears to be: θανάτου | . . . αἰαῖ | . . . βασιλέων | . . . γᾶν | . . . Ἅιδα. But alternative divisions are at-

COLOMETRY 143

tested: at λέγουϲιν | (VaRwZu) and φωνᾶι | (AdCrGMnRfSSaZc ZvTTp). In 1400–2 the inherited colometry appears to be λέγω | ... διδύμω |. But MAb also divide at δόμουϲ |. MnPrRSSa divide at δόμουϲ | too, but then at "Ελλανεϲ | instead of at λέγω |.

1407–17. Π¹⁸ shares division at ἡϲύχου | with MBOCKMnPRf SZZvTp, while AMtPrT divide at προνοίαϲ |,²⁶ and HVa+ write 1407a–b (-ῶν) as one line. In 1408 Π¹⁸ shares the correct division at ἔϲω | with only AbPrRfSa. The remainder divide at μολόντεϲ | (HMBOVa+) or later (ἔγημ' | FZu, τοξόταϲ | Rw, Πάριϲ | R) or earlier and later (πρὸϲ | ... ἔγημ' | MnS). At 1409 Π¹⁸ shares with HMBOVa+ division at Πάριϲ | (but, of the four which shared with Π¹⁸ the correct division at ἔϲω |, Pr divides at τοξόταϲ |, Rf at γυ- ναικὸϲ |). If (as its editor thinks possible) Π¹⁸ began 1411 and 1412 with πεφυρμένοι and ἔζονθ', it divided 1410 and 1411 at δακρύοιϲ| and ταπεινοί |, as do the majority (some run them together as a single line, FPPrSa divide at πεφυρμένοι |, AdMn at ἔζονθ' |). Π¹⁸ fails us after the beginning of 1412.²⁷ Only Sa (which divided 1411 at πεφυρμένοι |) divides 1412–13 at δὲ |. The remainder divide at κεῖθεν | ἄλλοϲ (except for Mn, which divides at ἄλλοθεν |). In 1414 HMBOVa+ divide after the dimeter at ἱκεϲίουϲ |, while AaAtPRw Zu divide at χέραϲ | and PrRS at γόνυ |. HOVa and some others then write ἔβαλον ἔβαλον 'Ελέναϲ ἄμφω as a single colon.

1427–30. The inherited divisions are αὔραν αὔραν | ... κύκλωι | ... ἀίϲϲων | ... νόμοιϲιν |. But VaFRw divide at βόϲτρυχον | instead of at αὔραν |, H divides at 'Ελέναϲ | 'Ελέναϲ (and next at ἀίϲϲων |), PrSa at πτερίνωι |, and FPrRwSa at βαρβάροιϲ |.

1431–43. Π¹⁸ is present for these lines. It shows no significant divergences from the norm, and the ancient colometry can be established with tolerable certainty:

1431–2 ἁ δὲ [Aa] λίνον [AbMnRfZvTp] ἠλα[S]κάται [T] δακτύ-
λοιϲ [PrSa] ἕλιϲϲε | [Π¹⁸HMBOVa+]
1433 νῆμα [MnS] δ' ἵετο πέδωι | [Π¹⁸HMBOVa+]
1434 ϲκύλων [AbPrSa] Φρυγίων [Cr] ἐπὶ τύμβον [AtFLMnRRf
RwSZbZcZmZuZvT] ἀγάλ|[Π¹⁸HMBACGKMtPZ]
1435 -ματα [AaAbPrSaξTp] ϲυϲτολίϲαι [VaT] χρήιζουϲα
λίνωι | [Π¹⁸ HMBO+]

²⁶ Willink accepts this division: wrongly, for it gives period-end before the final iambic metron (T. C. W. Stinton, *BICS* 22 [1975] 93).
²⁷ For the text and colometry of 1408–13 see *CQ* n.s. 40 (1990) 113–4.

144 COLOMETRY

1436a φάρεα [Pr] πορ[S]φυρέα | [Π¹⁸MBVa+]
1436b δῶρα Κλυταιμνήcτραι | [Π¹⁸HMB+]
1437 προcεῖπε δ' [AaPrSa] 'Ορέcτac | [Π¹⁸MBOVa+]
1438–9 Λάκαιναν [Z] κόραν [AbCrMnRfSZvTp] ΐΩ Διὸc παῖ |
   [Π¹⁸HMBVa+]
1440 θὲc ἴχνοc πέδωι [AbZb] δεῦρ' [MnST] ἀπο[R]cτᾶca
   [RfZvTp] κλιcμοῦ | [Π¹⁸HMBOVa+]
1441 Πέλοποc ἐπὶ [Zb] προ[MnS]πάτοροc [RfZv] ἕδραν [RTp]
   παλαιᾶc | [Π¹⁸⁾HMBO+]
1442–3 ἑcτίαc [VaFRw] ἵν' [MnS] εἰδῆιc λόγουc ἐμούc ||.

1431. It is surprising that Π¹⁸HMBOVa and the majority write
1431–2 as a single colon; and that only T divides at ἠλακάται |.
The division at ἠλακάται | may be original.²⁸
1434. Once again, division in mid-word has caused confusion.
1437–40. The ancient colometry appears to have divided the
nine bacchiacs as 2+3+4, in accordance with the most natural
rhetorical divisions. It is noteworthy, but not surprising, that no
manuscript divides, where division would be rational, at ΐΩ |.
1441–3. In 1443 the editor of Π¹⁸ (Haslam) reads only εμο]υc at
the end. If this is right, ἑcτίαc stood at the beginning of this line,
as in the majority, and not at the end of the previous line, as in
VaFRw. I agree with Haslam that this may be right. The alternative is to mark παλαιᾶc ἑcτίαc as a separate colon, as no manuscript
does. I should certainly not divide, with Willink, παλαιᾶc ἑcτίαc
ἵν' εἰδῆιc | (again, no manuscript does this), for a reason given
above.²⁹

1444–6. The correct division at ἐφεί|πετ' is found in only AMt.
The majority (HMBOVa+) divide at ἐφείπε|τ' or -ετ' | or -ετο |
(I ignore the divisions of an erratic minority). But AMt disappoint
us by their failure to divide next at ἔμcλ|λειν. No manuscript has
this division. The great majority divide at ἔμελλε(ν) |. Thereafter
the majority divide at ἰών | (HMB+) or not until Φωκεύc |
(OVa+), while AaPrZTp divide at κακὸc | and T divides at
ἔπραc|c'.
1448–51. We can recover the ancient colometry with the help of
attested divisions in mid-word:

²⁸ For the text and colometry of 1431–2 see CQ n.s. 40 (1990) 114–5.
²⁹ See n. 26.

1448a ἐκλήιϲε δ' ἄλλον ἄλλοϲ' ἐν [Z] ϲτέγαιϲ | [HMBVa+]
1448b τοὺϲ μὲν [JMn] ἐν ϲταθ[S]μοῖ| [HᶜMBA(Mt)P]
1449–50a -c[Hᵘᵛ]ιν [AdCFRfξZZv] ἱππικοῖϲι [OVa+] τοὺϲ δ'
        [AaPrSa] ἐν ἐξέδραιϲι [CCrJLMnRfSZZmZvT]
        τοὺϲ δ' | [HMBAMtP]
1450b ἐκεῖ[G]c' [AtKZb] ἐκεῖθεν [VaAbAdFRwZcT] ἄλλον
        [AaPrSa] ἄλ| [HMBOP]
1451 -λο[L]ϲε [AMtCCrJRRfSZZmZuZvξTTp] διαρμόϲαϲ
        [Mn] ἀποπρὸ [Rw] δεϲποίναϲ ||.

At 1448a the agreement in division at ϲτέγαιϲ | is striking. And
yet I should be loth to father on to the Alexandrians a line of five
iambi. This division becomes rational if we read ἔκληιϲεν (Zd²ᵞᵖ,
already conjectured by Willink), which gives bacchius, cretic,
iambic metron. 1448b is a hypodochmiac (see on 1376a above), and
division in mid-word has led astray all but HMBAMtP, which next
divide at (the second) τοὺϲ δ' |, giving an iambic trimeter. This
may not be the best way to divide these lines, but at least it is a rational one, and I assume it to be ancient. HMBP continue with an
iambic dimeter ending in another mid-word division at ἄλ|λοϲε,
and here they are joined by O, while AMt share the common divi-
sion at ἄλλοϲε |. Division at ἄλ|λοϲε gives two final dochmiacs.
And this division is a clear indication that the words ἄλλον ἄλλοϲε
(suspected by Wecklein, deleted by Murray) stood in the Alexandrian text.

1453–72. The manuscripts[30] treat Ἰδαία μᾶτερ (μᾶτερ) ὀβρίμα
ὀβρίμα as a single line (except that T divides μᾶτερ | ὀβρίμα and
O has Ἰδαῖα μᾶτερ Ἰδαῖα | ὀβρίμα ὀβρίμα), and αἰαῖ is appended
to this line by HMBO+, prefixed to 1455 by Va+ (except that
FAtZb do not divide between 1454 and 1455).

In 1455–6 the manuscripts, for the most part, present us with
two alternative divisions: (a) . . . φονίων παθέων | ἀνόμων τε κακῶν
ἅπερ ἔδρακον | ἔδρακον ἐν δόμοιϲ τυράννων HMBACCrLMtPRf
ZZv (and OAbξZmTp, which do not divide at παθέων |); (b) . . .
φονίων παθέων ἀνόμων τε κακῶν | ἅπερ ἔδρακον ἔδρακον ἐν δόμοιϲ
τυράννων AaGKMnRwSZcZuT (T also divides ἔδρακον | ἐν). The
remainder (VaAtFRZb) divide at παθέων | only and so do not help
us at the crucial point—the choice between κακῶν | and ἔδρακον |.

---

[30] I ignore the vagaries of PrSa in this passage.

Although ἔδρακον ἐν δόμοιc τυράννων would be acceptable (as a trochaic dimeter), ἅπερ ἔδρακον is an impossible ending to the colon which precedes. We must accept the division at κακῶν |, and then either analyse 1456 as an enoplian (Willink) or follow T's further division and take ἅπερ ἔδρακον ἔδρακον as a dochmiac.

In 1457–60 the almost universal colometry is ἀμφιπορφυρέων . . . cκότου | . . . ἄλλοcε | . . . τύχοι | (but VaAtF divide only at cπάcαντεc | and τύχοι |) and then ὀρέcτεροι | . . . cταθέντεc |. In 1467–70 the almost universal colometry (I interpolate the variants) is . . . πλαγᾶι | φυγᾶι δὲ [Pr] ποδὶ [Aa] τὸ χρυcεοcάνδαλον [SaZT] ἴχνοc | ἔφερεν ἔφερεν [AaAtFPrT] ἐc κόμαc δὲ [Sa] δακτύλουc | δικὼν Ὀρέcταc [AaṚT] Μυκη[Pr]νίδ᾽ [Sa] ἀρβύλαν [VaAtFZ] προβάc |. 1471 is divided surprisingly by HMBAC at ἀριcτεροῖ-cιν |: perhaps intended to be a catalectic iambic dimeter and hypodochmiac. In 1472a–b the correct division ἔμελ|λεν is found in only HMBAMtP. CT divide at ἔμελλεν |, the rest write as a single verse.

1478–84. The manuscripts (with few exceptions) divide at ἀλί-αcτοc |. Then HMBOACPZT isolate οἷοc οἷοc Ἕκτωρ | as a separate colon (MnPrSa, which divided at ἦλθε |, also divide here), (Aa)AbCrGKZv divide οἷοc οἷοc Ἕκτωρ ὁ Φρύγιοc |, while the rest do not divide until Αἴαc |. Division at Πριαμίcι |, cυνήψα-μεν |, διαπρεπεῖc |, and ἀλκάν | is almost universal.

1491–1502. There are many uncertainties in this passage. But the inherited colometry emerges clearly enough:

1491a ἐπὶ φόνωι [Mn] χαμαιπετεῖ ματρὸc [AaAbAtCCrRfRw ZbZcZuZvT] ἄ | [HMBALMtZm]

1491b νιν [GKPPrRSSaZ] ἔτεκεν [Mn] τλάμων | [HMBOVa+]

1492 ἄθυρcοι δ᾽ οἷά [S] νιν [AaAbPrRSa] δραμόντε [AtGK] βάκχαι | [HMBOVa+]

1493 cκύμνον [AbRS] ἐν χεροῖν [AaF] ὀρείαν [GKPrSa] ξυν-ήρπαcαν |[HMBOVa+]

1494a πάλιν δὲ [AaAtSa] τὰν Διὸc [Pr] κόραν | [HMBO+]

1494b ἐπὶ cφαγὰν [S] ἔτεινον | [HMBOVa+]

1495 ἁ δ᾽ [Sa] ἐκ θαλάμων [AbAtPrR] ἐγέ[S]νετο δια[T]προ [AaSa] δωμάτων | [HMBOVa+]

1496 ἄφαντοc [MnST] ὦ [Pr] Ζεῦ καὶ γᾶ [At] καὶ φῶc [Sa] καὶ νὺξ | [HMBVa+]

1497a ἤτοι φαρμάκοισιν | [HMBO+]
1497b ἢ μάγων τέχναις [VaAbLMnPrRSZvT] ἢ θεῶν [Sa]
       κλοπαῖς | [HMBO+]
1498   τὰ δ' ὕστερ' [S] οὐκέτ' οἶδα [VaAbLMnPrRSaZT]
       δραπέτην γὰρ [OAaCCrGKRfZcZmZuZvTp] ἐ||[HM
       BALMt PRwξ]
1499   -ξέ[SZ]κλεπτον [AtF] ἐκ δόμων [PrSa] πόδα | [HMBO
       Va+]
1500   πολύ [S]πονα δὲ [Aa] πολύπονα πάθεα | [HMBVa+]
1501a Μενέλαος [AaAd] ἀνασχόμενος | [HMBO+]
1501b ἀνό[GK]νητον ἀπὸ [AbR] Τροίας | [MBVa+]
1502   ἔλαβε [LRwZmZu] τὸν Ἑλένας γάμον ||.

I assume that the division in 1498 at ἐ|ξέκλεπτον is ancient.[31]
And I draw attention to the division of GK in 1501b at ἀνό |νητον.
What are the correct text and division of these final lines is uncertain. But K was found to have inherited uniquely a division in midword at 204.

I have assumed that correct division in mid-word is evidence of fidelity to the ancient colometry. It will be useful to review the instances which have been found, so that we can see the relative fidelity of our manuscripts in preserving these divisions: 204 γό|οισι Π⁵K; 325 ἐκ|λαθέσθαι Π⁷HMOVACrFGKPPrRSa ξZcT (ἐκλε|λαθέσθαι Ab, ἐκλα|θέσθαι BS); 326 φοιτα|λέου Π⁷HM BOVACGKξZc; 990 διε|δίφρευσε MBOAAtCKLPRfZZcZm; 1269 ἀμ|φὶ MBOAKLξZbZmZu; 1388 ἀπολ|λωνίων MBAGK Mtξ (ἀπολλω|νίων C, ἀπο|λλωνίων S); 1434 ἀγάλ|ματα Π¹⁸HMB ACGKMtPZ; 1445 ἐφεί|πετ' AMt; 1448b σταθμοῖ|σιν HMBAP (σταθμοῖσιν|σιν Mt, σταθ|μοῖσιν S); 1450b ἄλ|λοσε HMBOP (ἄλλο|σε L); 1472 ἔμελ|λεν HMBAMtP; 1498 ἐ|ξέκλεπτον HMB ALMtPRwξ (ἐξέ|κλεπτον SZ).

Here are the totals for each manuscript out of a possible maximum of 12 (9 for H), with additional near misses indicated after a plus sign. Ahead of the field come H (7), M (10), B (9 + 1), A (10). Next in order come K (7), P (7), O (5), ξ (5), G (4), C (3 + 1), L (3 + 1), S (0 + 4), Zc (3), Z (2 + 1), V (2), Zm (2). The rest score only one or none. Several performances are noteworthy. A scores as highly as HMB, while O falls short of these (but O tends to com-

---

[31] For the overlap see p. 138 n. 17.

bine two cola into one), and V/Va score very low. K and P and ξ emerge with credit. S (whose divisions are often erratic or non-existent) has a propensity for near-misses; but its usual partner Mn fails to score at all.

I now list a series of agreements in wrong division. For the most part our manuscripts show affiliations in colometry which match their textual affiliations.[32]

I begin with Θ:

MnS and (in the later part of the play, where they are twins) PrSa are commonly isolated in wrong colometry, and I need not cite examples. There are fewer examples of AbR and FSa isolated: 808 ἑλλάδα | AbR (et ZmTp); 817–19 αἵματος | . . . καλόν | FSa; 831 τίνα | FSa; 986 γενετόρας | FSa (et T); 1501 ἀπὸ | AbR. Other combinations of members of Θ: 839 ματρὸς | FMnSSa; 971 οἴχεται | MnSSa; 1306 δορὶ | AbMnR; 1372 τε | MnSa; 1376 αἰθέρ' | FMnS; 1379 ἑλίσσων | MnPrSSa; 1396 βάρβαροι | FPr; 1400 ἕλλανες | MnPrRSSa; 1414 γόνυ | PrRS; 1418 πεςὼν | PrS Sa; 1423 τὴν | PrSSa; 1432 δακτύλοις | PrRSa; 1434 cκύλων | Ab PrSa; 1459 γυναικὸς | AbPrSa; 1477 ξίφος | MnPrSSa; 1478 ἦλθε | MnPrSa; 1493 cκύμνον | AbRS.

Aa is often associated with members of Θ: 837 δινεύων | AaF Sa; 1001 πτερωτὸν | AaFSSa; 1410 ὄμμα | AaMnS; 1437 δ' | Aa PrSa; 1447 ξίφη | AaR; 1459 ἀντίοι | AaMnS (et Tp); 1463 κασιγνήτου | AaMn (et Tp); 1482 δ' | AaPrSa; 1488 δ' | AaMn; 1492 νιν | AaAbPrRSa; 1493 χεροῖν | AaF; 1495 διαπρὸ | AaSa.

Rf and Rw are closely associated with each other and with Aa: 201 βίου | AaRw; 343 πόνων | AaRf; 841 cφάγιον | AaRw; 1269 τίc | RfRwZ; 1285–6 cφάγια . . . εἰcακούουcιν | . . . κακῶν | RfRw (et Tp). And RfRw are commonly associated with Θ: 821 χρόα | AbFRwSa; 828 ματέρα | AaFPrRfSa; 831 δάκρυα | AaAbMnPrR RfS; 974 θεόθεν | MnPrRfS; 999 ἐγένετο | FMnRf; 1008 ἐπ-ώνυμα | MnRwSSa; 1408 ἔcω | Π[18]AbPrRfSa; 1409 τοξότης | PrRw; 1430 βαρβάροις | FPrRwSa; 1431 λίνον | AbMnRf (et ZvTp); 1438 κόραν | AbCrMnRfS (et ZvTp).

Cr has scarcely any unique agreements with members of Θ (1005 τε | CrMnS; 1490 ἔμολε | CrS; note also 1382a ἄcτυ | Π[17]CrMnSTp), but it sometimes joins company with Rf and Rw: 164 λοξίας | CrRw; 191 ἀπόφονον | CrRw; 349 ἕτερον | CrRfRw;

1002 ἅρμα | CrRw; 1388 περγάμων | Π¹⁷AaCrRf. Cr shows slight traces of a link with O: 181–2 cῖγα | cῖγα plurimi, no division OCr; 185 ἥcυχον | OAaCr; 195 μᾶτερ | OCr (et Rw(S)Zu); 205 ἄτε- κνοc | OCr.

V (Va) is the *uetus* most commonly found in agreement with Θ and associates: 815 τεκέων | VAbCrFMnRwSSa (et AAt); 1011 γενέτην | VMnRS (et T); 1364 πάριν | VaFMnPrSa (et ZbZu); 1371 κεδρωτὰ | VaFMnPrSSa; 1442 ἑcτίαc | VaFRw; 1447 cπάcαντεc | VaF (et At); 1470 ἀρβύλαν | VaF (et AtZ); 1489 ἔπιπ- τον | VaCrMnPrSSa (et AtZb); 1490 ἑρμιόνα | VaAa. GK are isolated at: 1467 κρᾶτα |, 1481 εἶδον | ἐν, 1482 φαc- γάνων |, 1483 δὴ |, 1501 ἀνό|νητον. They conspire with Θ and associates at: 196 τεκομένα | VAbGK; 983 χρυcέαιcι | AaCrGK PrRfSa (et O); 1269 ἄρ’ | VaAaFGPrRSa; 1444 νιν | AaGPrS; 1455 κακῶν | AaGKMnRwS (et ZcZuT); 1467 ἐμβαλοῦca | FGK (et AtZb); 1480 φρύγιοc | AaAbCrGK (et Zv); 1485 ἥccονεc | GKPr; 1493 ὀρείαν | GKPrSa.

ξ is almost never isolated and rarely agrees with a minority: 195 με | MnRSaξ; 204 μέροc | CRfξZu; 321 αἴτε | AbMnRSaξZTp; 974 εἷλε | Crξ; 1387 cκύμνον | AaGKξZcTp.

No member of ζ is linked to another member by any pattern of shared colometry. Members of ζ occasionally agree with members of Θ and associates: 149 ἀπόδοc | OAaCrRwSaZb; 986 ἐμέθεν | MnSZ; 997 ποιμνίοιcι | FRwSaZb; 1255 cταθεὶc | AdMnRfRw Zc; 1285 cφάγια . . . κακῶν | VaCrZm; 1366 γὰρ | PrSaZbZu; 1377 ταυρόκρανοc | Π¹⁷AaAbAtFZu; 1384 ἁρμάτειον | ἁρμάτειον FMnSZu; 1408 ἔγημ’ | FMnSZu; 1416 δὲ | MnZu; 1417 ἀμ- φίπολοι | FPrZu; 1440 πέδωι | AbZb; 1688 ἔcται | FJMnSaZ Zb; 1692 βίοτον | FJSaZZc.

Zv is closely linked with Rf: 1410 γυναικὸc | RfZcZv; 1441 προπάτοροc | RfZv; 1447 δ’ | RfZv; 1526 (this and the following passages are trochaic tetrameters) μῶροc | RfZv; 1533–5 δώμαcι | . . . διώκων | . . . ἐμήν | RfZv; 1547 τιc | RfZv; 1551–3 cυμπε- ραίνοντεc | . . . ἀτρεῖδαι | . . . πράccοντac | RfZv.

Ad rarely diverges from ξ: 1269 προcέρχεται | AdCrZcT (ἀμ|φὶ ξ); 1397 φωνᾶι | AdCrGMnRfSSaZcZvTTp (βαcιλέων | ξ); 1412 ἔζονθ’ | AdMn (ταπεινοὶ | ξ); 1416 δρομάδεc | AdSSa (ἔθορον ἔθορον | ξ); 1450b ἐκεῖθεν | AdVaAbFRwZcT (ἄλλοcε | ξ); 1501 μενέλαοc | AdAa (ἀναcχόμενοc | ξ).

At agrees with ξ in the early part of the play. Thereafter it commonly shares unique colometry with members of Θ and associates: 808 φρονοῦϲ' | AtFSa; 814 οἰκτρότατα | AtMnS; 839 μέλεοϲ | At AaCrRw; 1269 ὅδ' | AtMn; 1285–6 ϲφάγια | … (κακῶν) | AtAaF PrSa (κακῶν om. AtFPrSa); 1305 ἔκανεν | AtAaFPrSa; 1447 ϲπάϲαντεϲ | AtVaF; 1468 ἔφερεν ἔφερεν | AtAaFPr (et T); 1483 τότε δὴ τότε | AtAa; 1487 τραῦμα | AtPr; 1494 πάλιν δὲ πάλιν | AtAa; 1494 θαλάμων | AtAbPrR; 1498 ἐξέκλεπτον | AtF; 1633 τιμῶντεϲ | AtCrPrRfS. It also has two agreements with GK: 1449 ἐκεῖϲ' | (etiam Zb); 1492 δραμόντεϲ |.
For the colometry of Tp see pp. 105–7.

Does the evidence of colon-division shed light on the question whether our manuscripts are derived from a single ancestor of late antiquity or from more than one? The question has been addressed by Barrett and Mastronarde, and they have given different answers. Barrett has argued that our manuscripts are derived from a single ancestor, transcribed from majuscule into minuscule perhaps in the ninth century, and has attributed the variations in colon-division in the manuscripts of *Hippolytus* to a combination of corruption and deliberate adjustment. Mastronarde has argued that on occasion the manuscripts of *Phoenissae* offer more than one pattern of inherited colometry and that these are more likely to be derived from transcriptions of more than one majuscule ancestor. A telling piece of evidence is *Ph.* 182, where two papyri are available and their different divisions are reflected in the medieval manuscripts. I believe that there exists enough evidence in the colometry of the manuscripts of *Orestes* to support the belief that more than one majuscule ancestor survived into late antiquity.

In one place a single manuscript agrees with an early papyrus in what I have argued must be the Alexandrian colometry (204 γό|οιϲ(ι) Π⁵K). In another place a handful of manuscripts agrees in truth with a papyrus (1408 ἔϲω | Π¹⁸AbPrRfSa). In a few places the truth is preserved in only a handful of manuscripts, and those not the earliest (167 τάλαινα | MnRRfSaξT, 815 τεκέων | VAbAt FMnRwSSa, 1001 πτερωτὸν | AaFSSa). In several places a papyrus agrees in error with a handful of manuscripts (321 αἴτε | Π⁷ AbMnRSaξZTp, 814 θοινάματα | Π⁹CCr, 1378 ταυρόκρανοϲ |

Π¹⁷AaAbAtFZu, 1382a ἄcτυ | Π¹⁷CrMnSTp, 1383a ἱερὸν | Π¹⁷
MnSTp, 1386b καλλοcύναc | Π¹⁷CrTp, 1388 περγάμων | Π¹⁷Aa
CrRf). These agreements are not all of equal value. One might argue
that some, at least, of the agreements in error are such as might
have arisen independently in papyrus and manuscripts. One might
also attribute to chance the agreement in truth of papyrus and
manuscripts at 1408 ἔcω |. But no such explanation will serve for
204 γό|οιc(ι) Π⁵K. If we assume that our manuscripts are derived
from a single ancestor, that ancestor must have had γό|οιc(ι).
There are some of our manuscripts (above all S) in which the mid-
word division γό|οιc(ι) could be accidental. But the behaviour of
K rules out this possibility. If, then, we insist on the hypothesis of
a single transcription, we must assume that K is derived from a
very early copy of it, before its other descendants began to corrupt
the inherited reading. Such an assumption is tenable. But it is not
preferable to the assumption that K is derived from a different majuscule ancestor, which preserved the inherited colometry. And if
other correct colon-divisions exist (as they do) which, even if they
do not positively demand the assumption of a second ancestor, are
at least as naturally explained by such an assumption, we may wonder whether to insist on a single ancestor is not to sharpen Occam's
razor unnecessarily fine. It is perhaps no coincidence that all of the
divisions listed above (with the exception of γό|οιc(ι)) are found in
manuscripts which belong to or are associated with the class which
I call Θ. We have seen that Θ and its associates (which include V)
preserve good readings unknown to our older manuscripts. I assume that these derive from an ancestor which was not the ancestor
of MBO. We might, indeed, fall back on the assumption that this
ancestor was transcribed from the same majuscule ancestor as
MBO and the other manuscripts, and merely took a selection of
readings from the second majuscule source. But in such an assumption I see no advantage.

CHAPTER XVII

Conjectures in the Medieval Tradition

Mastronarde (50–61) has assembled an impressive list of readings in *Phoenissae*, outside of ξ and T, which he believes afford evidence of deliberate emendation. He finds such evidence even in the *ueteres* HMBOV. In addition, he has shown (61–5) that many adjustments in the text have been inspired by the application or misunderstanding of comments in the scholia.

It is often difficult to decide what is a deliberate emendation. Many adjustments may arise from a process of unconscious, as well as of conscious, thought. In the following lists I include only such adjustments as may be claimed with any plausibility to be deliberate responses to problems real or imagined. An asterisk indicates that the emendation is right or possibly right.

(i) *Emendation in HMBOV*

13 τ' post πόλεμον add. V¹ᶜSaζTᶻ (~T¹³). The addition was prompted by a misunderstanding of the construction, for which the scholia are evidence (97. 19–20 Schwartz πόλεμον καὶ ἔριν).

79* δ' om. B¹ᶜRw (coni. Porson). Prompted by the scholia (διὰ μέcου γὰρ (τὸ) ὅπωc ἔπλευcα [ita fere MBCCrRwSa, ὅπωc δ' V]), which either reflect a text without δ' or wilfully ignore it.

188 ἄλλο MBV+: ἄλλο γ' B¹/²ʸᵖO+: ἄλλο γ' εἶπαc H+. In B¹/²ʸᵖO+ γ' was added to eliminate hiatus and so may be termed a deliberate emendation. The addition of εἶπαc in H+ and similar additions in other manuscripts (εἴπω G(K), εἴποιc F, εἶπον S, εἴπηc R¹ˢ, εἶπεc Gʳˢ) is not so much conjecture as clarification; but, at all events, it is evidence of deliberate interference at an early date.

478 τὸ (alterum) om. BCrFSa. Perhaps a metrical adjustment, proceeding from failure to recognize the synecphonesis μὴ εἰδέναι (only LP have μὴ 'δέναι).

506 μητέρ' ἐγένετο Porson: ἐγένετο μητέρα MBOV+: γένετο μ- VJKZm, 'γένετο μ- P. Apparently a metrical adjustment, although γένετο for ἐγένετο reappears as a simple corruption at 493 (MBVA+) and 884 (A).

779 ἐcτι cωθῆναι κακῶν] ἐcτιν ἐκβῆναι κακῶν VCr. A banalization, affording a more obvious construction for the genitive. It is doubtful whether we should call this deliberate emendation.

1020 c' ἰδοῦc' ἐν Porson: ἰδοῦcά c' ἐν MBO+: ἰδοῦc' ἐν A+: ἰδοῦcά c' M¹ʸᵖB¹ʸᵖV+. The latter (like the reading of A+) could be a metrical adjustment, even though we may be surprised that the fifth foot anapaest should have caused offence.

1507* προcπίπτων] προcπιτνῶν OGJKZvT^t3, προcπεcών ξ. The latter is certainly conjectural; the former may be, but could equally be inherited truth.[1]

(ii) Emendation in later manuscripts (excluding ξ and T)

20* Μενέλεωc] μενέλαοc JKLP. Inherited truth is less likely than emendation. The same change was made by L, again apparently for metrical reasons, at 18 (Μενέλαοc ἐκ Κρήccηc τε μητρὸc Ἀερόπηc).[2]

82 γόνον] δόμον K²ʸᵖ (coni. Kirchhoff). Cf. 179 δόμον] γόνον ʸᵖV³Ab¹CrMnPrR¹SSa, 326 γόνον] δόμον <M>ZZa¹ʸᵖ (~M¹ᶜZʳʸᵖ Za), 1038 γόνον] δόμον Cr et ʸᵖΣᵐᵇᵛᶜ.

101 τοὺc post εἰc add. K. Prompted by the omission of δὴ in K+.

103 τ'] τῶ(ι)δ' RwᵘᵛZZcZmZu<Tᶻ?> (~Tᵗⁱ), τῶδε τ' Rwᶜᵘᵛ. Conceivably prompted by the scholia (108. 21 Schwartz πλεονάζει δὲ τὸ τέ).

111 τὴν ante θυγατέρ' add. G². Prompted by the omission of γε in G+.

118* τε] γε ZbZcTᶜ (coni. Benedict); om. Ms. If γε is an emendation prompted by the scholia (109. 18 Schwartz περιττὸc ὁ τέ· βούλεται δὲ λέγειν φόβωι ταρβοῦca), it is an admirable one (see Willink).[3] But it may be an accidental change.

231 ἀνακύκλει] κἀνακύκλει PZb³Zc<T'ᶻ> (~Tᵗⁱ/²) (καὶ Z²ˢ). This is only one of many instances which might be quoted of a copula interpolated to eliminate asyndeton. Emendation is not the right word for this activity.

249 τὸν om. MnSSa. Prompted by the scholia (124. 1 Schwartz περιccὸν δὲ τὸ ἄρθρον).[4]

---

[1] See p. 61. [2] Cf. J. Jackson, Marginalia Scaenica 64–5.
[3] See also above, p. 87. [4] See Mastronarde 62.

258 ἐν om. G. Prompted by the corruption of ἀτρέμα to -μας.⁵
266* οἳ (uel οἶ) ἐγώ] οἱ 'γὼ LPZmᶜ. Similarly 1018 (P), 1020
(PR), 1347 (P), *Ph.* 1274 (GᶜPVr).⁶
286 ἐπάρας] ἐπ' ἄρας V²ᐟ³AaR²ʸᵖ. A subtler way of introducing
a preposition than those devised by ξ and ζ.⁷
294 ἀνακάλυπτ' ὦ] ἀνακαλύπτου B²Tᵗ¹ᐟ², ἀνακάλυπτ' ὄμμ' ὦ F²
Rw (ὄμμα V³ᵍˡAaʳ). The change to the middle and the interpolation
of ὄμμ' were prompted by disquiet (Σᵐᵇᵛᶜ 128. 12–14 Schwartz)
over the reflexive use of ἀνακάλυπτε (disquiet which is consequent
on the corruption of κασιγνήτη to κασίγνητον).
303 τῷ ante χροΐ add. SXe (ˢAa³ᵍˡ). Possibly a metrical conjecture; but it may be simply the intrusion of a gloss-article.
348 καὶ μὴν βασιλεὺς ὧδε (ὅδε BOV+) δὴ στείχει ‹ποδί›. The
addition of ποδί (AdC²PXeZcZmZu) makes an iambic trimeter, if
we scan βασιλεύς.
398 μάλιστά γ'] γάρ ἐστιν Cʸᵖ. A banalization, perhaps proceeding from a scholiastic paraphrase explaining the ellipse of the
verb.
410 δ' ἀποτρέπου λέγειν] δὲ λέγειν ἀποτρέπου L. Although L
does have changes of word-order which are accidental rather than
deliberate (112 πάρος δόμων, 669 Ἕλλησι πᾶσι δάμαρτα, 865 συμφορὰς ἀδελφῷ, 1504 ἐκ προδωμάτων εἰσορῶ), this may be a deliberate attempt to restore metre, following the (widespread)
corruption of εὐπαίδευτα to ἀπαίδευτα (σεμναῖ γάρ ἄπαι|δεῦτά δὲ
λέγειν|ἀποτρέπου).
423 μητέρος] μρ̄ϲ AaAtFPrSaZZu, μρ̄ϲ αἱ P (μητρὸς αἱ Σᵛ 144.
19 Schwartz). The abbreviation was taken for μητρὸς.
479 ὡς ante δράκων add. Rw: cf. Σᵐᵇᵛᶜ λείπει δὲ τὸ ὡς, ἵν' ἦι·
ὡς δράκων.
491 οὐ ante σοφίας add. ‹Z›ZaZbZc²ZmᵗʸᵖTᶻ (~Zᶜ) et Xa²ˢ, ii
litt. spat. uac. P. The interpolation was perhaps prompted by
recognition of defective metre. The tenor of the scholia may have
suggested the choice of supplement.⁸
508 τόνδ'] τιν' Zu: cf. Σᵐᵇᶜ ἀντὶ τοῦ εἴ τινα.
537 Σπαρτιάτιδος] σπαρτιάδος AtCLRZcZu, τῆς σπαρτιάδος G.
549 λόγου] λέγειν AaᶜJMs: cf. Σᵐ ἀντὶ τοῦ· ἐξίστησι τοῦ λέγειν;
[Aa].

---

⁵ See p. 100.   ⁶ See Mastronarde 60.
⁷ See pp. 55 and 84.   ⁸ See p. 85.

156   CONJECTURES IN THE MEDIEVAL TRADITION

566* ἥξουcι] - cιν L⟨Tᶻ⟩ (~Tᶜ).

622 δὴ post τάδε add. G¹ˢ. Prompted by the omission of δὲ in AG.

686 θνῄcκοντα καὶ κτείνοντα τοὺc ἐναντίουc] κτείνοντα καὶ θνήcκοντα τοὺc ἐναντίουc CrF, κτείνοντα τοὺc ἐναντίουc καὶ θνήcκοντα Sa. One could hardly hope for clearer evidence of the influence of the scholia: ΣMBCPr (168. 15 Schwartz) ἀναcτρεπτέον· ἔcτι γὰρ κτ- τοὺc ἐν- καὶ θν-, ΣMnS πρωθύcτερον· πρῶτον γὰρ ἔδει εἰπεῖν κτείνοντα.

694 μὲν γὰρ] μὲν AAtXb¹ᶜ, γὰρ CrKSSagE. Two different remedies for the metrical fault.

861 ἀτὰρ τίc ἀγών (ἀγών Porson)· τίνεc ἐν Ἀργείοιc (M+: ἀργείοιc V+: ἐν ἀργείων ⟨B²⟩O: ἀργείων Bᶜ+) λόγοι] ἀτὰρ τίνεc λόγοι· τίc ἀργείων ἀγών K.

933 Δαναΐδαι] δαναΐδαι δὲ GKTᵗ¹/², δαναῖδαι XXaᶜ²Xb, δαναοίδε PrRf, δαναοὶ δὲ AaAtCrFPSaZbZm. The first of these is a metrical conjecture, and so probably are the others (δᾶν-).

960 αἷ αἷ ante κατάρχομαι An²J²MnPrRRfSSa¹ˢZm¹ˢ (post πελαcγία An⟨Cr²⟩). Prompted by Hec. 685 αἰαῖ, κατάρχομαι?

960* cτεναγμῶν] -μὸν ⟨K²⟩Pr¹ˢTᵗ3 (~K¹ᶜ). Presumably conjectural rather than inherited.

1005 δρόμημα (uel δράμημα) πλειάδοc BOVRw+: δρομήματα (uel δραμήματα) πλειάδοc M+: δρόμημα πελειάδοc KRw¹ᶜᵘᵛ. The latter is presumably conjectural.

1047* με τήξειc] μ' ἔτηξαc Zd¹ᶜ (coni. Bothe), με τήξαc ZdZu. Perhaps prompted by the gloss ἐξέτηξαc (ᵍˡV³AaʳMnZdZu).

1092 γ' post λέχοc add. K. Porson (following King) attributes the same interpolation to Arundel 522, which in fact has τὸ λέχοc, like Tᵗ3Ta.[9]

1125 τοῖcιδ' (τοῖcι(ν) A+, δ' FSa) ἔξομεν] τοῖcδ' ἔξοθεν Cr, τοῖcδ' ἐφέξομεν LXe. The latter appears to be a metrical emendation based on the corruption (in Cr) τοῖcδ'.

1169* ἔcχεν ὄν] ἔcχ' ὄν GK¹ᶜ (coni. Barnes), ἔcχεν RfRw (~Rf¹ˢRw²) (coni. Porson). The former will be conjectural, the latter could be a slip.

1235* μητέρα] μητέρ' VaGKZTᵗ3.

1236 ἐπεβούλευca] ἐβούλευca Cr, ἐπεκέλευca BVaAaAt, cυν-

[9] Arundel 522 is either a copy of Ta (Turyn 196; cf. Matthiessen 22 n. 17a) or a copy of a copy of T (Mastronarde, *GRBS* 26 [1985] 104–6).

ἐβούλευσα Aaʳˢ (coni. Kirchhoff). The latter is probably a metrical conjecture.

1238* οὐκοῦν] οὔκουν Prᶜ (coni. Brunck).

1323 μοι] με B³ˢAtJRfRw²ξZcZm¹ˢT't3 (~T'³ˢ). The accusative gives the more obvious construction (for the dative see KG 1. 443).

1380* ἔcθ' uel ἔcτ'] ἔcτιν (Π¹⁷)GKMtˢξᵍˡT't3. Probably conjectural in all but Π¹⁷.

1473* δῆτ'] δ' ἦτ'AtF²Rf⟨Rw²⟩ (~Rw²) (coni. Bothe). An excellent conjecture, if conjecture it is.

1607 οὔκουν uel οὐκοῦν uel οὐκ οὖν] οὐκ εἰ Pr (~Prᵞᵖ). The invention of a reader who was dissatisfied with the elliptical οὔκουν cύ γ'.

1648 ἐνθένδε δ' ἐλθών. Despite the reports (or the implications) of editors, no manuscript has this reading. The majority has ἔνθεν δε τ' ἐλθών, variously divided and accented. Possibly ἔνθεν δέ γ' (AAtCrGKMtSaZdᵞᵖ), ἐνθένδε γ' (C), ἐνθενδέ γ' (Zc) are conjectures, prompted by dislike of δέ τ'. But equally γ' for τ' could be a simple error. However, ἔνθεν δ' εἰcελθών (Rf¹ˢ) looks like a deliberate conjecture.

1677* καὶ ὁ] χ' ὦ GPrZTᶜ (~Prᵞᵖ), χ' ὁ Va.

While little evidence has emerged of deliberate emendation in HMBOV, there is substantial evidence of conjectural activity in the later manuscripts. The most striking instances are in the related manuscripts G and K, which show a remarkable attention to metre (G 111, 258, 537, 622; K 20, 101, 694, 861, 960, 1005, 1092, 1677; GK 933, 1169, 1235, 1380).[10] And these instances must caution us against too ready acceptance of the assumption (of Turyn) that, whenever G and/or K share metrical adjustments with ξ, these adjustments originated in the source of ξ (i.e. Moschopoulos, according to Turyn) and passed from that source into GK (such shared adjustments are hyp. 2.18, 439, 523, 594, 753, 782, 791, 798, 1094, 1607, 1609, 1622).[11] The attention to metre of GK is attested not only in readings which are conjectural but also in readings where GK side not with ξ but with a minority of other manuscripts in preserving the truth when the majority has destroyed the metre by a trivial slip. Here the distinction between inheritance of the truth and its restoration by conjecture is often impossible to make.

---

[10] G shows the same metrical expertise in *Phoenissae* (Mastronarde 57); K does not have that play.   [11] See pp. 53–6.

I list some of the more significant instances: 54 Ναύπλιον] ναυπλίειον GK² (et VACL¹ᶜRyξZ'ʸᵖZb²ʸᵖZm¹ʸᵖTᶜ), ναυπλ*ειον K,
ναύπλειον O; 81 γε καὶ] γε GK (et OVLPRfRyξZZcTᶻ); 235
ὑγείας] ὑγιείας GK (et BOVCrRyξZcTᶻᶜ); 515 ὡσίουν] ὁσιοῦν K
(et MS, ~M²), ὁσίουν ‹B›VC (~B²ᐟ³V²); 761 ἄστεος] ἄστεως GK
(et Π¹⁰Aa³L); 897 πόλεως] πόλεος GK (et HᶜMBATᵗ¹ᐟ², ~B²ᐟ³);
1507 προσπίπτων] -πιτνῶν GK (et OZvTᵗ³), -πεσών ξ.
Other manuscripts which are roughly contemporary with K and
Moschopoulos also show some awareness of metre (A 694; F 933;
Pr 933, 960, 1677; Rw 1005; Sa 694, 933). In later manuscripts
metrical awareness is shown by Aa (933, 1236), Cr (694, 933), L
(20, 266, 410, 566, 1125), P (20, 266, 348, 423, 933, 1018, 1020,
1347), R (1020), and S (303, 694). Conjectures which are prompted
by considerations other than metre are found, certainly or probably, in Cr (686), F (294, 686, 1473), K (82), Pr (1238, 1607), Rf
(1473, 1648), Rw (103, 294, 1473), and Sa (686).

CHAPTER XVIII

Truth Preserved in a Minority

I offer first a list (i) of 61 readings which I believe to be both right and inherited and whose preservation hangs by a slender thread—because they are attested by a single manuscript or by a handful of manuscripts or only as a variant.[1] Only a very few of these have any likelihood of being conjectural, or lucky slips, rather than inherited, or false rather than true. I then offer a list (ii) of 41 further readings which are also weakly preserved. I have included in this list readings which are either certainly or possibly true and which may be, but are not certainly, inherited rather than conjectural. For HMBOV I quote readings not only by the first hand but also by any correcting hands. For the later manuscripts I generally quote readings only by the first hand (including corrections and variants written by the first hand or the rubricator), but if there is doubt whether or not a correction or variant is by the first hand (the doubt arises particularly in the case of manuscripts which I have not inspected personally) I treat it as if it were.[2] I ignore MtRyZvTp and the gnomologies.

There follows a histogram (Figure 3) which shows the relative frequency with which the manuscripts preserve these 102 readings. The shaded part of each column shows the totals for list (i), and the unshaded part adds the totals for list (ii).

M emerges with greatest credit. Next come B and C, followed by O and V and A. The readings in list (ii) have boosted the totals of AdXXaXb up to the level of V and A. GK and MnS emerge with credit. T^t also scores highly. P emerges with more credit than L.

(i)

hyp. 1.5 τί δεῖ AaAbG^{1s}MnRSSa: om. cett.
hyp. 1.19 γυναῖκα] post λαβεῖν Π^{1}Ad, ante λαβεῖν Xa (see p. 71).
47 μήτε] μὴ δὲ AGK (μηδὲ Elmsley)

[1] Matthiessen (118–20) has performed a similar exercise for *Hecuba*, but confines himself to a smaller selection of very weakly attested readings (27). So too has Mastronarde (74–5) for *Phoenissae*.
[2] I include readings by F², since this is the hand of the original scribe (see p. 7).

61 cυμφοράν] -άc (Π³)AdGKSξ (see p. 52)
86 εἶ] ἡ VPT^t
91 ἀπείρηκ' ἐν] -κεν (Π³)MB(C)K
119 εὐμενῇ] πρευμενῆ M^{1γρ}V^{3γρ}C^{γρ}PS^{γρ}
128 ἀπέθριcε uel -ξε] -ιcεν MBO et Cyrill.
159 χαράν] χάριν A^{1s}
162 ἅ (uel sim.)] om. M^cOAdT^t
168 ἔβαλεc] ἐλάcαcα ^{γρ}M¹C (see p. 20)
186 ὦ om. AdAnAtξT^t (see p. 61)
212 γε] τε Π⁵AdAnRξ et Stob. et pars codd. Plut. (see p. 52)
238 ἐρινύεc] -ινύεc M‹B›OC
242 νεῶν] νεώc O
258 ἀτρέμαc] -μα BLZu et testes aliquot (see p. 100)
298 ἴcχα(ι)νε] ἴcχναινε M^{1γρ}C^{γρ}LP
303 cῖτον] cίτων MBCSa
314 νοcή(cηι)c] νοcῆ(ι) B^{3γρ}APrRf^{1s}
314 δοξάζη(ι)c uel -ειc] -ζη(ι) OA^{1s}G^{1s}Pr
400 θ' om. AaCLPRfRwZm
418 εἰcὶ(ν)] εἰcὶ(ν) οἱ AaPRfRwZb
515 ὁcίουν uel ὠc-] ὁcιοῦν MKS
602 καθεcτᾶcι] -cιν BOG
606 δυcτυχέcτερον] δυcχερέcτερον Z^{rγρ}Zm^{1s}Zu (see p. 86)
609 ἀνάξειc] ἀνάψειc AdAnF²Mn^cPSaξZZbZuT^c (see p. 60)
667 χρὴ] δεῖ B^{1s}V et Ar., Plut.
687 τὸ] τοῦ OLPRZZcZm‹T^{z?}›T^{ts}
693 προcήκομεν] προήκ- V
704 δὲ τυνδάρεών τέ coι] δ' ἐγώ coι τυνδάρεων ^{γρ}MC (see p. 21 n. 11)
710 cώζειν] cώιζ- M
758 δ'] om. VFP (coni. Brunck)
823 μεγάλη] ποικίλα fere M^{1γρ}C^{γρ}T^t
970 cτρατηλατῶν] -τᾶν MOVC
995 ἠϊόcιν] αἰόcιν O
1005 δράμημα uel δρομημα(τα)] δραμήματα MMnS
1011 γενέτην] -ταν VMnST^t
1022 λόγουc] γόουc M^{1γρ}AnMn^{γρ}PrRfSa^{1γρ}ξZb^{1c}
1039 κτανῶ] κτενῶ OMnSZb
1073 cὴν] cὺ ‹Π^{14?}›CrMn^{γρ}Pr (see p. 118)
1116 οὐ χάζομαι] οὐχ ἅζομαι BOAAt

1127 ἐκκλείcομεν uel sim.] -κλήιc- MB
1165 ἀνταναλώcωμεν] -ώcω μὲν V²ᐟ³A (coni.
Canter)
1263 εἶτ' ἐπ' ἄλλην] εἶτα πάλιν MBOC
1272 ἐχθροῖc εἰ (uel ἦν)] -οῖcι MAaC (-οῖcιν Porson)
1288 ἐν ὅπλοιc] ἔνοπλοc MnRRwᴵˢSTᵗ
1371 τέρεμνα] τέραμνα MBKZcZu
1382 καὶ Πᴵ⁷MOᴵˢAbMnRSZZc et ⟨Demetr.⟩: om. cett.
1468 χρυcεοcάνδαλον] -cάμβαλον fere HMBCK
1491 ἔτεκε] -εν MB
1507 προcπίπτων] -πιτνῶν OGJKTᵗ (see p. 61)
1516 κτανῶ] κτενῶ VMnS⟨Zbʾ⟩
1544 φόνου] πόνου CʸᵖPrSaZʳʸᵖZbZmᴵʸᵖ⟨Zu⟩
1545 θέλει] -η(ι) HMVAAtC
1567 κλείθρων] κλή(ι)θρων MBCFRf
1600 τε] γε AAdFPrSaξZZbZcZmTᶻ
1609 κτανεῖc] κτενεῖc AAtFJMnᴵˢPrRRwSᴵˢ
1611 κτανεῖν] θανεῖν A
1626 c' post Φοῖβοc Bᴵᐟ²ᶜAGKξZbZmTᶜ (see p. 54)
1650 βραβεῖc] -ῆc OᵘᵛAd
1689 υἱοῖc] ὑγρᾶc ʸᵖMᴵVᶾ

(ii)

hyp. 1.6 εἱcαπέcτειλε(ν) (ἀπέcτ- VAn)] εἱc ἄcτυ ἀπέcτειλε C.[3]
hyp. 1.19 cυνοικῆcαι] -ίcαι (Πᴵʾ)RfSa (see p. 117 n. 9)
hyp. 2.12 ὑπὸ μανίαc] post κάμνων K (coni. Kirchhoff, accepted
by West)
hyp. 2.14 δὲ] γὰρ C, δ' ἂν Ad (see pp. 71–2)
38 φόβωι] φόβον V³ˢ (coni. Willink)
138 ἐμοὶ] ὅμωc Π⁴ᵘᵛAbᴵʸᵖCr (see p. 118)
269 ἐξαμύναcθαι] -εcθαι MBAMnZmᴵᶜ (see Willink)
281 cε] coι AdAnAtAᴵˢJʳPrᴵˢRRwᴵˢξZZcZmZuᶜTᶻˢ (see pp.
58–9)
292 (ἔτ') ἤμελλε] ἔμελλε AbAdGJPRfRwZTᶜ
323 φόνον] φόνου BZuᴵˢ (see Willink)[4]
373 ἁλικτύπων] ἁλιτύπων AtJξ (see p. 61)
383 ἀφύλλου] -ουc V²ˢ (coni. Reiske)
406 Πυλάδηc ⟨γʾ⟩ SaZcZm (coni. Kirchhoff)
407 ἐκ φαcμάτων] φανταcμάτων AdJξ (see pp. 61–2)

---

[3] See ZPE 77 (1989) 4 n. 19.   [4] See also CQ n.s. 40 (1990) 109 n. 39.

429 νόμους] νόμον MCZmZu
475 χρόνιον] -ος MBCGKS
761 ἄςτεος] -εως Π¹⁰GKL
789 δὲ uel γάρ] γε VAb (coni. Lenting)
801 ἄςτεος] -εως ‹V?›L
897 πόλεως] πόλεος HᶜMBAGKTᵗ
922 ἀκέραιος] -ον FLPZZbZcZmZuTᶻ et Hesych., Chr. Pat. (see p. 123)
990 πελάγεςι] -εςςι MBOP¹ᶜ(Tᵗ) (see pp. 138–9)
1000 Ἀτρέως] -έος Pr¹ˢS (coni. Porson)
1027 ἀπ'] ὑπ' AaJMnSξZbZc
1038 γόνον] δόμον Cr et ᵞᵖΣᵐᵇᵛᶜ
1039 ἔχω] ἐγὼ AdJξ (see p. 62)
1094 ἀκρόπολιν] -πτολιν OAdGKXaXb (see p. 58)
1148 ςπάςω μέλαν] ςπαςώμεθα (V)CᵞᵖPrᵞᵖ(Zuᵞᵖ) (coni. Kirchhoff)
1156 τι] τοι MnS¹ˢ (coni. Willink), om. S
1186 ὑποτιθεις(α)] -τίθης AaAdF²GJPξZZbZcZuTᵗᶜᵘᵛ
1236 ἐπεβούλευςα] ἐπεκέλευςα BVaAaAt (see West)
1271 κεκρυμμένους] -νας M‹F?› (see Willink)
1278 ἔνθεν (ἐνθάδ' AaʳˢMnS)] ἐνθένδ' R
1311 κτύπου] κτύπον AaK¹ˢZZb (see Willink)
1447 ἀλλ' αἰεί (ἀεί)] ἄλλαι Aᵘᵛ (coni. Scaliger) (see pp. 45–6)
1449 ςτέγαις] ςτέγας Cr (coni. Willink), -ης AaJMnSξTᵗ (see p. 61)
1459 δίναςεν] δίνευον Aa (see Willink 362)
1591 τοῦδε] τῶδε AaʳˢAtG¹ˢK¹ˢPrˢᵘᵛRfRwᵘᵛ.⁵
1633 ἀπό] ὑπό MBOACR‹Tᶻ?›
1653 ἧ(ι)] ἧς CrG¹ᶜJξZc (see p. 58)
1684 Διός] ζηνὸς AdJξ (see p. 62)

---

⁵ It is surprising that τῶιδε has never been conjectured. The structure will be the same as *Andr.* 915 coὶ δ' ἦν τις ὅςτις τοῦδ' ἐκοινώνει φόνου; *El.* 1048 τίς ἂν φόνου coῦ πατρὸς (Denniston: π- c- φόνον L) ἐκοινώνηςέ μοι;. AaʳˢK¹ˢPr²Rwᵘᵛ (~Rw¹ᶜ) also have φόνω for φόνου.

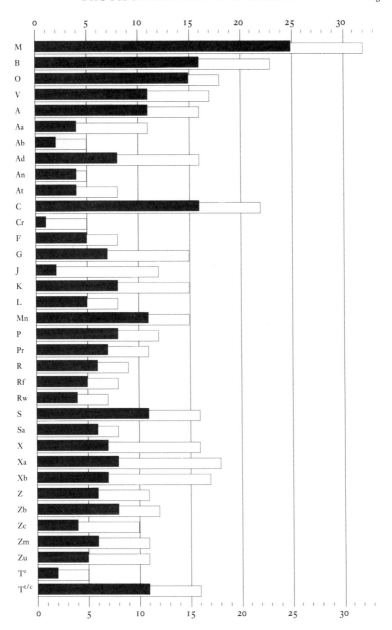

Figure 3

CHAPTER XIX

Conclusions

The editor of *Orestes*, if his apparatus criticus is not to exceed all reasonable proportions, must choose from the available manuscripts those which it is worthwhile to report consistently. It goes without argument that HMBOV(Va) must be reported. I should also report ACK, because of the generally high quality of their text. We might discard G, because it often duplicates K; but its contribution is impressive, and it might be retained. The group Θ (AbFMnPrRSSa) will be adequately reflected by a selection of about half these manuscripts. Since Mn is a close relative of S, and Ab of R, we can dispense with one of each pair. I judge that R and S have the edge on their partners. Of the trio FPrSa I should discard Sa, since it is related to F throughout and in part is a twin of Pr. The associates of Θ (AaCrRfRw) need not be cited, except on the rare occasions when they offer a good reading which is weakly attested. L and P, partly because their text is eclectic, partly because it is of generally good quality, deserve to be reported. The group ξ is adequately represented by X alone. One member of ζ is enough: I choose Z, because I have collated it from the original. It will be useful to report all of Triclinius' corrections, in the iambics and trochaics, as well as in the lyrics; and so it is desirable to report T^z, which, although it has little value in itself, may serve as an additional representative of ζ. Ry is perhaps worth reporting; but Tp may be ignored. We may ignore AdAnJ and the other manuscripts whose text is akin to ξ, as well as At, which, when it is not akin to ξ, duplicates others, and Mt, which duplicates A. Of the gnomologies, gV should be reported, because of its early date; gB and gE may be ignored.

In short, a more than adequate picture of the manuscript evidence which is available for the constitution of the text is provided by HMBOV(Va)ACFGKLPPrRSXZTgV. There will be few places where this evidence needs to be supplemented by the citation of other manuscripts.

Indexes

Subjects

Manuscripts

Manuscript Groups

Θ   19, 23–39, 42–3, 46–7, 70, 72, 73, 74, 75–6, 86, 90–1, 111–12, 113, 148–50, 151, 165
ξ   49–80, 89, 91, 96–8, 102–7, 147–8, 149–50, 157, 165
ζ   81–92, 95–6, 102–5, 111, 113, 149, 165

Papyri

Π¹ (P. Oxy. 2455)	49, 62, 71, 115, 117
Π² (P. Strasb. WG 307)	115
Π³ (P. Oxy. 1616)	52, 62, 115, 116, 117 (*bis*)
Π⁴ (P. Köln 131 = 252)	115, 117, 118, 119 (*ter*), 124, 132
Π⁵ (PL 111/308)	52, 62, 115, 116, 117, 119 (*bis*), 123, 132 n. 5, 133–4, 147, 150
Π⁶ (P. Columb. inv. 517A)	115, 116, 117 (*bis*), 120 (*bis*), 134 n. 9
Π⁷ P. Berol. 17051 et 17014)	115, 116 (*bis*), 134–6, 147, 150
Π⁸ (P. Vindob. G 2315)	115, 117, 120, 136
Π⁹ (P. Oxy. 1370)	116 (*bis*), 119 (*ter*), 136–7, 139, 140, 150
Π¹⁰ (P. Cairo inv. 56224)	116, 117
Π¹¹ (PSI 1475)	116, 120
Π¹² (P. Berol. 21180)	116
Π¹³ (P. Oxy 3716)	116, 117, 119, 137
Π¹⁴ (P. Geneva inv. 91)	116 (*quater*), 117, 119
Π¹⁵ (P. Ross.–Georg. 9)	116, 120
Π¹⁶ (P. Oxy. 1178)	116 (*bis*), 119, 120 (*ter*)
Π¹⁷ (P. Oxy. 3717)	116 (*bis*), 117 (*bis*), 119, 120, 124, 140–2, 150
Π¹⁸ (P. Oxy 3718)	116, 117 (*ter*), 119 (*bis*), 120, 143–4, 147, 150–1
Π¹⁹ (P. Mich. 3735c)	116, 119, 137

Greek Words

ἀλλ' ὅμως 118
(ἀ)πάνται 122
δαί 88
ἐc/εἰc 119
καλῶc κεκτῆcθαι/χρῆcθαι 125

νυν/νῦν 87 n. 27
ὄνειδοc with genitive 25 n. 5
τοι with imperative 124
ὑπαί 87 n. 28

Passages